# THE ADOLESCENT:
## HIS SEARCH FOR UNDERSTANDING

*THE PASTORAL PSYCHOLOGY SERIES,*
*NUMBER 3*

# THE ADOLESCENT:

## HIS SEARCH FOR UNDERSTANDING

*Edited by*

WILLIAM C. BIER, S.J.

FORDHAM UNIVERSITY PRESS · NEW YORK

# Table of Contents

D. EMOTIONAL ADJUSTMENT IN ADOLESCENCE

E. THE ADOLESCENT AND VOCATIONAL CHOICE

# Preface

The papers presented in this volume were given during the 1961 Fordham University Institute of Pastoral Psychology. This Institute was the fourth in a series, begun in 1955, and presented in alternate years since that time. These Institutes, intended to bring to the clergy the insights into pastoral problems provided by psychology and psychiatry, have all been structured in the same general way. They have been held each time from a Monday through a Friday of a week during the second half of June. Although sponsored by the Psychology Department, the conduct of the Institutes has been in the hands of a Committee appointed by the President of the University. Three members continued to serve on the Committee for all four Institutes, while the additional one or two members changed with each Institute, in keeping with its subject matter. In this way continuity of planning was secured, while fresh viewpoints and special competencies were provided by the special Committee members appointed for each Institute.

The Fordham Pastoral Psychology Institutes, unlike similar but less structured workshops conducted elsewhere, have been frankly problem-oriented. While bringing the clergymen into a face-to-face meeting with psychologists, psychiatrists, social workers, and other professional persons (which proves to be a very valuable experience for both groups), they did so with a view to treating previously selected and announced topics. The antecedent agreement on the subject matter for the Institute at once provides a common bond between the two groups, the clergymen by virtue of their interest in the topic to be discussed, and the professional people by reason of their competence in the areas in question. The particular topics selected for treatment were chosen because they posed genuine pastoral problems and also because they were in areas in which psychology, psychiatry and allied disciplines had something to offer to the clergy. Although this approach does not permit as much informal interchange between clergy and Institute faculty as would be provided in a less structured setting, it does have the advantage of lending itself to publication and thus making the work of the Institute available to a considerably wider group than could be present for the Institute itself.

The Fordham University Press has undertaken to publish the proceedings of these Institutes as a series in Pastoral Psychology. The present volume, containing as it does the proceedings of the 1961 Institute, is number 3 in the series. Volume 2 of the series, the outgrowth of the 1959 Institute, was published in the Spring of 1962 under the title: *Problems in Addiction: Alcohol and Drug Addiction.* The proceedings of the 1955 and 1957 Institutes were issued on a limited basis only and have long been unavailable. The best papers from these first two Institutes are now being readied for publication and they will form Volume 1 of the Pastoral Psychology series. Another Pastoral Psychology Institute will be held in June 1963, and the proceedings on publication will constitute Volume 4 in the published series.

The Institute whose proceedings are presented in this volume was conducted under the title: "The Clergy and the Teenager." It is clear that teenagers are a pastoral problem, and sometimes one of considerable magnitude, and it is evident also that the findings of psychology and psychiatry in this area have a contribution to make to the clergyman which can help him in his pastoral contacts with these young people. Consequently, in view of the aims of the Pastoral Psychology Institutes, as sketched above, the choice of the teenager as a topic for the Institute seemed appropriate and indicated.

Once the volume was assembled for publication, however, and could be seen in its entirety, it became evident that what our contributors had to say to the clergy about the teenager would also prove very helpful to parents, teachers, and others whose position brings them into contact with the adolescent. To publish the book under the title of "The Clergy and the Teenager" would have implied that these other groups would find little help from a reading of these pages, which we do not believe to be the case. In removing this restrictive implication from the title, we sought at the same time to direct attention in a positive way to what developed as a central theme in the papers of our contributors who see the adolescent as one who, most characteristically and above all else, is an individual in search of *understanding.* While we were at work in reshaping the title, we decided to do away with the slightly pejorative term "teenager" and to substitute for it the more objective designation "adolescent." The adolescent is a world-wide figure, while the teenager is, for the most part, an American phenomenon. We are, however, in these pages, speaking of the American adolescent, so that we are justified in this context in employing the two terms "adolescent" and "teenager" interchangeably, as our contributors do. So much for the metamorphosis which brought about the present title: *The Adolescent: His Search for Understanding.*

There were five divisions to the development accorded this topic in the Institute which may be clearly seen from the Table of Contents. The Institute began on a Monday afternoon and this first half-day was given over to an attempt to present a general perspective on adolescence which would furnish a suitable background and provide guidelines for the discussion of the more specific aspects of the question in the later phases of the Institute. Tuesday, the first full day of the Institute, was devoted to a consideration of sexual adjustment in adolescence, while Wednesday was given over to juvenile delinquency, and Thursday to emotional adjustment. The Institute concluded at noon on Friday, the morning session on this day being devoted to a consideration of vocational choice in adolescence.

The adolescent is, as our contributors consistently report, an individual in search of understanding. He is seeking, first of all, to understand himself, and there is much about himself that he does not understand. Prominent, of course, among things which he does not understand about himself is the entire area of sex with the newly discovered stirrings, urges, and impulses in this area receiving major attention in early adolescence, and the relationship to the opposite sex assuming an increasingly important role in later adolescence.

Another thing which the adolescent does not understand about himself is how to assert his independence, which he feels he must, without losing the security of the family, which he realizes that he still needs. Finally, in the area of self-understanding there is the profound and not infrequently soul-searching struggle to establish self-identity. The identity of boyhood, which was based on the say-so of parents and others, will no longer do, while the identity of manhood with its self-realized conviction is yet in the future. While the adolescent is still uncertain of how to conceive of himself in this period of transition, he is pressed to make a decision as to his vocational choice, what he will be in the future. Truly, the "mixed up adolescent," is one in search of self-understanding.

Precisely because he understands so little of himself, the adolescent experiences a great need of *understanding by others*. He craves to be understood by parents, teachers, and others who seem to him to possess all the maturity, stability, and self-identity which he is so painfully aware that he lacks. Yet, who is the adolescent who feels that his parents and his teachers really understand him? Actually, as Fr. Knott reports on the basis of his Tri-Une Conference work with adolescents and parents, the latter generally agree that they do not understand their teenage children, these "screwy" adolescents, whose behavior in an adult, as Dr. Blaine explains, "would be considered symptomatic of severe emotional disturbance," but which in the adolescent is "simply a normal part of that tumultuous period of life." In another context, our contributors who write about delinquency testify to how little the adolescent feels that he is understood by his elders. Small wonder, then, that we come to talk about "the isolation of the adolescent," as Dr. Edgar Friedenberg does in his paper.

It is because the adolescent feels such a compelling need to be understood, and because he does not find, or at least characteristically thinks that he does not find, this understanding on the part of his elders, that he turns to his contemporaries for understanding and support. This is the basic reason why the peer-group influences are so predominant in adolescence, and why, as Msgr. Paul Hanly Furfey explains, it is so difficult for adults to influence these groups particularly when they assume an anti-social form of behavior, as occurs in delinquency.

Dr. Alexander A. Schneiders, former Director of Psychological Services at Fordham University, was the Chairman of the Committee not only for the Institute whose proceedings are presented in this volume, but for the preceding three Institutes as well. His was a key role in planning the Institutes and he bore the major responsibility for the organization in each case. The conduct of the 1961 Institute was Dr. Schneiders' final contribution to Fordham since he left immediately after to assume new duties at Boston College. As Editor of the series in Pastoral Psychology, I have fallen heir to a very considerable degree to the fruit of his labors. I gladly take this opportunity to acknowledge the debt which the Fordham University Pastoral Psychology Institutes owe to him. Fortunately, he will be with us again for the 1963 Institute.

It is a pleasure to acknowledge as well the contribution to the 1961 Institute of the other two members of the Committee: Rev. Joseph G. Keegan, S.J., Director of the Counseling Center, and Dr. John M. Martin, Associate Professor of Sociology.

December, 1962                                      William C. Bier, S.J.

# The American Teenager

PAUL HANLY FURFEY

*Monsignor Paul Hanly Furfey received his A.B. degree from Boston College (1917), his M.A. degree from St. Mary's University, Baltimore (1918), and his Ph.D. from the Catholic University of America (1926). His first published book dealt with the adolescent and bore the title:* The Gang Age: A Study of the Preadolescent Boy and His Recreational Needs *(1926). He subsequently published another book in this area:* The Growing Boy: Case Studies of Developmental Age *(1930). From 1956 to 1961 he served as the Assistant Director of the Juvenile Delinquency Evaluation Project of the City of New York. It is clear that the adolescent has been a special area of interest and study for Msgr. Furfey for a period of 35 years. Although his doctoral degree was in psychology, his work in more recent years has been more in the field of sociology, and he has served for many years as head of the Department of Sociology at the Catholic University of America, a post which he holds at the present time. Msgr. Furfey is the author of at least fifteen published books and innumerable articles in professional journals in psychology, sociology, and allied fields.*

The topic assigned to me is enormously broad. Certainly the American teenager exists in an enormous variety of forms. However, the Committee has generously allowed me to narrow my topic a bit and talk

1

about the teenager who constantly forces himself on our attention in a most unwelcome manner; namely, the socially maladjusted teenager.

The socially maladjusted teenagers are a very variegated group. In fact, it is probably true that a good deal of confusion in our thinking is a result of our failure to take into account the enormous variety, both qualitative and quantitative, which teenage maladjustment can show. Oversimplification is an occupational disease of social planners.

Consider, for example, the enormous range of causes which may bring a teenager to the attention of law enforcement officials. The causes range between extremes. At one extreme we have a *teenage criminal.* Every newspaper is familiar with gruesome stories of adolescents who murder their parents, rape innocent girls, and commit various other revolting crimes. Scarcely less shocking are the young burglars, numbers runners, narcotics pushers, who seem quite deliberately to be serving an apprenticeship for a criminal career. At the other extreme we have the *socially confused teenager,* the child who does not fit into our educational system, or our general social milieu. Such adolescents may, indeed, become delinquents in the technical sense. They may be brought into courts as truants, as incorrigibles, for loitering or unlawful assembly, or some similar minor charge. However, they are less dangerous to society than to themselves. They should not be regarded as menaces, but rather as children pathetically in need of whatever help or guidance we can afford to give them.

It seems to me that a good deal of confusion in our thinking results from our failure to draw a clear distinction between the different types of teenagers who are brought into court and are classified legally as delinquents or offenders of some sort. There is a classic and continuous debate between law enforcement officials and crusading editors on the one hand, who advocate "cracking down" on the teenage offender and, on the other hand, the social workers and clinicians who advocate treating them with sympathy and understanding. Sometimes I get the impression that the two sets of disputants are really talking about different teenage offenders and that the dispute is more verbal than real.

On the one hand, the law enforcement officials and crusading editors are likely to have actual teenage criminals in mind when they talk about teenage offenders; we can hardly fail to agree that such criminals, in spite of their youth, can hardly be handled with kid gloves. A police officer must often risk his life when he sets out to arrest such a criminal. On the other hand, the social workers and clinicians are certainly right when they plead for sympathy and understanding for the teenager who is merely socially confused, whose offenses are minor and are directly traceable to his social confusion.

### LEGISLATIVE CONFUSION

Curiously enough, this unclear thinking, the lack of clear distinction between the different types of teenagers who may appear in court, is written into our legislation. Legal provisions for dealing with teenage offenders show a most startling diversity as between one jurisdiction and another. It would be utterly impossible to summarize this legislation in the space available at present. However, let me make one generalization: All states set a particular age limit, usually eighteen years, and define all offenders below that age as "juvenile delinquents," whereas those above the designated age may be treated as adult criminals. Thus two philosophies of treatment are separated by the tenuous barrier of a birthday. Juvenile courts are not very vitally concerned about guilt and innocence; rather, they ask whether this particular child needs help and supervision. Juvenile courts are designed to be helpful to the teenager who is merely socially confused. On the other hand, adult criminal courts deal habitually with more hardened criminals and deal with them, on the whole, rather sternly. The result is that a teenage criminal who needs energetic treatment may, on account of his age, be brought before a juvenile court and treated leniently, although his offense may be rape and murder. On the other hand, a teenager who is just over the juvenile-court age may be brought into a criminal court and treated with a rigor wholly inappropriate in his case.

There have been attempts to remedy this confusion, although they have not always been very satisfactory attempts. They fall into two classes. On the one hand there is a tendency to give criminal courts concurrent jurisdiction with the juvenile court over certain offenses and perhaps at certain ages. The result is that really serious criminal cases may be handled by criminal courts, even when the offender is below the maximum juvenile-court age. The other tendency is to modify, in some cases, the procedure of the adult criminal courts in treating selected offenders who are over juvenile-court age. Thus in New York, teenagers over sixteen (the maximum juvenile-court age in the state) may receive special treatment as "youthful offenders," as "wayward minors," or, in the case of females, as "girls for rehabilitation." In general, these exceptions represent an attempt to extend the philosophy of the juvenile court to the treatment of those over sixteen. In spite of all this, however, the confusion remains. In spite of a great deal of discussion, in spite of the multiplicity of legislation, teenage offenders are still very frequently treated either with more rigor and inflexibility, or else with more leniency and informality, than is appropriate in their particular cases (Tappan, 1960, pp. 387-401).

### UNDERSTANDING THE TEENAGER

The moral of what has been said so far is that socially maladjusted teenagers, like the socially maladjusted of any age, need individualized study and individualized treatment. To try to cure them all by the same treatment is as foolish as it would be if a physician should offer the same treatment for tuberculosis, a fractured femur, and schizophrenia. Distrust all those who are foolish enough to advocate some panacea for all forms of teenage social maladjustment. It is sheer foolishness to think that all forms of teenage misbehavior can be cured simply by greater severity or by more organized recreation or by better guidance clinics or by the elimination of sub-standard housing or by any other isolated remedy by itself.

The only strategy which offers the slightest hope of success is to gain a deep understanding of the individual teenager and his problems and then to discover the appropriate remedy which just those particular problems demand. Let us not underestimate the difficulty of this strategy. It is extremely difficult to gain really clear insight into the causation of any individual's behavior and, even when we do gain such insight, it is extremely difficult to find really effective remedies. This should not be news to any priest. We do indeed, all of us, I am sure, remember cases of very lax Catholics, leading demoralized lives, who have changed profoundly for the better. Yet how rare such complete conversions are! And when they do occur, how seldom can we credit the result to our own skill in spiritual direction! Yet in a matter of such importance we should not neglect any natural means which promises to smooth the way to good social adjustment of the teenager.

In trying to understand teenagers, whether they are socially maladjusted or not, we can rely to a certain extent on our own insight, our own experience, our own common sense. Yet it would be rash to neglect the very considerable help which the modern behavioral sciences can afford us. This help can be very real and practical.

### HELP FROM BEHAVIORAL SCIENCES

When I speak of the "behavioral sciences," I have in mind both psychology and sociology. It is one of my very strong convictions that both sciences are essential if one is to gain insight into human behavior of any sort, and that a great deal of confusion has been created by one-sided thinking which relies on one of these two sciences to the exclusion of the other. For example, to consider the particular problem at hand, there are sociologists who tend to explain delinquency almost exclusively in terms of environment. The absurdity of this view becomes clear when we realize that it fails to explain why different children react so differently to the same environment. The Central Harlem health-center district in New York City has the city's highest delinquency rates and the highest rates for almost any index of unhealthy social conditions that you can imagine. Yet only about nine percent of the youth population in this district are involved with the police even casually during a given year (New York City, Juvenile Delinquency Evaluation Project, 1961). If delinquency is determined by environment, what about the 91 percent of the youth in the district who keep out of trouble?

On the other hand, psychologists, too, can be one-sided. I have been present at case conferences where the psychiatrist discoursed most subtly on the mental mechanisms at work in the delinquent's psyche without any consideration of his social situation. Isn't it quite clear that, when delinquency rates are several times as high in one section of the city as in another, that environment must have *something* to do with delinquency?

It should be clear to every behavioral scientist as a very elementary truth that delinquent behavior is the reaction of a particular individual to a particular environment, and that, therefore, both the individual and the environment must be studied if one is to gain insight into the behavior. It is true that in a given case personality factors may loom larger than environmental factors, or vice versa. Yet in any case at all it would be rash to neglect to study both types of factors.

### IMPORTANCE OF CULTURAL FACTORS

Having recited my credo in the coordinate importance of psychology and sociology in the study of delinquent behavior, I hope I may devote the balance of my paper to the discussion of certain social factors without being accused of being an environmentalist. What interests me particularly in this connection is the importance of cultural factors. As you are doubtless aware, the word "culture" is here used in its anthropological sense. It denotes the sum total of all immaterial things that can be transmitted from man to man—beliefs, attitudes, folklore, etiquette, techniques, preferences, and customs of all sorts. Anthropologists have long been fascinated by the cultural differences among primitive tribes. More recently, both anthropologists and sociologists have come to realize that even within the unity of American civilization there are significant cultural differences which separate social classes, racial and ethnic groups, and the inhabitants of different parts of the country.

Obviously, the local culture of a neighborhood may have a very direct bearing on delinquency. For example, there exist in certain neighborhoods of New York City fighting gangs. These gangs operate in accordance with a very elaborate and conventionalized set of customs governing such things as membership qualifications, internal structure, their relations with other groups, the techniques for waging war and concluding peace, and many other activities (New York City, Juvenile Delinquency Evaluation Project, 1960; New York City Youth Board, 1960). In a word, these gangs form a part of the culture of certain neighborhoods. In many other neighborhoods, in New York City and elsewhere, fighting gangs do not exist. Thus it is that a boy, if he lives in certain neighborhoods, cannot join a fighting gang because such gangs do not exist there. In other neighborhoods he may live under social pressures which practically force him into a fighting gang.

As another example of the relation between culture and delinquency consider narcotic addiction. Not only in New York City, but throughout the country, addiction shows a very spotty pattern (New York City, Juvenile Delinquency Evaluation Project, 1961). It exists only here and there. Where it does exist, however, it has a profound and deleterious influence on the neighborhood culture. That is, the fact that heroin is available and that many are addicted to its use makes life in that neighborhood different. Possibilities of aberrant behavior exist there which are elsewhere absent. Probably all psychiatrists will agree that the drug addict is a particular sort of person who uses drugs to compensate for certain weaknesses in his personality make-up. Nevertheless, no matter what sort of a person he is, no teenager can become a drug addict unless drugs are locally available. It is only under such conditions that what has recently been called the "retreatist subculture" of the addict can develop (Cloward and Ohlin, 1960).

Fighting gangs and drug addiction illustrate in a crude and obvious way how neighborhood culture may be related to delinquency. However, these are very specialized phenomena with a very spotty distribution throughout the country. They are often involved in crimes which make the headlines; but they probably are involved in only a quite small proportion of run-of-the-mine delinquency through the country as a whole. The relation between individual delinquent acts and the special culture of high-delinquency areas is typically a much more subtle one.

### INFLUENCE OF SLUM CULTURE

High-delinquency areas are usually slum areas, characterized by overcrowding, substandard housing, low average income, high public welfare rates, high disease rates; in fact they are likely to be areas which compare unfavorably with the average of the city on almost any statistical comparison. A child growing up in such a neighborhood faces many handicaps.

The average middle-class teenager can reasonably anticipate a future which seems emotionally satisfying to him. He can go through college. He can qualify for a steady job with an income which will permit him to marry, raise a family, buy a house, and own a car. Because he is only an *average* middle-class teenager, he will never become rich or prominent. Probably he will be sensible enough to realize this before long; but nevertheless, middle-class life will probably yield him a reasonable satisfaction, as it does in the case of most of his fellows.

The average teenager from the slums faces a far different prospect. First, there is the difficulty of getting an adequate education. The culture of the slums does not always place such a high value on education as does the culture of the middle class. If the parents of the slum child do not encourage him in his school work, congratulating him on his successes and showing disappointment at his failure, he lacks an important incentive to study. Conditions for study are likely to be unfavorable in the crowded homes of the slums. Then there is the economic aspect of education. Free education is available to most American children, at least through high school. However, the child who attends school without paying tuition is nevertheless a wage earner lost to the family. Thus the tendency is for the slum child to drop out of school as soon as he is old enough to be exempt from the compulsory education laws.

When the slum child looks for a job, he finds himself facing new handicaps. Perhaps he is a member of some minority group and he find that intergroup prejudice is a barrier to the sort of job he wants. The very fact that he belongs to the lowest social class is a very real disadvantage to him. Putnam and O'Hern (1955) found in an ingenious experiment that hearers could very quickly and accurately identify lower-class speech when it was played from a tape along with specimens of the speech of other social classes in a random order. Thus the lower-class teenager, applying for a job, betrays his humble origin as soon as he opens his mouth. He finds that only monotonous, blind-alley jobs are open to him. Even in these unstimulating jobs, employment is likely to be irregular. Even in our prosperous economy, there are never enough jobs to go round. There is always some unemployment. No one is more likely to lose out in the competition for the available jobs than teenagers from the slums.

To put it in sociological terms, the slum teenager fits smoothly neither into our educational system, nor our economic system, nor our social system. To the average white-collar American, he is an outsider, separated by a cultural barrier of misunderstanding. The result is likely to be a deep, psychological dissatisfaction. The slum child knows that his opposite number in the white-collar class gets a good education and a good job—things which he himself is unable to obtain. He may feel cheated and become surly. Under the circumstances it is not particularly surprising if the slum teenager seeks a warped sort of self-realization in violence if he is a boy; nor is it surprising that the slum girl acts on the realization that her body has a monetary value. What *is* surprising, to me at least, is that a majority of slum teenagers lead law-abiding lives as respectable, if humble, citizens.

Another thing that makes delinquency easier in the slums is the attitude of slum culture toward it. This culture is likely to be more tolerant than middle-class culture toward infractions of the law. Arrest and imprisonment are less serious disgraces. The culture of slum dwellers may involve a certain resentment toward the rest of society. Infractions of the law may be viewed sometimes as a not unjustified protest against an unjust social system.

This paper has dealt at some length with the connection between slum life and delinquency. The result, I fear, has been an unduly unfavorable picture; for slum dwellers have their characteristic virtues as well as their characteristic vices. A colleague of mine, a sociologist who had lived for a long time in the slums as a participant observer, used to say that slum people had both startling virtues and startling vices, whereas white-collar people have pale virtues and pale vices. There is something in this. These people are apt to be extraordinarily generous with their few possessions, making room for a homeless relative in their already overcrowded homes or sharing their inadequate food with someone who has even less. Then too, they are apt to have great physical courage, bearing their rigorous living conditions without complaint. Sometimes I think that slum people are a bit like the pioneers of the Old West; they were often violent and immoral, but they opened up a continent. So too, the dwellers in our city slums are opening up a land of opportunity. Successive immigrant groups, Irish, Germans, Poles, Italians, did that in the past. Negroes and Puerto Ricans and Mexicans are doing it now. At the present moment their culture may appear out of adjustment and spotted with crime, but in the long perspective they seem destined to become triumphant.

In any case, our present duty is not primarily to pass moral judgment on the slum culture, but first and foremost to understand it. This may not be altogether easy. It is not easy for an educated man to see the world through the eyes of the illiterate. It is not easy for one reared in the white-collar class to understand the cultural setting of the slums. It is not easy for one who comes from a background of settled American tradition to see America as the recent immigrant sees it. It is not easy but it is vitally important. St. John Bosco was a country boy who exercised his priestly ministry in Turin, a city disorganized by the advent of the Industrial Revolution. It must not have been altogether easy for him to understand the teenagers of this strange city where life was so different from his native Becchi. Yet he succeeded magnificently, and because he succeeded, he was able to wield an incredibly effective influence. There is an example for us. It is not enough for us to have a sympathetic understanding of the upper class, the middle class, even the stable working class. We must also be at home among the dispossessed, the "subproletariat" (Walsh and Furfey, 1958), the unsettled and bewildered people who rank socially below the humblest stable workers. Only by deep understanding, only by a kindly empathy, only through the insight which a deep priestly charity yields, will we be able to help the maladjusted teenager in his problem.

## REFERENCES

Cloward, R. A. and Ohlin, L. E. *Delinquency and opportunity.* New York: Free Press, 1960.

New York City, Juvenile Delinquency Evaluation Project. *Dealing with the conflict gang in New York City.* New York: Author, 1960.

NewYork City, Juvenile Delinquency Evaluation Project. *Delinquency in the great city.* New York: Author, 1961.

New York City Youth Board. *Reaching the fighting gang.* New York: Author, 1960.

Putnam, G. N. and O'Hern, Edna. *The status significance of an isolated urban dialect.* Baltimore: Waverly, 1955 (Language Dissertation No. 53, Linguistic Society of America).

Tappan, P. W. *Crime, justice and correction.* New York: McGraw-Hill, 1960.

Walsh, Mary E. and Furfey, P. H. *Social problems and social action.* Englewood Cliffs, N. J.: Prentice-Hall, 1958.

# The Isolation of the Adolescent

EDGAR Z. FRIEDENBERG

*In his educational career, Edgar Z. Friedenberg has been associated with institutions in widely separated portions of the country. His undergraduate degree is from the South, from Centenary College in Shreveport, Louisiana. His master's degree is from the West, from Stanford University in California, while his doctoral degree is from the Mid-West, from the University of Chicago. Dr. Friedenberg is currently Associate Professor of Education in the East, at Brooklyn College, one of the corporate colleges of the recently formed City University of New York. He is the author, jointly with Julius A. Roth, of* Self-Perception in the University *(1954), and then on his own, of* The Vanishing Adolescent *(1959). Dr. Friedenberg is a frequent speaker on adolescence and adolescent problems at the meetings of professional organizations. He spoke on this subject in 1960 to the Child Study Association, to the Michigan Counselors Association, and to the College Entrance Examination Board's 8th Annual Colloquium, and in 1961 to the Society for Adolescent Psychiatry.*

The Isolation of the Adolescent is really a rather grim topic. The very fact that an Institute for the Clergy should have to discuss it is disturbing in itself. I was astonished, at first, to be asked to speak on

11

it, since it had not occurred to me that the adolescent could be re-garded as isolated. But a little reflection is sufficient to show that the idea makes sense.

It is not wholly a new idea, of course. Collier and Lawrence (1951) discussed the adolescent feeling of psychological isolation in a paper with precisely that title ten years ago; and, in a somewhat more gen-eral way so did Shakespeare, using as his case material a young Veronese boy and girl who had exceptional difficulty in communicating effectively with the adult world around them. But today we confront not just a feeling of isolation, or the special plight of certain isolated individuals, but what is held to be a social fact.

### REASON FOR ADOLESCENT ISOLATION

There is a good bit of evidence that it *is* a fact. I propose to examine this, and to discuss why I think the adolescent is becoming isolated. But first I should like to say why I find his isolation frightening. I think adolescents are quite right to resist adult infiltration and to institutionalize their defenses against it. In any case, they always have. What frightens me is that in our society, as I see it, there is a real foundation for adolescent distrust of adults. The way in which Ameri-can adult life has evolved makes our culture especially inimical to the essential developmental task of adolescence. The "isolation of the adolescent" then, is a specific response to a pervasive moral climate that adolescents find very destructive.

I am aware that there is an element of impertinence in presenting a problem in moral terms before an Institute for the Clergy. It is a little like trying to discuss health with the AMA; they simply don't take it seriously as a possibility. But sometimes, fortunately, an em-pirical analysis of the way a society functions leads to implications that can only be considered in moral terms. The way our society func-tions with respect to adolescents—the experience they have of grow-ing up in it—is a case in point.

In an earlier work (Friedenberg, 1959), I defined the central de-velopmental task of adolescence in this way:

> This task is self-definition. Adolescence is the period during which a young person learns who he is, and what he really feels. It is the time during which he differentiates himself from the culture; though on the culture's terms. It is the age at which, by becoming a person in his own right, he becomes capable of deeply felt relationships to other individu-als, perceived clearly as such (p. 9).

America in mid-century is not very hospitable to people who differentiate themselves from it, or who care too much. To adults who preserve the capacity to feel and to celebrate their unique perceptions of reality, this has long since become merely one of the facts of life. But adolescents must be free to feel and to make their own commitments if they are to grow. The institutions of any society, however, function to mold growing individuals into conformity with the norms of that society and to arrest by anxiety or atrophy such human development as tends to be excessively discordant. This is fully automatic, and, as stated, perfectly general. It is true of any society. But there is no *general* reason why a society should differentially stultify the essential emotional processes of adolescence. Ours, I think, does.

In any society that consistently impedes its members at a particular stage of their growth there will ultimately be a preponderance of immature adults. There manifestly is such immaturity in the United States today, and a considerable part of the deficiency that is so familiar to all of us has its origins in the experiences, or lack of them, and the anxieties that adolescents encounter. To defend their integrity as they create it, they quarantine themselves from the rest of society. But then they have nothing worthwhile to build themselves out of: no very significant symbols, no tested values to count on under stress. Ultimately, there is no refuge in triviality.

ADOLESCENTS AND ADULTS MISPERCEIVE EACH OTHER

In order to show this process of reduction in force through socialization in action, I have selected for comment a few recent publications that seem to me to shed specially revealing light on critical relationships between the adolescent and society. The first, and most innocent, of these is an ingenious study by Hess and Goldblatt (1957) entitled: "The status of adolescents in American society: A problem in social identity." Hess and Goldblatt used a very simple instrument, but they used it in a complicated way. The instrument was a rating scale of twenty polar pairs of adjectives: neat-untidy, cooperative-uncooperative, serious-frivolous, self-controlled-wild, grateful-ungrateful, and so on. They conducted a study among 32 upper-middle and middle class families in a metropolitan area, including 16 adolescent boys and 16 adolescent girls, 30 of their mothers and 24 of their fathers. Using this same simple rating scale, they obtained four sets of data from the youngsters, and four parallel sets of data from the adults.

The youngsters were asked to rate "the average teenager" on the scale, and to rate "the average adult" on it. They were also asked to predict how adults would rate "teenagers" and how adults would rate themselves. Similarly, the adults were asked to rate "the average teenager" and "the average adult"; and *they* were asked how they thought the youngsters would rate adults, and would rate themselves.

Hess and Goldblatt found that both adults and youngsters tend, on the whole, to rate "teenagers" rather favorably. But the youngsters believe that they will be rated very low by adults, even though, within the limits of the instrument they are not. The parents, in turn, believe that the youngsters will rate themselves much higher than they actually do, but the adolescents predict the parents' opinion of adults quite accurately.

The adolescents give the adults much higher ratings than the adults give themselves. The parents, however, believe that "teenagers" see them as *less* patient, grateful, considerate, and thoughtful than they rate themselves; though they expect "teenagers" to agree with their self-rating on traits like "moral-immoral" or "stable-unstable" that refer less directly to the kinds of parental behavior that arouse resentment in child-rearing.

Finally, adolescents whose mothers rate "teenagers" lower than they rate adults tend to expect "the average adult" to rate them low; and this is true of both boys and girls. But the father's attitude apparently does not matter much to either his sons or his daughters; it is not significantly related to the rating they expect from "the average adult." And *neither* parent's rating is related statistically to the youngsters *own* rating of "the average teenager."

The adolescents in Hess and Goldblatt's sample, in other words, mostly start with the conviction that adults are down on them, though this is generally a misapprehension. If, however, their mother really *is* down on them, their expectation of disapproval is increased, though they themselves do not go along with her judgment. But while the youngsters believe that adults "low-rate" them, the adults are convinced that the youngsters overrate themselves. The youngsters are more generous in their estimate of adults: they rate them higher than the adults do themselves, though the adults expect to be rated lower on those traits that are likely to give rise to family friction.

The importance of Hess and Goldblatt's study lies precisely in what it tells us about the degree to which adolescents and adults, even from the more articulate social classes, misperceive each other. Difficulties in communication must surely ensue. It is, of course, a hopeful sign that the adults in the study do not, by and large, rate "the average teenager" lower than adolescents do. But I am not greatly impressed by this finding for two reasons. People, it seems to me, are likely to seem a great deal more tolerant when reacting to a check list than they do if you actually have to live with them. Moreover, the pejorative image of the "teenager" is so well disseminated through our culture by every conceivable medium that I suspect the adolescents' original self-rating—their rating of the average teenager—is seriously depressed; and since all these interpretations are based on comparisons among ratings, it is impossible to judge the *absolute* level of approval or hostility toward "teenagers" from it. My hunch is that the level of hostility is high. Hardly anybody, since the death of Socrates, has really seen teenagers as they are.

### TEENAGE SUBCULTURES

If Hess and Goldblatt's findings are generally applicable, it is hardly astonishing that adolescents try to isolate themselves from adults who they feel disparage them; and one would expect the isolation to contribute to further misunderstanding and misappraisal between the two groups. Thrown back upon themselves, the youngsters would presumably build a world of their own, and this, to a large degree, is what they do. There is another recent research that I wish to quote which establishes this rather clearly: Coleman's (1961) study of "Social climates in high schools." The methodology is not as elegantly symmetrical as Hess and Goldblatt's—basically, it is an interview and questionnaire study with statistical analysis of the findings—but it is sound and clear enough.

Coleman studied ten very diverse high schools in Northern Illinois, ranging from very small town schools to Chicago and suburban high schools, including one working-class parochial school. Of the purport of his findings, Coleman says:

> The general point is this: Adolescents today are cut off, probably more than ever before, from the adult society. They are still oriented toward fulfilling their parents' desires, but they look very much to their peers for approval. As a consequence, American society now has in its midst a set of small teenage subcultures which focus teenage interests and attitudes on things far removed from adult responsibilities, subcultures which may develop standards that lead a child away from the goals toward which the schools are intended to lead (p. 7).

The subcultures Coleman identifies, however, seem mostly to lead the child, or adolescent, toward the goals the adult society *actually* values, though centering on symbols and objects—e.g., automobiles or athletic fame—that have special utility among adolescents. It is true that these are not the goals the school officially endorses, but what value is more characteristically American than a cynical and manipulative attitude toward official policy statements? If adolescents do not learn to ignore what the school says and attend to what it does they may grow up so naive that they believe White Papers are a guide to our foreign policy, which would impose on the State Department a crushing moral obligation that it is by no means ready to sustain.

Through most of his sample, Coleman finds that "personality," and "reputation" are what youngsters feel get them into "leading crowds" in schools and what they want to be remembered for; athletic ability is most highly prized in boys, popularity or social leadership in girls. Coleman asked the boys in his sample whether they would rather be pilots, nationally famous athletes, missionaries or atomic scientists; and the girls whether they would rather be actresses or artists, nurses, models, or school teachers. He interprets the fact that the most serious choices are least popular as a sign of immaturity: 31 percent of the boys pick "jet pilot" in contrast to only six percent who choose "missionary." But this seems fairly realistic; properly prepared, à la Congolèse, missionary is delicious, but in the jet age who has the time?

Coleman's findings *do* substantiate that direct efforts of adults to influence adolescent values hardly ever work, and that the better educated and more suburban the family is the less effective they are. The girls from the school he calls Executive Heights high school, for example, care least whether their parents disapprove of a club they wish to join. And he draws from the nearly universal lack of interest in scholarship the original and highly provocative inference that the top achievers in the American school system are probably very far from being the ablest, because the brightest and most perceptive youngsters learn quickly to shun this particular competition. This is terribly important, but it is also tricky to interpret, because it means that the ideal of scholarship that the school holds before the student will already be phoney in the first place, having been fixed by students who are partially self-selected in response to their own feelings of mediocrity. And I am not sure the really bright kids could make it to the top academically even if they wanted to; in many cases they would

get low marks just by threatening the teachers, who are not themselves from the highest end of the general intelligence distribution.

The widespread emphasis among boys on having a car and being
recognized as an athlete seems to me to be very often a sign of adolescent autonomy rather than of triviality or corruption. In our culture a
boy's car is much more than a means of transport *or* a status symbol;
it is his war stallion and his boudoir as well, and these are still the
necessities of chivalry. If he is an athletic attraction he does in reality
get more opportunity to use his automobile effectively in both these
functions. Moreover, some of the responses adolescents make to the
athlete are valid, and very moving. There is so much emphasis on de-
emphasizing athletics now that the particular good they do gets overlooked, and their defenders are not usually very clever in their choice
of reasons.

In the high school sports are likely to be a lot less of a fake than
classroom activity. Even if the teachers were of top intellectual calibre
they would be so much hemmed in by convention and social pressure
that they would still move as if in shackles much of the time. I have
seen boys from a small rural Louisiana high school who had nevertheless become champions of a league that included a major city and
several big towns come striding out of their locker room after the
game, dressed once more in their farm clothes, and they looked mag-
nificent. I have never seen how they look when they come out of their
class in Problems of Democracy, if they have one, but I expect they
look ashamed. They seemed to be the kind of boys who would know
when they had been cheated.

### DILEMMA OF ADOLESCENT ISOLATION

Coleman does establish the isolation of the adolescent, but the
most important thing he establishes about it is that it does not work.
It cuts the adolescent sub-culture off from the immediate impingement
of the adults who surround it, but then they do not have much of anything to work with that is really their own. Cars and Sports and Jazz
come closest, but if these are real to them they are also bait from
the adult world, proffered on its terms and presented in the context
of its values. Isolation, if it is to succeed, requires a kind of creative
autarchy. Adolescents are capable of this and I have often seen them
show it, though usually at some cost to their self-esteem since the
adult world had only enough idea of what they were doing to be

suspicious of it. The liberal youngsters at the University of Chicago during the late forties and early fifties, folk singing groups in Washington Square (though most of these are young men and women), or team members in an exacting but non-commercial sport like track —or in this country—soccer, are likely to have it. But Coleman's sample, by and large, have not got it.

One reason for this, probably, is that they are part of what Harold Taylor (1961) called the "teenage culture" of the public high school, instead of being what he called "shoe" or "progressive" youngsters. Both these groups come from the upper and upper middle class private schools and ivy colleges; and while they overlap the world of the teenager and show many of his characteristics their basic relationship to the economic and social system is likely to be different. They are, without much striving, its rightful heirs. Their schooling is designed, or has evolved, to fit them for a place in this system that is congruent with the rest of their experience, even though it may not be there any longer when they get there. Such a school is exacting but not alienating. They feel as if they belong in it, and as if the rewards it offers were the appropriate rewards. If these are the rewards they want, they go "shoe" and fit right in. If not, they go "progressive" and become critics or opponents of the system, but are still strengthened by the coherence of the culture in which they have participated rather than weakened by the unquestioned assumption that survival depends on being what other people need. The two heroes of really good contemporary literature about adolescents, as Taylor points out, are both "progressive" youngsters from "shoe" schools: Holden Caulfield of Salinger's (1951) *The Catcher in the Rye,* and the tragic hero, Phineas, of John Knowles' (1960) *A Separate Peace,* though Phineas, who fights for life and wholeness merely by being, does not know that he is a dissenter.

Indeed, it is Phineas' success in defining himself—his wholeness— that made him an intolerable threat. Understand this. It is the irony of the adolescent's plight in modern society that it is his integrity which ultimately isolates him. Toward the end of his account, the narrator of *A Separate Peace,* Finney's best friend and his killer says, quite simply:

> I never talked about Phineas and neither did anyone else; he was, however, present in every moment of every day. . . . Finny had a vitality which could not be quenched so suddenly. . . . During the time I was with him, Phineas created an atmosphere in which I con-

tinued now to live, a way of sizing up the world with erratic and entirely personal reservations, letting its rocklike facts sift through and be
accepted only a little at a time, only as much as he could assimilate
without a sense of chaos and loss.

No one else I have ever met could do this. All others at some point
found something in themselves pitted violently against something in the
world around them. . . . When they began to feel that there was this
overwhelmingly hostile thing in the world with them, then the simplicity
and unity of their characters broke and they were not the same again.

Phineas alone had escaped this. He possessed an extra vigor, a
heightened confidence in himself, a serene capacity for affection which
saved him. Nothing as he was growing up at home, nothing at Devon,
nothing even about the war had broken his harmonious and natural
unity. So at last I had.

.   .   .   .   .   .   .   .   .   .   .   .   .   .   .   .   .   .   .   .

I never killed anybody and I never developed an intense level of
hatred for the enemy. Because my war ended before I ever put on a
uniform; I was on active duty all my time at school. I killed my enemy
there.

Only Phineas never was afraid, only Phineas never hated anyone.
Other people experienced this fearful shock somewhere, this sighting
of the enemy, and so began an obsessive labor of defense . . .

All of them, all except Phineas, constructed at infinite cost to themselves these Maginot lines against this enemy they thought they saw
across the frontier, this enemy who never attacked that way—if he ever
attacked at all; if he was, indeed, the enemy (pp. 183-186).

But what, finally, is this overwhelmingly hostile thing? Different
authors, from Kierkegaard to Fromm or Tillich, have called it by
different names, but they all seem to agree that it exists. One of the
best and simplest of recent statements, that of Paul Goodman (1960),
identifies it implicitly in his title. The danger is that of *Growing Up
Absurd*.

Among the several merits of Goodman's work from our point of
view is that it is the only work I have cited that deals specifically and
primarily with the plight of the working class adolescent, though Goodman insists, quite rightly, that the plight of the college boy is not
usually very different but his race is run for higher stakes. The problem, basically, is the falsification of experience by the suppression or
denial of those aspects of it that impair the individual's quest for
social goals.

If this suppression or denial were simply dissimulation it would
be disagreeable, but not destructive. The problem is that the victim,
in order to avoid anxiety about his destiny, becomes the unconscious

ally of society. Our society provides its richest rewards so exclusively to persons who are more concerned with means than with ends, and with symbols rather than realities, that perception itself becomes a threat. It is getting very difficult for most mothers to answer the question, "But what does daddy do?"; though it makes it much worse still if the next question is "Why?" And this does not apply merely to what daddy does to make a living: with equal force it applies to other things that daddy does that seem quite obvious, like getting on the 5:23 after only one martini and coming home.

Multiple choice items are often abused, though they are not quite as bad as they are now being painted. But there is one series of them that goes rather like this, which every adolescent had better get right:

When I grow up I would like to be:

A. an executive of an electric company;

B. a soldier;

C. the Director of the Central Intelligence Agency;

D. none of the above;

E. the premise is false; I do not even like it now.

It isn't easy.

## REFERENCES

Coleman, J. S., Jonassohn, K., & Johnstone, J. W. C. *Social climates in high schools.* Washington, U.S. Office of Health, Education and Welfare, Cooperative Research Monograph No. 4, 1961.

Collier, R. M., and Lawrence, H. P. The adolescent feeling of social isolation. *Educ. Theory,* 1951, *1,* 106-115.

Friedenberg, E. Z. *The vanishing adolescent.* Boston: Beacon, 1959.

Goodman, P. *Growing up absurd.* New York: Random House, 1960.

Hess, R. D., and Goldblatt, Irene. The status of adolescents in American society: A problem in social identity. *Child Develpm.,* 1957, *28,* 459-468.

Knowles, J. *A separate peace.* New York: Macmillan, 1960.

Patterson, F. K. *The adolescent citizen.* New York: Free Press, 1960.

Salinger, J. D. *The catcher in the rye.* Boston: Little, Brown, 1951.

Taylor, H. The understood child. *Sat. Rev.,* 1961, *44,* 47-49, 66.

# Peer-Group Influences in Adolescence

PAUL HANLY FURFEY

*Monsignor Paul Hanly Furfey received his
A.B. degree from Boston College (1917), his
M.A. degree from St. Mary's University, Baltimore (1918), and his Ph.D. from the Catholic
University of America (1926). His first published book dealt with the adolescent and bore
the title:* The Gang Age: A Study of the Pre-
adolescent Boy and His Recreational Needs
*(1926). He subsequently published another
book in this area:* The Growing Boy: Case
Studies of Developmental Age *(1930). From
1956 to 1961 he served as the Assistant Director of the Juvenile Delinquency Evaluation
Project of the City of New York. It is clear
that the adolescent has been a special area of
interest and study for Msgr. Furfey for a period
of 35 years. Although his doctoral degree was
in psychology, his work in more recent years
has been more in the field of sociology, and he
has served for many years as head of the Department of Sociology at the Catholic University of America, a post which he holds at the
present time. Msgr. Furfey is the author of at
least fifteen published books and innumerable
articles in professional journals in psychology,
sociology, and allied fields.*

Dr. Friedenberg has made abundantly clear to us the psychological
isolation of the adolescent from the adult world. May I add a fact that
will surprise nobody, but which is nevertheless important? The ado-

21

lescent is isolated not only from the adult world, but from the pre-adolescent world as well.

Many years ago I was doing some research with a group of pre-adolescent boys in a Washington parish (Furfey, 1930). I found it convenient to organize the experimental group as a troop of Boy Scouts; and, since we had a very gifted Scoutmaster, the troop was successful and interest ran high. Yet the older Scouts kept dropping out of the troop. A lack of interest would develop, the boy would become irregular in his attendance, and finally he would drop out altogether, publicly expressing his opinion that Scouting is only for "little boys." It was found that this sudden discovery of the childishness of the Scout movement was only one of the more visible signs of a quite thoroughgoing alteration in the boy's social attitudes. It was the beginning of adolescence.

Of course in the case of girls the change is even more dramatic. The tomboy who starred in the corner lot baseball playground suddenly becomes a young lady. You meet her balanced precariously on her first high heels applying lipstick inexpertly but very, very seriously. Definitely, her tomboy days are over and she does not care to associate with tomboys.

We gathered some evidence in these early studies—it is conveniently summarized in Carmichael (1946, pp. 649-650)—that the changes in interpersonal attitudes which occur at the threshold of adolescence are closely correlated with the biological changes of puberty. The point is irrelevant here, except in so far as it suggests that the gap between adolescence and preadolescence is far from artificial. It may be, after all, that high heels and lipstick have ultimately an endocrine basis!

Since the adolescent is isolated from the adult world, and since he is also isolated from the world of preadolescence, he is thrown back on his coevals for company. Hence the importance of the peer-group. It is only here that the adolescent feels truly at home. It is only here that he finds self-realization.

### ADOLESCENT PEER-GROUPS

The social structure of the adolescent peer-group is a matter of very great importance; for the adolescent must adapt himself to this structure, and, in doing so, he acquires habits in interpersonal relations which are likely to affect him profoundly throughout life.

It is too bad we know so little with scientific accuracy as to how adolescent peer-groups are structured. One fact seems certain. This is that there exists no standard form of social structure common to all these groups. On the contrary, there is great variety. This is what makes the scientific study of these groups so difficult. We would have to study an enormous number of adolescent peer-groups existing under all sorts of social conditions in different socio-economic classes, in different ethnic groups, in the city and in the country, in various parts of the country, before we could make valid generalizations about the group life of American adolescents.

One variable which deserves close study is the extent to which the peer-group structure is formalized. When it is formalized to a considerable extent, the group can appropriately be called a "gang." It seems clear that gangs are not a universal phenomenon of adolescence. It seems difficult to predict under what social conditions they will occur. A friend of mine who runs a boys' club in Brooklyn told me that boys never join his club as individuals. Either a gang joins his club as a unit, or else nobody from the gang joins. Yet in nineteen years at Fides House in Washington, where the local social conditions seem roughly similar, I never saw anything similar. There were no gangs. There were groups which organized themselves into a basketball team or a quartette, there were numbers of boys who seemed on particularly good terms with one another, but there never appeared that close social cohesion, that formality of structure, which characterizes a genuine gang.

### UNSTRUCTURED PEER-GROUPS

Probably our best information about the interpersonal relations within the unstructured peer-group, the peer-group which is in no sense a gang, comes from the technique known as *sociometry*. The technique is rather simple. It is typically applied to such groups as the pupils in one school grade, the student nurses in one class in nursing school, the boys in a camp, the children in a child-caring institution. Each subject is asked to name his best friend, or his three best friends, or the two boys with whom he would prefer to share a room—in any case, some question designed to reveal personal preferences. On the basis of the answers a diagram called a *sociogram* is prepared. Each subject is represented, say, by a circle. If $A$ chooses $B$ as one of his choices, then an arrow is drawn from $A$'s circle to $B$'s circle. If $B$ also chooses *A,* then the arrow is double-headed, showing graphically that the choice is a mutual one (Moreno, 1934).

If a genuine gang is present in a group studied sociometrically, it will reveal itself as a group of circles on the sociogram which are interconnected by a great many arrows. This is often the case. However, as I have said, the sociogram may also reveal the interpersonal pattern of an unstructured peer group. Because the group *is* unstructured, the sociogram will appear very irregular and complex. There will be popular group members with several arrows pointing toward them. There will be social isolates with no arrows pointing in their direction. There will be dyads and triads connected by double-headed arrows. It is interesting to add that when a sociometric test is repeated on an unstructured group after a few months, the sociogram is often very different from the original one. This, of course, is an indication that interpersonal relations tend to shift. The irregular and shifting pattern of an unstructured group's sociograms really yields no basis for generalizations except the purely negative one that such a peer-group shows no definite and enduring pattern of interpersonal relationships. In other words, it really *is* unstructured.

### STRUCTURED PEER-GROUPS: GANGS

At the other extreme is the definitely structured peer-group, the gang. One point to grasp about gangs is that they are not necessarily antisocial. Even in New York City which is all too well known for its fighting gangs, many, many other gangs are entirely law-abiding. This has been observed frequently. Thus, for example, Padilla (1958, p. 225), after studying the structured peer-groups in a congested Puerto Rican section of the city, says: "Social cliques are those that emphasize recreation and outspokenly make claims of avoiding violence. Fighting clubs may have a recreational purpose but emphasize violence and war as a method of solving conflicts." Thus both types were definitely present.

It is unfortunate that in the behavioral sciences we tend to emphasize pathology, and this is true in the study of gangs, as elsewhere. The result is that a great deal more effort has gone into the study of delinquent gangs than their law-abiding counterparts. This fact is responsible for serious gaps in our knowledge. Moreover, to make the picture still more one-sided, social scientists tend to concentrate on the study of the *lower-class* delinquent gang, rather than on delinquent gangs in general. As the authors of a recent study remark:

> Rarely in sociological literature are middle-class adolescent groups referred to as gangs, irrespective of their similarity to their lower economic-class counterparts. . . . As far as the commission of delinquent acts is concerned, middle-class adolescents, singly and in groups, participate in a variety of delinquent episodes, including such illegal activities as auto theft, operating a motor vehicle without a license, disorderly conduct, and a wide variety of other lawbreaking activities (Bloch and Niederhoffer, 1958, pp. 7-8).

Our knowledge, biased and fragmentary as it is, does at least permit us to see how highly structured an adolescent peer-group may become, as illustrated by the delinquent gang. The New York City Youth Board (1960, pp. 12-59) reports a gang divided vertically by age into Seniors, Juniors, Cubs, and Midgets, ranging in age from 14 to 20 with an additional group, the Tots, for younger boys. Some gangs have girl auxiliaries (Debs). In addition, there are horizontal groupings, that is, parallel sections in different blocks, or neighborhoods, or parts of the city. It is usual for each gang, and each division within the gang, to have officers—commonly a president, a vice-president, and a war counselor; some, in addition, have a secretary and a treasurer. It is usual for each gang to have its own territory, certain blocks where its members are free "to live and play without fear from invasion." For one gang to invade another's territory is regarded as a provocative act. Within its territory the gang will have a hangout, which is very frequently a candy store, which might seem to be an incongruously innocent place for a criminal gang to congregate. A gang is likely to have a very definite code of conduct. Some gangs may prohibit drinking or the use of narcotics. There may be rules against associating "with persons of particular religious, ethnic or cultural backgrounds, or persons from certain neighborhoods." It would be possible to add many details, but perhaps enough has been said to bring home the essential point which is that in some cases at least the adolescent peer-group may take the form of a very highly structured group.

### THE CRIMINAL GANG

The criminal gang certainly needs the attention of society to wean it away from its illegal activities. Even law-abiding groups could usually profit by the understanding interest of a friendly adult. However, it is difficult for an adult to gain the confidence of the teenage groups for the reason already discussed, namely, the phenomenon of adolescent isolation. However, we should remember that this isolation, though very general, is by no means absolute and inevitable. With skill, patience, and a generous amount of empathy, the exceptional adult can penetrate it. If the barriers were absolutely impenetrable, no priest could give effective spiritual direction, no psychiatrist could give effective therapy, no teacher could be effective in the fullest sense, when dealing with adolescents.

The barrier may be penetrated, but it is not easy. The adult must be prepared to meet the adolescent on his own terms. He must be prepared to be thoroughly tested before he is accepted. The price of success may be high. This is well-illustrated by the work of the "detached workers" who have had a good deal of success with the fighting gangs of New York City (New York City Youth Board, 1960; Crawford, Malamud, & Dumpson, 1950). The detached worker simply approaches the gang hangout, meets the gang members, and tries to gain acceptance. At first, of course, he is received with profound skepticism. Sooner or later, he is perhaps able to do some gang member a favor, to get him a job, or secure needed medical treatment. By doing such favors but, above all, by proving himself an understanding human being, a good worker will gain acceptance. The job of the detached worker is one of the toughest in all social work. It means unremitting toil. If the gang reaches a crisis at two o'clock in the morning, the worker must anticipate it and be present. However, the example of these workers is encouraging. If the protective isolation of these anti-social gangs can be penetrated by a skillful and persistent worker, it should *a fortiori* be possible to gain the confidence of less extreme types of adolescent peer groups.

### CONCLUSION

The moral, I suppose, is plain. As priests, we have to deal with groups as well as with individuals. In fact, in the case of the closely knit adolescent peer-group, we can often gain the confidence of the individual only by gaining the confidence of the group as a whole. To do this we must first of all learn to understand the characteristics of these groups in their different forms and what they mean in the life of the adolescent. Then we must have the skill and patience to penetrate the barrier of the adolescent's characteristic isolation. It is difficult, but it can be done.

## REFERENCES

Bloch, H. A. and Niederhoffer, A. *The gang.* New York: Philosophical Library, 1958.

Carmichael, L. (Ed.). *Manual of child psychology.* New York: Wiley, 1946.

Crawford, P. L., Malamud, D. I., & Dumpson, J. R. *Working with teen-age gangs.* New York: Welfare Council of New York City, 1950.

Furfey, P. H. *The growing boy.* New York: Macmillan, 1930.

Moreno, J. L. *Who shall survive?* Washington: Nervous and Mental disease Publishing Co., 1934.

New York City Youth Board. *Reaching the fighting gang.* New York: Author, 1960.

Padilla, Elena. *Up from Puerto Rico.* New York: Columbia Univer., 1958.

# Sex and the Teenager

## ROBERT J. CAMPBELL

*Robert Jean Campbell, III, M.D. is Chief of the Out-Patient Psychiatric Service of St. Vincent's Hospital; Instructor in Psychiatry, Columbia University, College of Physicians and Surgeons; and Adjunct Associate Professor, Fordham University Graduate School. Prior to assuming his post at St. Vincent's Hospital, Dr. Campbell was Senior Clinical Psychiatrist at the New York State Psychiatric Institute. After graduating from the University of Wisconsin, Dr. Campbell received his M.D. degree from Columbia University. He is a diplomate, American Board of Psychiatry and Neurology, a contributor to various medical journals, and is currently editor of Hinsie & Campbell's Psychiatric dictionary (1960). Dr. Campbell has been the most consistent contributor to the Fordham Pastoral Psychology Institutes, the current Institute being the third in which he has participated as a faculty member.*

Sudden change can be a serious threat even to the stable, mature adult, despite his experience and his armamentarium of smoothly-working, ordinarily adequate defenses. But to the teenager, limited by his inexperience and as much hampered by tenuous defenses as by the internal drives against which they were erected, the abrupt pubertal shifts—in endocrine balance, in the reproductive apparatus, and in the demands the environment places upon him—typically spell

28

chaos. There is nothing to which he can anchor for long. The family structure that may once have offered him asylum becomes an intimidating, dangerous enemy; his equanimity is battered by unwelcome surges of new, forbidden feelings; even his body changes, and he finds that he is a stranger to himself. Small wonder that in the face of such internal and external revolution he should seem to side with anarchy, and indulge in turbulent, violent behavior that is unpredictable, contradictory, and often self-defeating.

Can we discern a pattern in this melee, a thread of sense or meaning in this nonsense? Can we relate the adolescent's behavioral disarray to the relative balance of his recent childhood years or to the relative stability that we hope will characterize his adult life? As we shall see, a tentative yes can be answered to both questions, but to understand adolescence as a normal maturational step we shall have to go back, in time, to describe psychic structure and functioning in childhood.

### EARLIER STAGES OF SEXUAL DEVELOPMENT

Because sex plays so prominent a role in adolescence, we are especially curious about its forerunners in childhood. But a look at the immediate preadolescent years will be disappointing, for they provide few overt signs of sexuality. Instead, we see that sexuality has taken a subordinate position and has more or less lain dormant during the latter half of childhood, and thus we understand why Freud called this the period of latency. To find the forerunners of adolescent sexuality we must delve still deeper, to the period of infantile sexuality. It is only here that the palimpsest which is the mind will reveal the traces that we seek. At the layer of the Oedipal period, we uncover ample evidence that sexuality has been struggled with before, and that the child has set precedents for himself to follow when he must struggle with it again in adolescence. Let us see, then, what these older layers of the mind tell us, and, just as the adolescent does when he must once more meet his sexuality head-on, let us recapitulate briefly the history of the mind's development.

*Origin of sexual energy.* We can begin very simply with an operational definition of mental ontogeny—the result of the inborn needs or instincts or drives (or, if you will, species-specific, inborn, sensorimotor patterns) adapting to environmental demands. Our next step should be to identify the human drives and trace their vicissitudes.

Time will not permit any adequate consideration of the weighty arguments for or against Freud's hypothesis that there are only two drives in man—Eros and Thanatos. If for no more than heuristic reasons we shall, at least for the moment, accept this view and proceed with our sketch of mental development. The impetus or force of the drives is no doubt determined by the subject's genetic endowment, and their source probably lies in the physiological functioning of the organism. We can do nothing, then, to control their appearance; at a practical level, we can only work with the aim and the object of the drive, that is, with the ways in which it manifests itself and the direction it takes in seeking discharge.

I think it worthwhile to emphasize this point, for our concept of the mind as a dynamic unit whose energy arises from the very fact of life itself has far-reaching consequences. In the area of sex and the teenager, for instance, it means that, whether desirable or not, sexual energy is present and is no more removable or banishable than the biological energy that makes the hair grow or the heart beat. Yet in psychiatric practice it is alarming how many otherwise intelligent adolescents interpret the statement: "Man is a rational animal," to mean that intellectual control not only can, but must, remove him from his biological being. For such youngsters, all feelings and emotions must be excluded, for the rational man does not feel; total abolition of all drives seems to be their goal, but the quest is doomed to failure.

*Human drives.* To return, now, to the drives themselves. The drive Eros, which is sometimes referred to as the sexual drive and whose energy has been given the name libido, has as its aim the preservation of the object, while Thanatos, the destructive or aggressive drive, has as its aim the total destruction of the object. The drives are present from the very beginning of life and at first are amorphous energy potentials in the undifferentiated psyche. Since there are no object relationships at birth, these energies are, perforce, directed to the infant himself. This is the period of autoeroticism, when no distinction is made between the self and the non-self, when little if any heed is paid to the external environment. The chief danger at this time, since all energies are invested in the self, is that the destructive energy will outweigh libido. To escape this threat, aggression must be directed away from the self; this will restore balance, at least, and at best it will tip the scales in favor of life-preservative libido. Such external deflection of aggression is accomplished by means of a new psychic structure called the ego, our name for that part of the mental apparatus that mediates between the self and the outside world. The drive energies ascend from the tenebrous recesses of the mind—the portion we call the id—and must pass through the ego before they can be deflected from the self.

*Development of the ego.* The ego is, in a way, the sense organ of the mind. Increasing neurophysiological maturation allows the ego to perceive that things go on outside the self. It begins to see, and hear, and feel the environment, and it begins also to develop awareness that things are happening within the self—the stomach is empty and it senses a discomfort we call hunger, the bowels and bladder are full and a sense of urgency is perceived. Slowly the ego begins to see a self apart from all else in its as yet tiny world, and this step in maturation marks the beginning of narcissism. What is pleasant and pleasurable—contentment, satiety, warmth—is considered self; whatever is unpleasant and distressing is considered non-self or non-ego. With this delineation arises the possibility of deflection of destructive energies away from the self. The representation of what is perceived as unpleasant is energized (cathected) with destructive energy (such as the desire, if we could speak of it as such in so young an organism, to do away with the bad, frustrating object), while the pleasant is cathected with libido and becomes the good object.

Increasing experience with frustrating and also gratifying reality, and continuing neurophysiological development, allow the ego to broaden its scope of operations. Not for long does it remain little more than a passive way-station between id tensions and environmental conditions, for it becomes ever more active until finally it achieves some degree of mastery and control. While in the beginning ego and id were as one seeking immediate outlet for the slightest drive tension, the ego gradually schools itself to tolerate more and more discomfort, at least temporarily. It learns that external reality can exert pressure that is just as uncomfortable as the demands of the id; it begins to test the environment to see what is allowed, and it begins to apply the brake of temporization to the energies of the drives. "Not now, but later" it comes to say when it finds that temporary control of impulses can often bring more complete satisfaction eventually. Even though its ultimate aim coincides with the id's plea for discharge of drive tension, the ego's obedience to reality demands and prohibitions puts it in opposition to the id. This tug of war between ego and impulse is the essence of neurotic conflict, the most common concomitant of which is a particularly unpleasant emotion we term anxiety. The capacity to develop anxiety, like the drives themselves, is biologically determined, and this capacity is perhaps the most powerful weapon the ego has at its disposal. Anxiety appears as a warning signal to the ego that an id demand is not realizable, and that discharge of the drive would be dangerous. For reasons too complex to detail here, the sounding of this danger signal provides the ego with reinforcements in its attempts to check or inhibit the dangerous id impulses. The ego's ways of holding the id at bay we term defense mechanisms, which we shall pay particular attention to when we consider how sexuality is handled by the teenager.

*Oral phase of development.* Now that we have seen how the developing ego comes to control the drives, let us follow their development through the various stages in human growth. Probably for biological reasons, the main energies of the infant are concentrated first in the mouth area—feeding is his most important function and reality demands little else of him. We may accept mounting evidence from ethology and believe that the sexual drive as we recognize it in the adult is not a unitary biological force pressing inexorably for discharge but represents, rather, a progressive synthesis of inborn sensorimotor patterns which reach their final integration as a result, at least in part, of learning during the course of maturation (Kaufman, 1960). According to this view, we would then say that orality represents one of the steps in learning, and at this stage in ontogenetic development stress and distress stem primarily from the complex physiological processes that produce hunger. Gratification is then seen to be a result of stimulation of the mouth area, and oral stimulation is what the infant seeks because of the pleasure it provides.

It is important to remember that even though maturation will propel the infant into other stages of development, no stage is completely disposed of or eliminated. Rather, the frustrations and gratifications of every developmental level foster specific ways of handling reality that are carried over into later life as character traits. Gratification at the oral stage, for instance, generally is associated with such adolescent and adult-life traits as optimism ("I have been adequately fed in the past so I have full confidence that this will continue in the future"), generosity ("I have been given enough and can afford to share"), and sociability (which represents generosity with one's social self). Frustration in the oral period, on the other hand, may produce contrary traits—greed ("As in childhood, I seek constantly the stimulation and food that were denied me"), an extractive and manipulative parasitism ("You, society, must make up for what was denied me"), envy ("Everyone should be denied, as I was"), niggardliness ("I dare not part with what little I have"), and frequently such recognizably oral habits as aggressive and obstinate talking, over-eating, smoking, alcoholism or drug addiction.

*Anal phase of development.* Whatever the later holdovers of orality may be, the next step in development is the anal phase. We Americans are a bathroom-conscious people, and as soon as his physical maturation allows it, the child is "trained." That this is an important stage there can be no doubt (even though it has perhaps been overemphasized in psychoanalytic writings). For this is the time, at least in our culture, when the child is first presented with specific prohibitions and demands, and his reaction to these may forever color his attitudes to and relationships with authority. Of equal significance is the step forward in object relations—largely in response to the value mother so clearly gives to the child's excreta. He passes, at this time, from autoeroticism through narcissism into a stage of object love. There are objects *outside* the self than can be good, and the child comes to learn the meaning of possessions, of something of his own that he can dispense freely or adamantly withhold. In general, two kinds of reaction are possible at this stage—a reaction of defiance to the demands of mother, or a reaction of compliance in order to win her praise and keep her love. Later we see evidence of these extremes in such character traits as ill-tempered obstinacy, miserliness, all sorts of collecting manias, or general messiness and untidiness; and, on the other side, meticulous attention to order and personal hygiene, pedantic overinsistence on logic and formality (such as the specialist in trifles, or the author who has been described as a footnote fetishist), and an obsession with time and schedules.

*Phallic phase of development.* It is in the next stage—the phallic period—that we find the libidinal and aggressive energies concentrated mainly in the genital area. This is due in part to increasing physical maturation, but also to the child's increasing awareness of and natural curiosity about the difference between the sexes. Manipulation of the genitalia has certainly been seen before, but masturbation now is characteristically accompanied by phantasies which relate to the use of the penis as an executive of libido and/or aggression. Object love in the phallic period is very close to what it will be in adolescence and adulthood, but there are two factors that decisively limit sexuality to a still infantile level. One is physiologic immaturity, and maturation here will have to wait until adolescence; the other is the danger attendant upon the choice of the love object. The child is restricted in his social contacts, and the mother who has been more or less the only other actor on his stage retains her leading role. She will be the object of his psychic energies here, just as she was in earlier days; this is the relationship we term Oedipal. The dangers of this relationship—rejection by mother, retaliation by father, and the rest—necessitate a strong blockade against libidinal impulses. The ego achieves this by mobilizing aggressive energies against the id. In effect, then, libidinal energies are repressed (we have already referred to this result as the latency period), and aggressive energies are redirected into elaborating a more effective web of defenses, including the superego, and into increasing mastery in the social sphere, in socially condoned and desirable competitiveness, conquest, and domination.

*Summary of early sexual development.* What has happened, in other words, is that development has occurred in spurts. In the infantile years, libidinal forces are more in evidence as they are deployed in various areas in accordance with physiologic growth. With the appearance of the Oedipus, these forces must be held in check and the aggressive forces of the ego acquire greater prominence. They are used as front line combatants to prepare the way for later reappearance of libidinal energies. We are now in a position to survey the problems of adolescence from the point of view of psychic dynamics, to see what happens to these two more or less separated forces.

### ADOLESCENT SEXUALITY

The chief task of adolescence is to effect a stable integration or fusion of the two drives, and then to direct them into acceptable channels—which in our culture means outside the family and onto an object of the opposite sex. Following the guide lines of a more mature ego, now bolstered by the work of the latency years in developing defenses (not the least of which is the superego), the adolescent is able to allow libidinal impulses to reassert themselves. The sexual development of early childhood is recapitulated in condensed form, and the Oedipus complex is reactivated.

The biological intensification of sexual impulses at the time of puberty presents a new challenge to the ego, which must adapt itself to and somehow come to accept sexuality. The task of adaptation is complicated by several factors: (1) the intensified impulses have no satisfactory outlet as yet, since genital primacy is not established; (2) because the impulses are similar to those of the Oedipal period, the conflicts of that stage are reactivated; (3) fear of the new forms of the drive encourage regression to older, more familiar forms of infantile sexuality; (4) during latency, the ego and superego developed attitudes antagonistic to sexuality and thus productive of more guilt and anxiety than was present in childhood (Fenichel, 1945); (5) not only are the id impulses dangerous and anxiety-provoking, but the very existence of love objects constitutes a danger (Freud, 1958).

The adolescent, then, is a house divided against itself, with conflicts between the newly strengthened drive and the ego defenses against its manifestations. Because of cultural conditioning, the child came to recognize his sexual impulses as dangerous; at puberty, he returns to just that point in his sexual development where he had abandoned it earlier, and the fears and guilt connected with the Oedipus complex reappear in the form of hostility to his own urges, and a generalized asceticism whose point seems to be not only the suppression of sexuality but of everything pleasant as well.

The conflicts for a time center consciously about autoeroticism. Sooner or later, the increased sexual drive of puberty finds expression in masturbatory activity, about which we shall have more to say in a later paper. Then appear certain features of later infantile stages. In the oral area, for instance, the adolescent becomes argumentative or complaining; he goes through food fads and at other times eats barely enough to keep a bird alive. He becomes rude and almost intolerable in conversation. He starts to smoke and may develop the habit of grinding his teeth. Certain holdovers from the anal stage appear next. The nice, gentle lad of ten changes into the rough, untidy boy of thirteen; he is extravagant, obstinate, with a tendency to procrastination and a passion for collecting. And finally, elements of the phallic phase are seen in the characteristics of bumptiousness, conceit, overweening cocksureness, or as the reverse, as self-depreciation, uncertainty, and lack of confidence.

This passes gradually into the homosexual phase, about which we shall reserve comment for the panel on Special Problems in Sexual Adjustment. But we might note that some overt sexuality is allowed to creep in at this period, and finally, at about sixteen or seventeen, the adolescent desexualizes his relationship with all but one person of the opposite sex and the stage of heterosexuality is reached (Josselyn, 1959). By this age, the social and cultural taboos have relaxed to permit freer expression of attraction to members of the opposite sex, and courtship is culturally approved.

The normal adolescent should have the strength to weather the storms of this period of sexual development, and most adolescents do, in fact, battle their way through. Some, however, force themselves on the attention of others by their oppositional, defiant behavior, while others withdraw or otherwise show signs of emotional disturbance. The chief danger signals of this period include preoccupation with physical development, anxiety over the sexual role the adolescent feels he must adopt, hostility, excessive shyness, antisocial behavior, sudden or gradual loss of interest in the environment, excessive feelings of inadequacy, and excessive feelings of guilt and failure in school.

## UNHEALTHY ADOLESCENT DEFENSES AGAINST SEXUALITY

We can now look more closely at some of the defenses we find in adolescents, and at the way in which these danger signals come into being. Just as optimal results of adolescent upheavals will depend upon the adequacy of defenses marshalled against id impulses, so will adolescent (and later) pathology be an expression of inadequate or inappropriate use of these defenses.

The first defense I should like to mention is displacement of libido. The adolescent may avoid the danger of infantile object ties by transferring libidinal energies to parent substitutes. While this may seem at first glance a most workable defense, its danger lies in the type of substitute chosen, and particularly so in a culture such as ours which affords no heroic figures as substitutes. To escape the dangers of his infantile object choice, the adolescent must choose a new object who is the diametric opposite of the old one. Such oppositeness may reside in sociocultural characteristics—as with the boy who falls in love with a girl of different race, creed, education, or social background. It may be determined by ethical or moral standards—joining a delinquent gang or becoming a deviate overachiever with underachievement in acceptable areas (Gardner, 1959). It may be determined by age, leading to a pressing for acceptance by a peer group or peer leader. Or it may hinge upon physical sexuality, and a homosexual object choice will be made (Josselyn, 1959). Whatever the object choice, once it is made the adolescent may physically remove himself from his family or, more commonly, he will remain in the home a detached, inconsiderate, non-paying guest.

Displacement may also be directed against the libidinal impulses, which lose their more patently sexual characteristics and appear instead as substitute activities—"hot-rodding," stealing and other anti-social acts, intellectual preoccupations and pseudophilosophizing, and any number of mannerisms and stereotypes (and this in part explains the seeming need of adolescents to develop a language of their own, whose vocabulary to the uninitiated seems repetitive, sterile, and inappropriate). We can also include here many of the fetishes, which fairly obviously represent a displacement of interest from genital to non-genital areas.

A second major defense is reversal of affect, or reaction-formation. This is a way of escaping the dangers of Oedipal attachments by changing the associated emotions into their opposites: love into hate, dependency into an intolerable hubris that is often expressed in an almost compulsive flaunting of all codes and laws. This is a less workable defense than displacement, for the unleashed aggressivity in time becomes as threatening to the ego as the libidinal impulses had been originally, and the churlish defiance brings punishment from without as well. So the hostility itself must be checked, and if projection is used the parents are transformed into persecutors. The adolescent who uses this defense may go so far as to develop paranoid delusions. Another way of defending against hostility is to turn it inward, upon the self. This leads to spells of intense depression and guilt, often expressed in self-pejorative thoughts, loss of interest in the environment, accident-proneness (another factor in "hot-rodding"), or even attempts at suicide. A third way of handling dangerous aggression is to deny that any feelings at all are present—the "ascetic" or "uncompromising" types described by Anna Freud. Such denial may be extended

> . . . even to the fulfillment of the physiological needs for food, sleep, and body comfort. (This defense) . . . leaves no room for the finer distinctions between vital or merely pleasant satisfactions, the healthy or the morbid, the morally permitted or forbidden pleasures. Total war is waged against the pursuit of pleasure as such. Accordingly, most of the normal processes of instinct and need satisfaction are interfered with and become paralyzed (Freud, 1958, p. 274).

One expression of such asceticism with which you are familiar is scrupulosity, about which we shall hear more from Father Riffel.

A third, and still more pathological, defense is withdrawal of libido to the self. When the withdrawn libido invests the ego and superego, megalomaniacal trends appear—the adolescent phantasies himself omnipotent, at the very least an expert in some field of endeavor and, at the other extreme, he develops grandiose delusions with Messianic overtones. If the withdrawn libido instead becomes attached to the body organs, hypochondriacal preoccupation and feelings of body change will appear. This augurs ill and may be the first sign of impending schizophrenic decompensation.

We could certainly detail many more defenses, but these are perhaps enough to indicate the inner turmoil that rages in the adolescent. Since none of his defenses is fully adequate to deal with the anxieties produced by his impulses, he must shift from one to the other and his behavior shifts accordingly. At one point he may appear neurotically inhibited, at another he seems schizophrenic, at still another he shows bursts of creativity, or delinquency, or perversion. But this is the quiddity of adolescence, and the teenager who upholds a steady equilibrium is abnormal.

> While an adolescent remains inconsistent and unpredictable in his behavior, he may suffer, but he does not seem to me to be in need of treatment. I think that he should be given time and scope to work out his own solution. Rather, it may be his parents who need help and guidance so as to be able to bear with him (Freud, 1958, p. 276).

## REFERENCES

Fenichel, O. *The psychoanalytic theory of neurosis*. New York: Norton, 1945.

Freud, Anna. Adolescence. In Ruth Eissler *et al.* (Eds.) *The psychoanalytic study of the child*. New York: International Universities, 1958, *13*, 255-278.

Gardner, G. E. Psychiatric problems of adolescence. In S. Arieti (Ed.). *American handbook of psychiatry*. New York: Basic Books, 1959. Pp. 870-892.

Josselyn, Irene M. The psychoanalytic psychology of the adolescent. In M. Levitt (Ed.). *Readings in psychoanalytic psychology*. New York: Appleton-Century-Crofts, 1959. Pp. 70-83.

Kaufman, I. C. Some theoretical implications from animal behavior studies for the psycho-analytic concepts of instinct, energy, and drive. *Int. J. Psychoanal.*, 1960, *41*, 318-326.

# Sex and Scrupulosity

## PIUS A. RIFFEL, S.J.

*Father Pius A. Riffel, S.J., received his A.B. degree from Loyola College, Montreal, and did graduate study at Fordham University. He is currently a doctoral candidate in clinical psychology. He has made a special study of scrupulosity, his master's dissertation being on the topic: "Scrupulosity as Related to Age and Sex," one of the few empirical studies on this subject. For the academic year 1959-1960, Fr. Riffel served as a staff psychologist at the St. Charles Guidance Clinic in Brooklyn, and during this time he collaborated with a psychiatrist on the clinic staff, Dr. Wayne M. Weisner, on a paper which appeared in the* American Journal of Psychiatry *for October, 1960, under the title: "Scrupulosity: Religion and Obsessive-Compulsive Behavior in Children." Fr. Riffel is continuing his work on scrupulosity in his research for his doctoral degree, which is on the topic: "Personality Characteristics of the Pastorally Scrupulous."*

The term scrupolosity is well known to those devoted to pastoral work. It has both theological and psychological aspects. It may be taken to mean an unhealthy and morbid kind of meticulousness which hampers a person's religious adjustment. Early spiritual writers looked upon continuous scrupulosity as a malady of the soul. The present attitude stresses rather the fact that scrupulosity means fear and insecurity which tend to make an individual see evil where there is no evil, serious sin where there is no serious sin, and obligation where there is no obligation. Thus, scrupulosity is not seen as due to lack of knowledge but to emotional factors (Hagmaier and Gleason, 1959). There is evidence of a disturbance of judgment in that the scrupulous person considers something as important which in reality is trifling and negligible. This results in unending consultations with many priests, a state of endless doubt and involvement with trivialities. All of these together constitute in varying degrees a scrupulous state.

### SCRUPULOSITY FROM THE PSYCHOLOGICAL POINT OF VIEW

Among the first to classify the scrupulous person from a psychological point of view was Janet (1908). He viewed scrupulosity as a manifestation of psychasthenia in that it was a particular form of this disorder with moral implications and religious background. Eymieu (1933) pretty well followed Janet's theory. Briefly, in this theory, a lowering of psychic energy renders an individual incapable of forming judgments with certitude in the moral and religious area and the individual falls prey to the pathological doubts, phobias and obsessions which characterize scrupulosity.

Differing from Janet, the psychoanalytic interpretation explains scrupulosity as the result of deep unconscious conflicts (Odier, 1948; Mahoney, 1957; Mora, 1957). In his unconscious, the scrupulous person is in conflict and cannot satisfy his pathologically high ideals. Anxiety breaks through to disturb his equilibrium and the scrupulous person then channels his anxiety into obsessive preoccupation with possible sin, past, present and future. Thus the healthy drives and inhibitions become exaggerated and the normal desire for holiness and sinlessness becomes a pathological self-destructive avoidance of sin. The ego of the scrupulous person is caught between the contradictory forces of the id and the superego (Fenichel, 1945). He has the ambivalence associated with regression to an earlier stage of personality organization and uses the defense mechanisms of reaction formation, isolation and undoing, which are characteristic of obsessive-compulsive behavior (S. Freud, 1926; A. Freud, 1946; Odier, 1948; Mahoney, 1957; Mora, 1957; Weisner and Riffel, 1960).

In the psychoanalytic interpretation, then, scrupulosity is explained by postulating that an over-rigorous, excessively demanding superego, which was formed in childhood through the introjection of the parents' attitudes, has taken over or is blocking the functioning of the moral conscience (an ego function) of the scrupulous person. Consequently, even if the intellect of the scrupulous person possesses the theoretical knowledge, it is prevented from forming a practical judgment on the goodness or sinfulness of an act. In the scrupulous person, the infantile, irrational, unconscious superego rather than functioning harmoniously with the conscious, rational conscience, is functioning as an independent system and dominating the individual's activity.

This interpretation attempts to make a distinction between the superego and the moral conscience as understood in the traditional Christian sense. It suggests that man possesses a double register of morality; that is, the moral imperatives of an individual are derived from two sources: one unconscious, the superego; and the other conscious, the ego. These two levels of morality easily intermingle so that it is difficult at times to distinguish between the genuine morality of the moral conscience and the pseudo-morality of the superego (Weigel, 1955; Mahoney, 1957). The scrupulous person is said to be more under the influence of the superego than the non-scrupulous person.

Two kinds of guilt are said to be experienced in relation to conscience and superego (Odier, 1948; Zilboorg, 1955; Mahoney, 1957; Mora, 1957). First, there is the conscious sense of guilt related to the conscience with the acknowledgment of having done something wrong, with accompanying regret, anxiety, confession, penance, restitution and finally the relief of anxiety. Second, there is the unconscious sense of guilt, related to the superego, which is more an unconscious need for expiation and self-punishment. It is postulated that this need for punishment is developed as a result of the accumulation of excessively hostile feelings in the building up of the superego. Through an unconscious sense of guilt, the individual is punishing himself. Thus, there is a continued need to confess, to do penance, but following this, there is no relief, only repetition of the process. This is the guilt predominant in the scrupulous person.

From the above, it may be seen that the scruple is a *product of anxiety*. The scruple does not cause the anxiety, but rather the anxiety brings on the scruple.

## DEGREE OF SCRUPULOSITY

The degree of scrupulosity is all important when it comes to determining the pathology of the scrupulous person (Doyle, 1955; Weisner and Riffel, 1960). Anyone trying to lead a sound moral life will have fleeting reactions of concern for sinfulness bordering on near excess. All suffer on occasion from anxiety, depression, frustration, daydreams and scrupulous thoughts. Scruples are not unique. But scruples do become a major problem when the concern over committing sin becomes the main concern of the day and disrupts the healthy flow of emotions.

Many adolescents undergo a mild and transitory form of scrupulosity which is not necessarily indicative of any severe pathology but rather indicative of a still immature and developing conscience. This is particularly true of earlier adolescence.

Though accurate figures on the extent of scrupulosity among Catholic adolescent students are hard to obtain, the data of several reports are available. Mullen (1927) reported in a study of 400 Catholic high school girls that 26 percent of them admitted to habitual scrupulosity. A Fordham study (Riffel, 1958) corroborated this earlier report of Mullen. This study was based on 490 students divided between sophomore high school and sophomore college years. In this study, the students were asked to rate themselves with reference to a definition of scrupulosity. They placed themselves into three categories in relation to scrupulosity: (1) currently scrupulous; (2) formerly scrupulous but not now; (3) never scrupulous. Of the high school students, 26 percent admitted to current scrupulosity, but in college this number had declined to 14 percent. It is generally believed that women are more frequently scrupulous than men. The Fordham study (Riffel, 1958) does not support this impression. Boys and girls were included in the sample and the percentage of boys admitting to scrupulosity was almost precisely the same as that for girls. In fact, the findings of the Fordham study would suggest that scrupulosity is more significantly related to age than to sex. A further indication of the prevalence of scrupulosity is the report of Doyle (1955) that 30 percent of the students who came for counselling help to the Fordham Psychological Services Unit were diagnosed as being troubled with some form of scrupulosity. True enough, students seeking counselling help in college are a select group and are not representative of the general college population, but the combined data emphasize the prevalence of scrupulosity among adolescents as a common pastoral problem.

## TRANSITORY SCRUPULOSITY

Adolescent scrupulosity is often referred to as "short lived," "passing," and "clearing without any specific therapy." The above-mentioned Fordham study (Riffel, 1958) attempted to obtain further clarification on the duration of adolescent scrupulosity. Twenty-five percent of the formerly-scrupulous high school boys estimated the duration of their past scrupulosity as having been a year or less, and 60 percent estimated their past scrupulosity as having been from two to three years in duration. Among the formerly-scrupulous high school girls, 55 percent reported their scrupulosity as lasting a year or less and 36 percent estimated it to have lasted from two to three years. Of the formerly-scrupulous college boys, 18 percent were scrupulous a year or less, while 51 percent had been scrupulous between two and three years. Fourteen percent of the formerly-scrupulous college girls reported being scrupulous a year or less and 63 percent were scrupulous from two to four years.

In summary, it may be said that the duration of transitory scrupulosity in adolescence is relatively long; one-, two- or three-year duration not being unusual.

The Fordham study also obtained data on the age of onset of scrupulosity. In general, it may be said that it confirmed the generalization of Mullen's (1927) study that the age of onset of scrupulosity is scattered across the developmental period from early childhood to late adolescence with a peak at puberty for both boys and girls. In the Fordham study (Riffel, 1958), 31 percent of the sophomore high school boys and 35 percent of the sophomore high school girls who were scrupulous said they became scrupulous between the ages of six and ten, that is, prior to puberty; 58 percent of the sophomore high school boys and 52 percent of the sophomore high school girls placed the onset of their scrupulosity between the ages of 11 and 13, i.e., at puberty; and only 10 percent of the sophomore high school boys and 12 percent of the sophomore high school girls placed the onset of their scrupulosity between the ages of 14 and 15.

The Fordham study also indicated that half of the currently-scrupulous college boys had not yet overcome the scrupulosity that began at puberty. This fact is even more strikingly evident in the case of the currently-scrupulous college girls, *none* of whom have been scrupulous less than six years. The college students currently scrupulous for more than eight years (approximately 25 percent of the group), have been scrupulous since childhood, i.e., before puberty. The data on the currently-scrupulous college students, both boys and girls, clearly demonstrate the relationship between the onset of scrupulosity either in early childhood or at puberty and its persistence into the college years.

It is frequently thought that the scrupulosity of the adolescent is due to a lack of sufficient knowledge of the moral principles involved in making a moral judgment. The Fordham study indicates that this is not so. The students who were scrupulous and those who were not scored the same on a religious knowledge test, but the students who were scrupulous scored significantly higher on a test designed to measure scrupulosity.

The students taking part in the Fordham study were asked to give the reason why they felt that they were scrupulous. The results are shown in Table 1. They indicate the basic difficulty of making satisfying and firm decisions in the moral area. This difficulty was not due to lack of knowledge.

## TABLE 1

### STUDENTS' REASONS FOR SCRUPULOSITY

| Reasons | Percent |
|---|---|
| Inability to decide between mortal and venial sin | 27 |
| Constant fear of doing wrong in everything | 24 |
| Present and/or past difficulties in deciding what is a sin in matters pertaining to sex | 20 |
| Feeling that every offense is a mortal sin | 15 |
| Worry about past and/or present confessions | 5 |
| Feeling that venial sins must be confessed as mortal sins to be sure | 4 |
| Doubts arising from an inability to decide between temptation and sin | 3 |
| Doubts about faith | 2 |

The Fordham study also asked the formerly-scrupulous students why they felt they were no longer scrupulous. The results are shown in Table 2. It may be noted that the spontaneous remission of scrupulosity is generally accompanied by the ability to make satisfying and firm decisions in the moral area.

TABLE 2

STUDENTS' REASONS FOR RECOVERY FROM SCRUPULOSITY

| Reasons | Percent |
|---|---|
| Better understanding of the conditions for mortal and venial sin | 27 |
| Increased confidence gained in deciding between mortal and venial sin | 26 |
| Religious counsel from priests | 13 |
| Courses in religion at school | 11 |
| Just grew out of it | 7 |
| No longer fear sex | 5 |
| Help received from teachers | 4 |
| Better understanding of God | 3 |
| Help of a retreat | 3 |
| Reading religious articles | 1 |

From the data obtained on the transitory scrupulosity of the adolescent, it may be said that this type of scrupulosity in adolescence is a sign of an immature conscience and decreases as the conscience matures. The development of a mature conscience may be considered as consisting in widening the domain of conscience at the expense of the superego. A person with a mature conscience is one in whom only unimportant actions may continue under the guidance of the superego.

### SEVERE SCRUPULOSITY

It must, however, be pointed out that severe scrupulosity among children and adolescents can be an indication of pathology. A study (Weisner and Riffel, 1960) was made of 23 children who had been referred to the St. Charles Child Guidance Clinic in Brooklyn over the past ten years because of continuous and chronic scrupulosity. The group consisted of 12 boys and 11 girls between the ages of 10 and 17, the mean age being 12 years and 9 months. Fourteen of these children were referred by priests and six by doctors. Thirteen of them were referred specifically for scrupulosity. Typical initial referrals were: "A bad dose of scrupulosity"; "Scruples—most acute anxiety"; "Abnormally scrupulous"; "Compulsive thoughts of killing mother and beginning of scruples"; "Overly religious"; "Very disturbed—concerned about right and wrong."

These children were from families who were intact and practicing their religion. For the most part, they were of better than average intelligence with IQ's ranging from 100 to 135 with only five of them below 110. Scholastically, they functioned well, school averages being in the 90's. Furthermore, they were considered exemplary students, generally receiving A for conduct. Three were only children. Typical school reports were: "Tops in class"; "Fine scholastic record, energetic, splendid altar boy."

On initial referral, the mothers of these children were frequently very upset. Because of their own anxieties, the mothers tended to minimize the symptoms and emphasize the predominantly religious aspect, namely, the scrupulosity which they tended to view in a privileged way. This made it difficult for the mothers to look upon their children as suffering from an emotional disturbance and consequently follow through on treatment.

On arrival at the clinic, the children showed their scrupulosity in many different ways. Accompanying complaints included problems about food ("finicky eaters," "food having lost its appeal," "permission required to eat,") or thumb sucking and hand chewing. There was also concern about breathing ("breathing is a sin," or "breathing is stealing air that belongs to others"). Coughing and spitting were likewise sinful because someone might in this way contract germs and die. Another group of symptoms involved obsessive-compulsive tics and rituals such as hand washing, touching the walls or stepping on cracks, the latter being regarded as a mortal sin. Difficulties in handling possessions also appeared; moving and kicking furniture was sinful as property was destroyed. There were also fears of injuring, brushing against, or killing someone.

The sexual area particularly presented many problems for these children. There was much concern with impure thoughts and with mixed parties at which kissing games were played. There also seemed to be over-concern about bodily functions, and there were many problems relative to touching one's body. In some girls, menstruation was equated with sinfulness. One girl felt compelled to take her bath with the light out. Television and other pictures, because of their sexual implications, also were of great concern to some of these children. There was over-concern about modesty and dress in the case of girls for fear that they might be sexually seductive to others.

One girl was concerned lest her parochial school uniform might be too sheer.

In general, these children were looked upon as very good children and more religious than average. Their scrupulosity showed itself in specifically religious behavior in various ways. There were many indecisions about right and wrong and fear of wrong in everything. They were continually consulting the priest and re-examining their consciences frequently throughout the day. The problem about Confession showed itself in various ways and was frequently quite dramatic. They felt that past sins were either not properly confessed or were not properly understocd by the priest. They were afraid they had omitted something and there were endless ruminations and repetitions of the same sin and of all the trivial circumstances surrounding their actions with inability to arrive at a satisfactory decision. Many found it difficult to go to Communion because of their inability to resolve their doubts about sin on their souls.

The precipitating event which triggered an acute phase of scrupulosity was generally an intense situation emotionally linked with their conflict. In the cases making up our study, we found the following kinds of precipitating factors:

    A. The introduction of sexual material as, for example, the first mixed party or kissing game; learning about the processes of birth from a friend; seeing dirty words on a lavatory wall.

    B. Special religious events, such as the beginning of Lent or the making of one's Easter Duty.

    C. A traumatic event such as a sudden separation from the mother or mother substitute; physical injury; hearing a story about someone being possessed by the devil.

The personality picture of these children as presented by the mothers appeared as follows. The children were usually seen as perfectionistic, overly clean, always prim and fussy, and extremely neat. They were also studious and too thorough, spending much time on their homework with a need to excel (which in fact they did). One youngster was described in the following terms: "Prays, works and studies intensely for long periods of time." Others were described as being "too good," "always a good child," and "requires little correction." These children were described as shy, over-sensitive, serious, and nervous with a tendency to worry and depression. Socially, there was poor adjustment. They seldom had close friends and thus appeared withdrawn, seclusive and lonely. The mothers felt that their children were over-attached, needed their approval for being good and made them their chief confidants. However, remarks from the mother on sex and sin were disturbing to the children. In brief, there was a very close mother-child relationship which characteristically developed into overprotection on the part of the mother and overdependence on the part of the child.

Psychological testing indicated much immaturity and dependency. The scrupulous children appeared introverted, fearful, sensitive, anxious, critical and perfectionistic. They were frequently guarded, evasive, and cautious. There was lack of spontaneity, a preponderance of obsessive-compulsive traits and constriction or rigidity of function. Ambivalence and the seeking of inner controls was in evidence with chronic doubt, sexual conflict, guilt and poor self-identity.

Seven boys and four girls received treatment at the clinic. The approach to therapy depended in part on the diagnosis: some had been diagnosed as having an underlying schizophrenic personality structure or as functioning on a pre-psychotic level. Although scrupulosity was their most prominent (and frequently most dramatic) symptom, the scrupulosity itself seldom became an issue and treatment stayed on the supportive level. Consequently defenses were seldom attacked. Much of the progress in therapy appeared due to the relationship established.

In the pre-psychotic child with an underlying schizophrenic personality tendency, our goal was to ward off an acute psychotic break and to maintain functioning at the level where attendance at school and living in the community could be continued. There was little interpretation other than to clarify reality and help the child to see the emotional problem. Initial psychotic episodes, if any, were short-lived and quickly walled off. At the beginning of treatment, it was frequently advisable to use Thorazine, Compazine, and Miltown to tide the children over their acute anxiety or disturbed ego-organization; in the less disturbed children Librium was used.

In the more obsessive-compulsive neurotic child, treatment was less dramatic and the symptomatology alternated between periods of mild remission and exacerbation with diminishing intensity. To assure treatment, it was equally important to have the parents recognize that their child was undergoing a primarily emotional disturbance which required professional help. The parents were aided in handling the more open aggression of their children as the treatment progressed and were instructed to view this as an encouraging sign. With the cessation of the more obvious scrupulous behavior, the parents frequently wished to terminate treatment at once. This was not surprising since they had difficulty in accepting treatment for the child's scrupulosity in the first place. The emotional flexibility and spontaneity of the child which resulted from treatment were an important aid to more positive, comfortable and constructive adjustment in the religious life. Follow-up studies indicate that many of these children were able to maintain this newly acquired adjustment throughout high school and college.

SUMMARY AND RECOMMENDATIONS

This paper presented the psychological aspects of adolescent scrupulosity. The psychoanalytic interpretation explains scrupulosity by postulating that an over-rigorous, excessively demanding superego has taken over or is blocking the functioning of the moral conscience. The guilt predominant in the scrupulous person is that experienced in relation to the superego, which is described as an unconscious need for punishment. The scruple is a product of anxiety and not the cause of anxiety.

The degree of scrupulosity is all-important in determining the pathology of the scrupulous person. It was seen that the mild and transitory form of scrupulosity of many adolescents is not necessarily indicative of pathology, but rather of an immature and still developing personality. A mature conscience develops by widening its domain at the expense of the superego.

The Fordham study (Riffel, 1958) gives further data on the incidence, duration, and age of onset of scrupulosity. It also shows that scrupulosity is not due to a lack of knowledge. Twenty-six percent of the adolescents reported current scrupulosity. The formerly-scrupulous adolescents give evidence that transitory scrupulosity lasts an average of two to three years. The age of onset of scrupulosity extends across the developmental period from early childhood to late adolescence with a peak at puberty. The students felt that their scrupulosity showed an inability to make satisfying and firm decisions in the moral area, and that this ability improved with the decrease of scrupulosity. One conclusion with reference to pastoral treatment coming from the Fordham study is that the priest who would work with the scrupulous adolescent would need to have a good understanding of the psychological development of the moral conscience.

The clinical study (Weisner and Riffel, 1960) presents a picture of severe adolescent scrupulosity as a pathological condition. Children referred to a clinic for their scrupulosity are seriously disturbed. These children present a consistent picture in terms of symptoms and basic personality traits. Their scrupulosity generally appears as an obsessive-compulsive disturbance involving fear and doubt. However, the constriction and inhibitions of these scrupulous children are frequently indicative of a schizoid personality, and, in some cases, of an underlying schizophrenic condition. Psychotherapy with these latter patients was frequently accompanied with the use of Thorazine, Compazine and Miltown. Follow-up studies indicate that a good number of these children are able to maintain their newly-acquired adjustment throughout high school and college.

Since the priest is generally the first to become aware of the scrupulous nature of the troubles experienced by the penitent, he should attempt to clarify the personality of the penitent to himself. The basic question in this respect is the following: Is the scrupulosity of the penitent an indication of an immature and still developing conscience, or is it a manifestation of obsessive-compulsive tendencies, or a symptom of a schizoid or schizophrenic personality?

Therapeutically, the role of the confessor in severe cases is clear and the decision relatively simple. They are mental cases and they should be referred to the psychiatrist. The situation is less clear in dealing with less severe cases. Even when dealing with a basically neurotic and non-psychotic type, the services of the psychiatrist can be beneficial and may also be necessary. In this connection a few factors should be mentioned. The manner in which the scrupulous person learns that his troubles need the intervention of a psychiatrist is most important. Also critical in this connection, is the attitude which the priest himself has toward the problem of scrupulosity and toward the psychiatrist and his work. This attitude is, of course, greatly influenced by the cultural environment in which both the priest and the scrupulous person live. If the priest's attitudes are negative, they can considerably hinder the scrupulous person in need of psychiatric help even when the scrupulous person is already in treatment. It should perhaps also be mentioned that even though the scrupulous person is receiving psychotherapy it does not mean that he will necessarily be *rapidly* cured of his troubles. Even after a long treatment, he may still retain his basic personality and the effect of treatment may be merely to teach him how to live with his scrupulous tendencies.

## REFERENCES

Doyle, T. L. The problem of scrupulosity in pastoral work. In A. A. Schneiders (Ed.). *Proceedings of the institute for the clergy on problems in pastoral psychology.* New York: Fordham Univer., 1955. Pp. 75-81.

Eymieu, A. *L'obsessions et le scruple* (33rd ed.). Paris: Librarie Academique, 1933.

Fenichel, O. *The psychoanalytic theory of neurosis.* New York: Norton, 1945.

Freud, Anna. *The ego and the mechanisms of defense.* New York: International Universities Press, 1946.

Freud, S. *The problem of anxiety.* New York: Norton, 1936. (First German edition, 1926).

Janet, P. *Les obsessions et la psychathanie* (2nd ed.). Paris: Alcan, 1908.

Hagmaier, G., C.S.P. and Gleason, R. W., S.J. *Counselling the Catholic.* New York: Sheed & Ward, 1959.

Mahoney, V. P. Scrupulosity from a psychoanalytic point of view. *Bull. Guild Cath. Psychiatrists,* 1957, *5,* No. 2, 12-14.

Mora, G. The psychotherapeutic treatment of scrupulous patients. *Cross Currents,* 1957, *7,* 29-40.

Mullen, J. J. Psychological factors in the pastoral treatment of scruples. *Stud. Psychol. Psychiat. Cathol. Univ. Amer.,* 1927, *1,* No. 3.

Odier, C. *Les deux sources conscientes et inconscientes de la vie moral.* Neuchatel: Editions de la Bacconiere, 1948.

Riffel, P. A., S.J. The detection of scrupulosity and its relation to age and sex. Unpublished master's dissertation. Fordham Univer., 1958

Weigel, G. A., S.J. Comment on paper of Dr. Gregory Zilboorg. In A. A. Schneiders (Ed.). *Proceedings of the institute for the clergy on problems in pastoral psychology,* New York: Fordham Univer., 1955. Pp. 25-26.

Weisner, W. M. and Riffel, P. A., S.J. Scrupulosity: religion and obsessive compulsive behavior in children. *Amer. J. Psychiat.,* 1960, *117,* 314-318.

Zilboorg, G. The sense of guilt. In A. A. Schneiders (Ed.). *Proceedings of the institute for the clergy on problems in pastoral psychology.* New York: Fordham Univer., 1955. Pp. 75-85.

# Masturbation and Homosexuality

## ROBERT J. CAMPBELL

*Robert Jean Campbell, III, M.D., is Chief of the Out-Patient Psychiatric Service of St. Vincent's Hospital; Instructor in Psychiatry, Columbia University, College of Physicians and Surgeons; and Adjunct Associate Professor, Fordham University Graduate School. Prior to assuming his post at St. Vincent's Hospital, Dr. Campbell was Senior Clinical Psychiatrist at the New York State Psychiatric Institute. After graduating from the University of Wisconsin, Dr. Campbell received his M.D. degree from Columbia University. He is a diplomate, American Board of Psychiatry and Neurology, a contributor to various medical journals, and is currently editor of Hinsie & Campbell's* Psychiatric dictionary *(1960). Dr. Campbell has been the most consistent contributor to the Fordham Pastoral Psychology Institutes, the current Institute being the third in which he has participated as a faculty member.*

We can define masturbation as direct self-manipulation of the genitals, most commonly by the hand, accompanied by phantasies that are usually of a recognizably sexual nature, and having as its aim the discharge of sexual excitation. We can also recognize "psychic" masturbation, where phantasy alone is sufficient to effect sexual discharge without any direct physical manipulation. The masturbatory act, then, has two aspects—form (the physical manipulations) and content (the nature of the accompanying or provoking phantasy).

As thus defined, masturbation first occurs in the phallic period, although we can certainly find autoerotic activity that includes the genitalia and many other areas of the body from the earliest days of life. But in the phallic period, the major portion of psychic energy is invested in the genital area, and autoerotic activity now comes to be associated with oedipal phantasies and so can be termed true masturbation. At the height of the Oedipus complex, castration and other retaliatory fears necessitate the relinquishing of sexuality as such, and the energies that earlier had been employed primarily for libidinal gratification are redirected into furthering object relationships and promoting adaptation to the external world.

*Frequency of adolescent masturbation.* But the tremendous resurgence of libidinal energy at puberty forces the adolescent to cope with sexuality once more; he returns to just that point in his sexual development where he had abandoned it earlier, and masturbation again becomes prominent.

In a previous Institute for the Clergy, I made the following statement:

> It is recognized that all children masturbate during the infantile period, most do during adolescence, and some do during the latency period. Masturbation, then, can be considered psychologically normal during childhood, and is a major avenue for the discharge of instinctual tension. Under present cultural conditions, masturbation can also be considered psychologically normal during adolescence, and to some extent even in adulthood when gratification of a physical and emotional relationship with a member of the opposite sex is not possible (Campbell, 1957a, p. 106).

Remembering the rather heated discussion which followed the 1957 symposium, I should like to take the time to repeat a footnote that I later added to the record of that symposium:

> The term "normal" as used herein is meant to refer to that which is usual, typical, and/or common as inferred from whatever empirical observations are available and without reference to whether or not what is so termed complies or conflicts with the natural or moral law. The term "normal," then, is used somewhat in a statistical sense to refer to what is found in a majority of cases, and

specifically to indicate behavior which in itself is not considered pathognomonic of severe psychiatric or emotional disorder (Campbell, 1957a, p. 106).

From such a statistical point of view, how "normal" is masturbation? The figures I am about to quote are based on Kinsey's findings (1948), but we might note that other studies in the area of sexual behavior almost universally confirm, rather than contradict, his results.

Masturbation occurs in 92 percent of American males and accounts for first ejaculation in 68 percent (the remainder experience first ejaculation with nocturnal emission or with coitus). Age of onset varies, with a peak in the years 10-12. Also variable is the frequency of masturbation; the average in adolescence is between two and three times a week, but 17 percent have frequencies of six to seven per week, and the group with the highest frequency averages 23 per week in early adolescence. In this last group, incidentally, frequency drops to 15 per week by age 20, to 6 per week by age 50, and to once every fortnight by age 60.

*Guilt associated with masturbation.* Probably the most constant concomitant of masturbation is the guilt the adolescent feels about it. His guilt, by the way, is but very little related to his training—whether his home and school have been uncommonly permissive in their attitude to sexual activity, or whether they have been more than usually prohibitive, seems to make little difference. The boy in either event feels that masturbation is wrong and at least for a time is mainly concerned with trying to give it up. When he succeeds, he feels relieved, "manly," and perhaps even too pleased with himself. But when he fails, he sinks almost to the level of despair and upbraids himself unmercifully with having caused all sorts of damage to himself—pimples, insanity, weakness, impotence, feeblemindedness—to name a few. Faced with such a guilt-ridden adolescent, we might first think that reassurance about harmful consequences might at least remove this secondary burden from his shoulders. But we should be surprised and perhaps also chagrined to find that our reassurance had little effect. For his guilt stems not from what his parents or teachers or peers might think about masturbation, but from within himself. To understand his refractory guilt, we must remind ourselves once more of his psychosexual development, and remember that adolescent masturbation, at least at first, is an expression of the same libidinal strivings that characterized the oedipal phase. His masturbatory phantasies, in other words, are derivatives of his oedipal phantasies, and they are even more dangerous now than they were then. The almost delusional conviction that masturbation is a terrible thing, and resistance to enlightenment about its harmlessness, are the chief mechanisms used by the ego to maintain control over the unconscious incest phantasies. If the adolescent were to believe that masturbation is harmless he would have to resurrect these phantasies and would have to face the desires responsible for his guilt. Instead, he keeps his guilt and diverts his energies to controlling the act of masturbation.

Rarely is he successful in this, as we know, and the few who are tend to be severely disturbed persons whose prognosis in psychotherapy is notoriously poor. More commonly he is only partially successful in his struggle and there occur periodic eruptions of masturbatory activity. He tries to enlist the aid of faith and prayer, but recurrences of the act may strain his faith to the breaking point. He will often develop a one-sided concept of the Deity as a merciless, punishing figure—and at least in part this is a derivative of fears of his own father's retaliation for incest phantasies. The danger is that, unable to conceive of God as forgiving, benevolent, and merciful, the adolescent will be left only the alternative of fleeing the field of conflict, and will run away from God as he would run away from the father. Other adolescents search for a loophole in the law and/or use rationalization to an almost pathological degree to deny responsibility for their actions. This, too, can assume dangerous proportions, for searching for loopholes can backfire into scrupulosity, and excessive use of rationalization impairs reality testing and favors a withdrawal from object relationships. Another way to escape the dangers of masturbation is to plunge prematurely into heterosexual activity; such promiscuity, while more common in girls, can be seen also in boys who feel uncertain about their sexual role.

*Substitute gratification.* The problem of masturbation is further complicated by the fact that libidinal impulses are not the only ones that find discharge in such behavior. Aggressivity, too, must be controlled, and masturbation may afford a means of regression when object relationships prove unsatisfactory. When love and affection are lacking in the adolescent's world, he may withdraw psychic energies onto himself and his body functions, and masturbation becomes a general pacifier or a substitute gratification for a non-genital need. Time does not permit a more extensive discussion of what masturbation may come to represent; I would refer those of you who are interested in this aspect to the transcript of my remarks on Habitual Masturbation in the 1957 Institute for the Clergy (Campbell 1957b).

*Illustrative cases.* We might now turn to a very brief consideration of some of the more patently pathologic reactions to masturbation, and specifically to substitute or derivative expressions of masturbatory activity. It is obvious that we can hardly cover all the possibilities, but the following two cases illustrate the sort of symptom formation that may replace the entire masturbatory process, or the associated phantasy, or the physical act alone.

*Case 1:* Repression of libidinal impulses producing amnesia.

A 32-year-old, single, tax lawyer was referred with complaints of feelings of inferiority in his work, episodes of dejection, and difficulties in concentration. These symptoms had been present for the preceding five years, but as his responsibilities and professional commitments increased, he found himself more and more limited in his work by his inability to retain memory of the voluminous research required by each case. He developed an elaborate system of note-taking and with this was able to keep his head above water for a time, but in the few months before admission he found himself "going blank" at important conferences with his clients. It would sometimes take him as long as six hours of uninterrupted study to feel that he could remember the contents of only two or three paragraphs of tax law, but even so he would forget it all in a week or two. His colleagues had begun to notice his poor performance, and he was on the verge of giving up his practice entirely when he came into treatment.

After some months of psychotherapy, it became clear that what the patient labelled concentration difficulties had begun in mid-adolescence and followed shortly upon what he described as "finally getting the upper hand over my animal self. I had had the habit of self-abuse, but when I got older I saw that my confessor was right. If I kept it up I would ruin myself mentally and physically, and if I didn't stop it he said he couldn't give me absolution. So I did stop it, but I guess not soon enough. I'm afraid the damage was already done, and I suppose that's what explains this trouble I have. I think I must have damaged my brain." It turned out, further, that in order to stop masturbation, the patient had had to avoid all possible sources of temptation. He stopped going out with girls, he withdrew from his male friends since they talked so much about sex, and his whole life other than his school work and later his profession revolved about various regimens of spiritual betterment. The therapist suggested that even though he might not give in to temptation, it seemed unlikely that he never had any thoughts about sex. He staunchly maintained that the only expression of his "baser self" was an occasional nocturnal emission, but that no dreams ever accompanied such experiences. After a few weeks more, he reported one or two dreams with fairly obvious sexual referents, but he denied that such dreams could really be expressing his wishes and claimed that since it was all a dream responsibility for the images could hardly be imputed to him. Soon thereafter he experienced a return of many fleeting sexual thoughts; probably correctly he concluded that if he gave any rein to these thoughts he might be tempted to masturbate. So at night he forced himself to get out of bed, and although it was mid-winter at the time, he took a cold shower and forced himself to spend the rest of the night on the bathroom floor as punishment for his evil thoughts.

For our purposes, this is probably as much material as we need, although the case had numerous ramifications too complicated to detail at present. From the above information, however, we can rather easily formulate the dynamics of his presenting symptoms of inability to remember. In adolescence, external reality, ego forces, and superego defenses had joined together in a massive blockade against libidinal impulses. The patient used the mechanism of repression, and forcibly, although unconsciously, cut out that portion of his mind which gave rise to sexual phantasies. Unfortunately, repression so selective as this is almost impossible to maintain; rather than admit defeat, however, his defensive forces attempted to take more and more under their control, so that by the time he appeared in a psychiatrist's office he was not only pushing sexual thoughts from his mind, but other memory presentations as well.

*Case 2:* Conversion of libidinal impulses and the defenses against them into somatic symptoms.

A 28-year-old male was referred because of inability to speak under certain conditions. He could carry on normal conversations with one or two friends, but he could not speak in public (even though this was a large part of his job). His symptoms had really begun some three years previously with the thought, "What if I should mispronounce a word in front of my audience?" The words that he had particularly worried about were such that the change of one or two letters would convert them into an obviously sexual word—luck, knock, hunt, etc.—but the patient himself denied awareness of any such associations. Subsequent sessions revealed that the patient had many conflicts over "solitary sinning," and that his symptoms had not appeared until one or two years after he felt he had this problem under control. His was a more elaborate defense than that used by the first patient, and the formation of his symptoms occurred as follows: he repressed libidinal impulses that had for a time been expressed in masturbation; having repressed them, he displaced them onto the function of speaking. He became as concerned about his voice and its functions as he had originally been about his genitals. But as libidinal pressures mounted, displacement was not enough and the impulses threatened to break through into awareness. He then was forced to immobilize his genital substitute (his voice), and the defenses that had originally been mobilized against sexuality were turned now against the use of his voice, especially in public where his "solitary sinning" could be witnessed by all.

## HOMOSEXUAL

In current usage, the phrase "overt homosexuality" is used to refer to physical, sexual contact between members of the same sex, while latent homosexuality refers to impulses and desires toward a member of the same sex which are unconscious or, if conscious, are not openly expressed. Some writers differentiate between homogenitality (genital relationships); homosexuality (sexual relationship, but not expressed genitally); and homoerotism (erotic relationship which is well sublimated). The term inversion is also used synonymously with the term homosexuality.

*Incidence of homosexuality.* Homosexuality is probably the most common disturbance of sexuality in the male, but data on its incidence are difficult to obtain. It is commonly said that incidence of male homosexuality is between two and five percent of the total population, but such estimates are biased by the belief that to qualify as a homosexual the person must be exclusively homosexual. Kinsey's (1948) data are based on sexual contact resulting in orgasm; that is, his statistics do not include those who engage in sexual activity without achieving ejaculation, or those who are erotically aroused by a homosexual stimulus without ever having overt relations. As thus defined, Kinsey found that 37 percent of the male population had some homosexual experience between the beginning of adolescence and old age; and of unmarried males who are 35 years of age or over, almost 50 percent have had a homosexual experience since the beginning of adolescence. In line with the older estimates, Kinsey reported that four percent of the white male population are exclusively homosexual throughout their lives.

*Dynamics of homosexuality.* Accidental homosexuality (faute de mieux—for lack of anything better), that kind of homosexuality seen in prisons and on ships when women are not available, indicates that most males are probably capable of a homosexual object choice. But the true homosexual must exclude women as his object choice for some other reason. Factors predisposing to homosexuality include fixation at pregenital (and especially anal) levels, fear of castration, intense oedipal attachment to the mother, narcissism and narcissistic object choice, and readiness to substitute identification for object relationships as is seen in identification with sibling rivals with secondary overcompensatory love for them. The sight of the female genitalia provokes castration anxiety by providing concrete evidence that castration is a reality and, through association with old oral anxieties, by perception of the genitalia as a castrating instrument. Such castration anxiety favors retirement from rivalry with the father by a denial and renunciation of all women.

Of course, castration anxiety is seen in non-homosexuals too; the difference is the reaction of the child to castration shock. The homosexual is characterized by a refusal to have anything more to do with such frightening sights. Similarly, intense attachment to the oedipal mother is seen in non-homosexuals as well as in homosexuals, but characteristic of the homosexual is that castration anxiety makes the mother and the female genitalia disappointing as a love object. Following such disappointment, there is regression from object love to identification with the object, and the homosexual identifies with the frustrating mother in a particular aspect—like his mother, he loves men. Then, if his fixation is predominantly narcissistic, he will choose as love objects young men or boys who represent himself, and he loves them in the way he wanted his mother to love him. These are so called subject-homoerotics, one of whose conditions of love is often that the homosexual object be of the same age as the person himself when the change into overt homosexuality occurred. If, on the other hand, the fixation is predominantly anal (i.e., passive-receptive), he will choose the father or masculine father substitutes as love-objects and attempt to enjoy sex in the same way as his mother did. These are the object-homoerotics, who cover with superficial passivity and submissiveness the idea of depriving the object choice of their "secrets," viz., the genitals. Narcissistic and anal fixations may, of course, occur in the same person, in which case a combination of the above types would be seen.

Kallman (1953) presents evidence that the major factors in such a development as outlined above are genetically determined. Male homosexuality shows one of the highest one-egg concordance rates of any behavioral abnormality studied, and the identical twins studied rated at least midway on Kinsey's scale of degree of homosexuality. But two-egg, fraternal twins show concordance in only 40 percent, and only 11.5 percent of these were rated as high as 5 or 6 on Kinsey's scale of homosexuality. Interestingly enough, the role of twins in homosexual activities was strikingly similar, and there were no instances of mutual sex relationships between the twins in Kallmann's studies. It might be noted, additionally, that there is no evidence that any treatment so far available changes the direction of the sexual drive in the true homosexual; at best, successful treatment will reduce the frequency of contact.

*Significance of adolescent homosexual experience.* For our purposes, then, it would be pertinent to consider briefly the prognostic import of homosexual experiences in the teenager. From the high incidence of such experiences we can readily see that most of them are without serious, long-term effects. One of the tasks of the adolescent is to overcome his inherent bisexuality and identify with the sex role appropriate to his biology, and it is hardly surprising that homosexual tendencies will remain even in his overt behavior until that task is complete. Our culture, with its taboos on childhood and early adolescent heterosexual play, tends to impede progress in sex identification and favors the banding together of adolescents in homosexual groups. And, at least for a time, these groups can offer reassurance to the teenager who suffers acutely from masturbatory guilt. For in the group, he finds he is no worse than his peers, with whom he swaps stories about sexuality and with whom he may indulge in mutual or group masturbation.

Clinically speaking, occasional overt homosexual relationships, particularly in early and mid-adolescence, are better ignored than made much of. More deserving of attention are the few adolescents who give indication that their homosexual experiences are more than a passing phase and instead represent definite blocking or fixation at this developmental stage. Unfortunately, we have little very definite knowledge in this area, but most would agree that the following are danger signals:

1. the boy whose homosexual experiences separate him from rather than integrate him into a peer group—the sort of boy whose classmates call a "fag" or "queer" and who avoid him as much as possible;
2. the boy whose homosexual contacts persist into late adolescence and who avoids any excursion into the heteroerotic field—such as the 19-year-old who is still too "shy" to date;
3. frequent episodes of active performance of fellatio or submission to anal intercourse—while either of these may be tried experi-

mentally by the teenager, usually his homosexual experiences will be confined to mutual masturbation;

4. a history of overt sexual experiences that continued uninterruptedly throughout the latency period;
5. homosexual contacts with adult males—no matter how much overt homosexuality is allowable in the teenager's peer group, experiences with older men are absolutely taboo even among delinquents (Fraiberg, 1961).

## REFERENCES

Campbell, R. J. Sexual development and pathology in the second decade. In W. C. Bier, S.J. and A. A. Schneiders (Eds.). *Proceedings, second institute for the clergy on problems in pastoral psychology.* New York: Fordham Univ., 1957. Pp. 99-113 (a).

Campbell, R. J. Habitual masturbation. In W. C. Bier, S.J. and A. A. Schneiders (Eds.). *Proceedings, second institute for the clergy on problems in pastoral psychology.* New York: Fordham Univ., 1957. Pp. 195-198 (b).

Fraiberg, S. H. Homosexual conflicts. In S. Lorand & H. Schneer (Eds.). *Adolescents.* New York: Hoeber, 1961. Pp. 78-112.

Kallmann, F. J. *Heredity in health and mental disorder.* New York: Norton, 1953.

Kinsey, A. C., Pomroy, W. B., & Martin, C. E. *Sexual behavior in the human male.* Philadelphia: Saunders, 1948.

# The School and Sex Education

## L. AUGUSTINE GRADY, S.J.

*Father L. Augustine Grady, S.J., received his A.B. degree from Georgetown University and his M.A. degree from Fordham University in the field of counseling and guidance. He is a member of the American Psychological Association, the American Catholic Psychological Association, and a professional member of the National Vocational Guidance Association. Fr. Grady has specialized in the area of college counseling, and he speaks from a background of more than ten years of experience as Director of Student Counseling at St. Peter's College in Jersey City.*

Over the past forty years there has been a growing concern about sex education in both public and parochial schools. Many constructive steps have been taken and any elucidation of the ideal role of the school in sex education should be prefaced by some account of what experience has taught.

### SEX EDUCATION IN PUBLIC SCHOOLS

Around the beginning of the present century, the notable increase in sexual delinquency and the rising divorce rate brought many proposals that the schools do something about the situation. As one writer reports:

Each group of influential citizens wanted to attack some special evil with its own set of lessons or projects. Tell children the facts of life, some said, so they will not be led astray by curiosity. Tell them the dangers of venereal infection. Tell them the miseries they invite if they act contrary to the rules of the church or the law (Gruenberg, 1946, pp. 8-9).

Sporadic attempts were made in various courses to meet specific needs. Here and there biology teachers taught the "facts of life," teachers of hygiene managed to include instruction about venereal disease, and physical education teachers spoke of personal cleanliness. Those who tried to improve the situation shared the same convictions: sex education was a new subject that must be added to the curriculum, and that instruction was all that was needed (Gruenberg, 1946).

By 1920, sex education had become a common concern of educators. In that year the National Education Association recommended that social hygiene become a part of teacher training, and that teachers cooperate with parents "in the instruction necessary to the inculcation of sound ideas and attitudes in children and youth" (Gruenberg, 1946, p. 12).

By 1938, more explicit prescriptions were in order. The American Association of School Administrators (1938) declared it a duty of educators to treat problems of sex. Along with this concern of educators, there grew the realization that mere information is not enough, that sound attitudes and ideals are even more important (American Association of School Administrators, 1941). Consequently, specific courses in sex education are no longer recommended. Rather it is agreed that stress should be put on the development of character throughout the entire curriculum (Gruenberg, 1946).

In 1942, a survey was conducted to determine the status of sex education in the public schools of the United States (Baker, 1942). It was found that 27 states gave little or no attention to sex education in their schools, while 9 states allowed local school boards to establish courses as they pleased. Only 10 states had made sex education a part of their state course of studies or had encouraged it on a statewide basis.

As New Jersey was listed as one of the 10 states most favorable to sex education, it seemed that it would be informative to investigate the present situation there. New Jersey's encouragement of sex education is contained in its Official Curriculum for Health Education in the Secondary Schools (New Jersey, 1955, p. 99). The matter is considered under the heading of "Personal and Family Living" and the objectives as stated are to:

> Develop an understanding of certain aspects of adolescent development.
>
> Build wholesome attitudes towards the many drives, feelings, and urges that frequently are present during the adolescent period.
>
> Develop ethical and socially satisfying ways of associating with the opposite sex and in planning for marriage and parenthood.

Under the heading "Content Material" the New Jersey Health Curriculum goes on to make the following recommendations:

> In most secondary schools, the separation of the boys and girls for physical education sets a pattern for separation of the sexes in health class. In these separate classes there is provided a normal situation for the discussion of the intimate facts of human reproduction as well as consideration of many other matters of healthful living in which one sex may find a greater opportunity for free discussion when apart from the other sex.
>
> Knowledge of the facts about the process of human reproduction is of course only one area of study in learning about home and family living. While it is important, attention to it should not be allowed to become out of proportion to the many other aspects of family life, particularly the part played by adolescents in the home (New Jersey, 1955, p. 102).

Investigations were made in several New Jersey public high schools to see how the state recommendations were being implemented. Not a single one was found that included even the most general type of sex education in its health curriculum. One principal reported that even in the physiology course the pages treating of human reproduction had been removed from the textbook.

The reluctance on the part of the schools to implement official recommendations is due to difficulties that have hampered the sex education movement from its start. Studies (Kearney, 1958) have indicated that these difficulties arise from the following sources:

1. *The parents and general public.* A representative study (Baker, 1942), however, has shown that parents usually cease to object when school authorities explain to them the true nature of the course.
2. *The Church, especially the Catholic Church.* In view of the balanced approach of modern educators, this opposition is at present negligible (Baker, 1942). As one writer has observed, "Catholic leaders advocate essentially the same basic principles regarding sex educa-

tion as have been formulated by non-Catholic psychologists and educators" (Gruenberg, 1946, p. 14).

3. *The schools themselves.* Herein lies the true source of the difficulty. One principal in New Jersey put it this way: "We have a health teacher, an ex-coach who has an M.A. in education, who is a nice fellow. But I would not want him to tell my son the facts of life, so how can I let him teach sex education in my school?" There is evidence that most current objections to sex education in the schools boil down to the inability of the teachers to perform the task (Gruenberg, 1946).

At present, public educators agree that sex must be taught as part of character education, and urge that teachers be trained to stress personal and social ideals in all of their courses. Some writers (Kearney, 1958) feel that perhaps the best course of action is to continue along the present lines in the hope that the new attitude being imparted to teachers will gradually bring favorable results. Meanwhile, even the most optimistic observer must admit that young people today are more muddled than ever in matters of sex, and that sexual promiscuity and marriage failure are on the increase (Gruenberg, 1946).

### SEX EDUCATION IN CATHOLIC SCHOOLS

Early attempts at sex education were viewed with reservations in Catholic circles. These reservations were expressed by Pius XI in 1929, in his encyclical on Education. He decried the error of those who propagate sex education ". . . falsely imagining that they can forearm youth against the dangers of sensuality by means purely natural, such as a foolhardy initiation and precautionary instruction for all indiscriminately, even in public . . ." The Pope adds that ". . . evil practices are the effect not so much of ignorance of intellect as of weakness of a will exposed to dangerous occasions and unsupported by the means of grace" (Pius XI, 1929, p. 25).

Catholics never felt that the Papal warnings meant to exclude all instruction concerning sex from the schools. The encyclical insisted upon two points: that sex education is primarily the function of the parents, and that mere information is no substitute for virtue. Commenting on the encyclical not long after its publication, Fr. Paul L. Blakely, S.J. (1931), presumes that the school may supplement the parents in the task of sex education. He also makes mention of sex instruction that "lays the primary emphasis upon the acquisition of virtue."

Over the years the same needs that were felt in public schools have prompted Catholic educators to include some kind of sex education in their programs. In a survey of 66 Catholic high schools around metropolitan New York City made in 1957, Fr. J. Franklin Ewing, S.J. (1957, p. 128) found that 11.9 percent had special courses concerning sex, 30 percent had a series of lectures, and 81.8 percent provided instructions on sex during the annual retreat.

A spot check indicates that in 1961 the situation is about the same. The majority of Catholic schools still rely upon the annual retreat to impart sex information. In schools where small groups of seniors make a closed retreat this situation is far more conducive to proper instruction than where 500 boys are crowded into a church. Even here it would seem that information should be given before the senior year.

Some Catholic schools are making an admirable attempt to provide sex instruction. In one high school for boys the freshmen are given a pamphlet on sex and instructed to discuss it with their parents. The parents are alerted beforehand by mail and are invited to contact the student counselor if their sons do not consult them.

One high school for girls provides a course in home economics for first year students in which an attempt is made to provide the girls with enough sex information for that stage of their development. In junior year, a six weeks' course in marriage, taught by a local priest, is included in the religion course.

Even public educators admit that some of the best organized work in the field of sex instruction is being done in Catholic schools (Gruenberg, 1946). The Church did oppose the first crude efforts at sex instruction thirty years ago, but the very principles that Pius XI enunciated then have led to the present Catholic attitude. As mentioned above, the Pope insisted that:

1. *Sex education is primarily the right of the parents.* But so many parents fail to exercise their right that one cannot help but wonder whether neglect is the whole story. In Fr. Ewing's (1957) study, one respondent felt that children find it difficult to confide in those to whom they owe obedience. Moreover, any counselor knows how difficult it is to advise those with whom one is emotionally involved. At any rate, experience would certainly in-

dicate that parents need a great deal of help in the matter of sex education, and that this condition is not likely to change.

2. *Mere information is not enough.* This principle of Pius XI has been embraced with equal fervor by public educators, who insist that sex must be taught in the context of personal values and ideals (Gruenberg, 1946). Catholic educators have come to realize the extraordinary advantages they have in the implementation of this principle. First, in the Catholic school there is total agreement on the concept of the person and the nature of his ideals, and a total commitment to these ideals may be presumed. Second, the Catholic has at his disposal supernatural motives and the supernatural help of the sacraments.

### CONCLUSION

Experience has established a definite role that the school should play in sex education. It is generally agreed that the school should concern itself with the entire outlook of the person, and that essential to this outlook is a positive attitude towards sex and marriage. This attitude is best imparted not by a special course, but by all courses, insofar as they have a bearing on personal and social ideals.

Catholic educators agree that sex education should form ideals, but must insist that these ideals recognize the spiritual nature of man. Some of the most enlightened and helpful of the writers on sex education ignore the spiritual side of man and see him as a purely material being, meant to live in total harmony with his natural instincts and surroundings. Chesser and Dawe, for instance, present much helpful advice and information for parents and teachers, but reveal their limited view of human nature by remarks like the following:

> If we could conceive of some happy state in which children had an entirely normal and natural home background, where there were no false morals and no unhealthy inhibitions to be acquired, where life was lived genuinely close to, and true to nature, with no false modesties and conventions to influence the child, the sexual urge would express itself in a proper and healthy manner (Chesser & Dawe, 1946, p. 5).

Some writers, like Bibby (1946), are willing to recognize the value of religion, but more as a single source of motivation than as a prime shaper of human ideals. Others, like Dorothy Baruch, tend to exaggerate the place of sex among human values. One of her illustrations depicts a young couple gazing fondly at their infant and exclaiming: "Just think! His sex education's already begun" (Baruch, 1959, p. 10). Sex education should not mean sex preoccupation, and one wonders if many of the precocious sexual concerns of the children whom Dr. Baruch describes were not prompted by the training they received.

It is important then, that Catholic educators recognize their duty to impart sexual attitudes worthy of the highest Christian ideals. They must realize, as do secular educators, that mere prohibitions are useless without a positive concept of sex and marriage. Since sex education is almost always conducted by priests or religious, they must make special efforts to understand and appreciate the vocation to married love, which they have not themselves experienced, and not to limit their teachings to warnings and threats.

Sex instruction will tend to be negative if based upon a moral theology which is chiefly concerned with sin and occasions of sin. An excellent exposition of the Catholic ideal of sex and marriage is presented by Dr. August Adam in his books, *The Primacy of Love* and *The Sixth Commandment*. He emphasizes the place that sex and marriage play in the Christian ideal of love, and presents moral theology in the light of this ideal.

Catholic teachers have often been open to the accusations of placing emphasis only upon the religious vocation. Sex education, properly understood, is an ideal remedy for this deficiency. It can enable Catholic schools to impart a true sense of vocation not only to future religious, but also to those who will serve God in the married state.

## REFERENCES

Adam, A. *The sixth commandment.* Cork, Ireland: Mercier, 1955.
———. *The primacy of love.* Westminster: Newman, 1958.
American Association of School Administrators. *Youth education today.* (16th Yearb.) Washington: Author, 1938.
American Association of School Administrators. *Education for family life.* (19th Yearb.) Washington: Author, 1941.
Baker, J. N. *Sex education in high schools.* New York: Emerson, 1942.
Baruch, Dorothy W. *New ways in sex education.* New York: McGraw-Hill, 1959.
Bibby, C. *Sex education.* New York: Emerson, 1946.
Blakely, P. L., S.J. Education for marriage. *America,* 1931, *44,* 408-409.
Chesser, E., and Dawe, Z. *The practice of sex education.* New York: Roy, 1946.
Ewing, J. F., S.J. The school in sex education. In W. C. Bier, S.J. and A.

A. Schneiders (Eds.). *Proceedings, second institute for the clergy on problems in pastoral psychology.* New York: Fordham Univ., 1957. Pp. 125-134.

Gruenberg, B. C. *How can we teach about sex.* New York: Public Affairs Committee, 1946. (Public Affairs Pamphlet No. 122.)

Kearney, N. C. Sex education in the public schools and factors affecting it. *Educ. Dig.,* 1958, *23,* 34-36.

New Jersey, State Department of Education. *A guide for health education in the secondary school.* Trenton: Author, 1955.

Pope Pius XI. *Christian education of youth.* New York: Paulist Press, 1929.

# The Role of the Parish in Sex Education

HENRY V. SATTLER, C.SS.R.

*Father Henry V. Sattler, C.SS.R. was ordained to the priesthood in 1943. From 1944 to 1947 he devoted himself to doctoral studies in philosophy at the Catholic University of America earning his Ph.D. in 1948. Fr. Sattler is the author of two books:* A Philosophy of Submission (*1948*), *and* Parents, Children, and the Facts of Life (*1952*), *and a number of pamphlets, among them* The Challenge of Chastity, *and* Educating Parents to Sex Instructions. *He was the author of a column, "A Course in Courtship" in* Our Sunday Visitor *for the years 1958 to 1960, and is the editor of the volume* Together in Christ: A Course in Marriage Preparation (*1960*). *Fr. Sattler is also a consistent contributor to journals and a frequent lecturer on topics dealing with marriage, sex instruction, and family living. He was awarded the Pontifical Medal, "Bene Merenti," by the present Holy Father, Pope John XXIII, in 1960. Since 1957, Fr. Sattler has been Assistant Director of the Family Life Bureau of the National Catholic Welfare Conference.*

The parish is a family of families. It is the social organism of Catholicism, immediately above the fundamental cell of the individual Catholic family. In our modern pluralistic society, the parish is the center of instruction, education, and formation of the parishioner families.

It cannot rest content to be the service station for the distribution of the sacraments. It must defend the families of which it is composed from the impact of the general secularism of American society. It must promote the optimum of Christian family living, since Christians must not merely maintain their Christian position in a "value-ghetto" but must also be a leaven for society.

Every *want* shows a basic *need,* though the need may not be apparent. A child may *want* his Dad's razor blade. He might *need* attention, a toy, a spanking. Society's preoccupation with sex shows a tremendous hunger. Perhaps this hunger indicates a real need for supernatural love. Perhaps it merely masks a need to understand the fullness of role between husband and wife, father and mother. But whatever the need, it is the parish that must discover and satisfy it for Catholic families.

### PARISH PROGRAM OF SEX EDUCATION

The matrix of good sex education is a program of positive family living, in which sexual experience is recognized as good, not merely permitted but fully approved by God. The parish must, therefore, provide a program for its families which will restore the hierarchy of Christian family values including those values of sex within the vocational concept of Christian marriage. Cana conferences, family retreats, family novenas and family missions would be of great value in restoring this concept. We must beware of preaching a negative approach to sexuality. If Christian concepts were fully integrated into life, we could preach against sin and get a hearing. Today, tirades against contraception, abortion, premarital experiences and steady dating will do little good unless positive values are inculcated. People want to know why. Evil is only hated when it is shown to be a threat to a highly cherished value. The value of Christian married love must be appreciated before sin will be avoided. The threat of hell is valid but remote.

Since chastity education is best provided indirectly by priests, the chief function of the parish is good leadership. Leadership will give parents the best possible tools for this home function. Modern parents can find more leisure to come to meetings than the parents of the past. They are intensely concerned with their children's welfare, which is witnessed by the rapid growth of parent-teacher or home-and-school associations. A good program for such an organization should be provided about every four years to meet the changing needs and population.

The parish is composed of priests, teachers, and laymen. Therefore all three should plan the program. A program for the home-and-school association should include a series of lectures, visual aids, and extensive discussion. The discussion should be between parents. A mere question and answer period is not discussion. Many parents are delinquent because they are not comfortable with the right words. If they compare notes, or use role-playing, they will develop better attitudes.

A year's program could encompass the following:

1. A lecture by a parish priest on the obligation of parents to give adequate sex instruction (Sattler, 1953, Chap. III).

2. A talk by some local educational expert on the principles which should govern chastity education (Sattler, 1953, Chaps. IV, V, IX).

3. A nursery school teacher could lecture on the sexual problems of preschool children (Odenwald, 1960; Sister Marie de Lourdes, 1951; Sattler, 1953, Chap. XI).

4. For the pre-puberty child, a speaker could present to the parents the natural curiosities of children of this age (Sattler, 1953, Chap. XI; film*; record †).

5. The problem of incipient adolescence could be handled by a local psychologist, who might help parents in dealing with the first physical changes of adolescence (Haley, 1948; educational programs‡).

6. The moral principles of the sixth and ninth commandments could be presented by a priest (Sattler, 1953, Chaps. VII, VIII; Mission Helpers, 1961; Kelly, 1941).

7. The pressures of steady dating and premarital petting should be explained by a sociologist (Kelly, 1960; Griffith, 1961).

8. The local marriage counselor should give, to the parents, some ideas concerning qualities of a marriage partner (Clemens, 1957).

* *Human beginnings.* E. C. Brown Trust Fund, University of Oregon, Eugene, Oregon.

† *Christopher Recordings on Sex Instruction.* The Christophers, 18 East 48th St., New York 17, N. Y.

‡ Available from manufacturers of feminine hygiene products, as for instance, Modess, Kotex, *et al.* This literature will facilitate the mother's explanation.

## PARISH LEADERSHIP OF TEACHERS

Not only should the parish instruct parents, but it should also inspire the teachers of parochial schools. Too frequently our teachers have hesitated to do anything about chastity education, because they have not been encouraged by the clergy. On the other hand, pastor and curate have bogged down for fear that teachers would be uncooperative or antagonistic. The leaders have waited for the followers, and the followers have waited for the leaders!

The parish should provide insight into the local problem of sexual maturation for the teachers. Sometimes teachers have implied that physical sexuality is only for those "without a vocation," a mere concession to lust. Occasionally their treatment of "the girl in trouble" has been unnecessarily harsh, unsympathetic, and un-Christian. School modesty programs are sometimes unrealistic to the extent of banning as seriously sinful what would be, at the most, a venial fault.

Some positive education program should be set up within the parish for the teachers. Together with their priests and parents they should work out effective methods of teaching the principles for the sixth and ninth commandments. Their positive formation should give them a respect and love for the sexual act so that this attitude might be transferred to the children almost without words. They should know clearly the environmental and cultural situation in which their people live. Married couples, doctors and other professionals should be asked to work with nuns and lay teachers.

## CRITICAL EVALUATION OF THE TEENAGE PROGRAM

A committee of priests, teachers, and effective laypeople should critically evaluate all work for adolescents. They should attempt to answer the following questions: Is it possible to have effective teenage programs without demanding, or occasioning steady dating? Are our programs providing "baptized" secular competition for activities about which we are most dubious? What social approval can be provided by way of teen codes to solve the perennial complaint: "but everybody does it"? How should parents, teachers, scout leaders, etc. treat the early "crush"? What type of conferences, religious activities, retreats, etc., should be provided to the teenage population?

## MARRIAGE PREPARATION PROGRAM

In view of the sexual preoccupation of young people entering marriage, it is imperative that the parish provide Christian education for marriage. Some general preparation can be worked out within the youth program by means of Teenage Forums, Tri-Une conferences, etc. In larger parishes a Pre-Cana conference or a marriage preparation course (e.g., Together in Christ), can be supplied within the parish. In less populous areas the marriage preparation course can be given on a Deanery level or by correspondence. Perhaps a number of couples within the parish could be trained to give adequate marriage preparation.

However, no program will ever fully substitute for the effective instruction given personally by the parish priest or his assistants (Canon 1033). Most priests of my acquaintance are very dissatisfied with themselves in this area. Very few dioceses provide detailed guides for their priests to follow in this important, personal instruction. Too frequently we are content to administer the premarital investigation, present a few inspirational thoughts, and take the couple over to the church for the wedding practice. Priests who tell the couple "Well, you know all about this" should examine their consciences.


## COUNSELING

The most effective work in chastity education is accomplished by counseling, either in or out of the confessional. True, the priest in the confessional should not spontaneously initiate instruction in the areas of sex (Canon 888 Sec. 2.; Private Response of Holy Office, May 16, 1943; Bouscaren, 1954, pp. 379-383). Nevertheless, when the needs of the penitent clearly indicate an ignorance or a false attitude which could be an occasion of sin, the confessor should not hesitate to elucidate. Outside the confessional, though he should be most circumspect lest he be labled a "sexpert," he should not hesitate to meet the needs of those who come for help. Since he cannot presume competence in all areas, referrals to competent psychiatrists, psychologists, or trained lay couples should be provided. The areas where counseling is most necessary are the following:

1. Male or female masturbation, whether on an intermittent or habitual level.

2. The problem of seduction whether homosexual or heterosexual.

3. The Christian approach to seminal emission for boys.

4. Problems of premarital experience by way of petting, intimacies, etc.

5. Principles regarding the choice of a possible marriage partner.

6. Methods of counseling the unwed mother-to-be.

7. General principles regarding sexual adjustment and disunity within marriage.

### CONCLUSION

Our modern families are suffering tremendous sexual pressures in modern American society. They will never successfully solve their adaptation to the American scene without clear and effective leadership and organic example on the parochial level. The occasional "diocesan institute" by a visiting lecturer, or single "drive" toward this goal will not be satisfactory. All of the cells of the parochial organ of the Mystical Body must be tied into the effort of providing an integrated program. Priests, teachers, youth leaders, responsible lay leaders and parents must all join in bringing about an effective family program. Only in such a parochial context will parents, priests, teachers, and counselors educate young people to Christian sexuality and chastity.

### REFERENCES

Bertocci, P. A. *The human venture in sex, love and marriage.* New York: Association Press, 1951.

Bouscaren, T. L., S.J. *Canon law digest.* Vol. III. Milwaukee: Bruce, 1954.

Bruckner, P. J., S.J. *How to give sex instruction.* St. Louis: Queen's Work, 1937 (pamphlet).

Buckley, J. *Christian design for sex.* Chicago: Fides, 1952.

Catholic Woman Doctor. *Growing up: a book for girls.* New York: Benziger, 1940.

Cervantes, L. F., S.J. *And God made man and woman.* Chicago: Regnery, 1959.

Clemens, A. H., ed. *Marriage education and counseling.* Washington: Catholic Univer., 1951.

Clemens, A. H. *Marriage and the family.* Englewood Cliffs, N. J.: Prentice-Hall, 1957.

Griffith, Jeanette. *Dearest Kate*. Philadelphia: Lippincott, 1961.

Haley, J. E., C.S.C. *Accent on purity*. Chicago: Fides, 1948.

Juergens, S. P., S.M. *Fundamental talks on purity*. Milwaukee: Bruce, 1941 (pamphlet).

Kelly, G., S.J. *Modern youth and chastity*. St. Louis: Queen's Work, 1941 (pamphlet).

Kelly, G. A. *The Catholic youth's guide to life and love*. New York: Random House, 1960.

*Listen, son!* Chicago: Franciscan Herald Press, 1952 (pamphlet).

Marie de Lourdes, Sister. *Baby grows in age and grace*. Norwalk, Conn.: Gibson, 1951.

A Medical Woman, a Girl, and a Wife. *Into their company*. New York: Kenedy, 1931.

Mission Helpers of the Sacred Heart. *Vital steps to chastity*. Towson, Md.: Author, 1961.

*Mother's little helper*. Chicago: Franciscan Herald Press, 1952 (pamphlet).

Odenwald, R. P. *How God made you*. New York: Kenedy, 1960.

Pope Pius XII. *Guiding Christ's little ones*. Washington, D. C.: National Catholic Welfare Conference, 1942 (pamphlet).

Sattler, H. V. *Parents, children and the facts of life*. Paterson, N. J.: St. Anthony Guild, 1953.

Sattler, H. V., ed. *Together in Christ*. Washington, D. C.: National Catholic Welfare Conference, 1960.

Schneiders, A. A. *Personality development and adjustment in adolescence*. Milwaukee: Bruce, 1960.

Trevett, R. F. *The church and sex*. New York: Hawthorn Books, 1960.

Watkin, A. *The enemies of love*. New York: Kenedy, 1958.

# The Home and Delinquency

## FABIAN L. ROUKE

*Fabian L. Rouke received his A.B. degree from Boston College (1934) and his M.A. (1937) and Ph.D. (1942) degrees from Fordham University. Prior to World War II he was a psychologist at Lincoln Hall, Lincolndale, N. Y., a school for delinquent boys. During the war he was a psychologist at the U.S. Naval Prison at Portsmouth, New Hampshire. Since 1950, Dr. Rouke has been professor of psychology and head of the Department of Psychology at Manhattan College. Prior to assuming his present post, he taught at City College of New York and New York University. In addition to his work at Manhattan, Dr. Rouke has been chief psychologist at the Youth Center, Ossining, N. Y., from 1957 to the present. Dr. Rouke is a fellow of the American Psychological Association and a diplomate in clinical psychology of the American Board of Examiners in Professional Psychology. He has contributed articles on lie detection, problems of criminal motivation, and delinquency to various scientific journals.*

### DIFFERING APPROACHES TO DELINQUENCY

At the very start of our discussion it should be pointed out that the clergy must become aware of the differing approaches to the study of delinquency. On the one hand there are those investigators who analyze groups of delinquents. They study delinquency as a process and then apply the findings of their studies to other groups. This is an approach which needs an understanding of the statistical nature of things—at least in the broad sense—and gives us information about the central tendency of the group studied. On the other hand there is the approach to delinquency where the clinician studies and works with the individual person, an individual who may or may not be one who represents the central tendency of the group.

The parish priest needs an appreciation of both approaches. In planning parish activities for delinquency prevention he must be aware of group findings, but in counseling the boy in trouble he must have at his grasp an appreciation of the individual approach.

Other speakers on today's program will cover group approaches, so in my discussion of the home and delinquency, I will dwell more on an individual approach.

### ACCEPTING AUTHORITY AND CONTROL

Where is the main contribution of the home to the problem of delinquency? To my mind it resides in the twin areas of accepting authority and developing control (Rouke, 1950). The child who learns to accept authority comfortably is rarely in any delinquent difficulty. The child who is delinquent, in almost every case, has undergone great difficulty in his developmental years in learning to accept and adjust to parental authority. Whether this be the responsibility of the child or the parent is not the point at issue here. I think we can safely assume that even where it is the responsibility of the parent, the parent is rarely "doing it on purpose."

In order to understand just what happens when a developing child encounters authority, let us review briefly the beginnings of personality. As we all know, people are different. The difference begins at the instant of conception when the varying hereditary potentials are set for each of us. These differences are magnified by variations in prenatal environment. Even at the moment of birth, therefore, people are different. This difference depends upon each child's hereditary potential and upon the assortment of physiological drives and needs which have developed during the child's prenatal period. At birth the child's first response to external stimulation depends completely upon these physiological factors. In psychoanalytic terminology this collection of drives is named id. The id drives are completely selfish and demand immediate gratification. The id operates entirely at the unconscious level and is not restricted by considerations of time, space and logic. At birth a personality is completely id. But even in the first few days of life many of the id drives cannot be gratified immediately and thus frustration ensues. Therefore, as reality is encountered this interaction of the id drives with reality generates a product which is called *ego* and thus the psychological aspect of personality begins (Coleman, 1960).

The ego is the "me" or the "self" in which the individual differentiates himself from his surroundings and through which the integrating core of the personality is formed. During the first few months of life the ego continues to develop as it interacts with reality and the child seems to sense in some way that all frustrations are reality frustrations. At about the age of eighteen months to two years, however, something else occurs. The child begins to sense that some of the frustrations of his needs are not inevitable and due to reality, but are due to the wishes of his parents. Consider for example the toddler who enjoys tearing bright colored pictures out of a magazine and throwing them on the living room floor. His parents will stop this activity either by removing him, by removing the magazines, by verbal instructions, or by physical punishment. Quite soon the child can be observed to reach toward the magazine, but then hold up his activity as he looks at the parent and shakes his own head, "No, No." He has now absorbed into his own personality one of the controls of parental admonition. Thus begins another aspect of the personality which is given the name *superego*. It is the first mechanism of inner control that the child develops. However, the control of the superego is not one dictated by what is right or what is wrong, but is rather an immature and defensive measure to protect the child against the fear of the loss of parental approval. As such it can be conceived of as a predominantly negative force and yet at this stage of development it is a very normal and necessary aspect of personality. Superego, as it grows, has to do with the feelings, or affective life, and it becomes largely unconscious.

A few years further along in development, when the child begins to gain the use of reason, another mechanism of control comes into being. This is the *conscience,* or the knowledge of what is right and wrong according to moral standards.

All feelings of guilt are derived from the superego and/or the conscience. Although many authors use the terms interchangeably, superego may be distinguished from conscience as follows: The superego is a set of attitudes derived from internalized social values which are used by the individual to evaluate his own behavior. It is affective, irrational, largely unconscious, and the source of emotional guilt which may be neurotic or pathological. The superego is adopted by the child from parental sanction without reflection upon, or insight into, the meaning of his own experience. Conscience, on the other hand, involves intellectual judgment concerning right and wrong; it is conscious and self-reflective, and is the source of normal moral guilt (e.g., a normal reaction to sin in the theological sense). Conformance to the demands of the superego represents a childish and dependent mode of behavior; responses to the dictates of conscience represents a mature evaluation of realistic duties and responsibilities (Bulatao, 1957).

These two factors of control exist side by side in the growing person. In the preschool child superego is naturally ascendant, but as conscience begins to develop the relationship should be that of the elevator and the balance weight. As the one increases the other should decrease. You might even say that a good measure of maturity is the degree to which an individual's behavior is controlled by the conscience rather than by the superego.

### SELF-CONTROL AND DELINQUENCY

The discussion may have seemed a bit off the direct topic of the home and delinquency but to my mind it is close to the heart of the problem, namely, the control of behavior. Where mature control develops we can expect a low percentage of delinquency. Where controls remain immature we may have either one of two reactions. We may have a withdrawal into illness or we may have the rebellion of antisocial behavior. The key period for all of this lies early in the life of the child in the home when he is first learning to meet authority. If he meets authority at the hands of parents who are benevolent and loving, and who, even though their discipline is consistent and firm, never let him feel that he is not wanted, he will be able to accept authority and perhaps even gain a measure of gratification from a life lived according to the dictates of authority. However, if on the other hand his first meeting with authority is at the hands of parents who are cruel, harsh and even brutal, or in a home where the parents are confused and inconsistent, the acceptance of authority will always be a problem to him. To refer to the two directions of possible development mentioned above, delinquency is not inevitable under such circumstances, but it may be a consequent of this pattern.

## REFERENCES

Bulatao, J. C., S.J. Conscience and superego. *ACPA Newsletter,* 1957, *8,* No. 2 (Supplement No. 26).

Coleman, J. C. *Personality dynamics and effective behavior.* Chicago: Scott, Foresman, 1960.

Rouke, F. L. Delinquency. In E. L. Hartley & Ruth E. Hartley (Eds.). *Fundamentals of social psychology.* New York: Knopf, 1952. Pp. 341-368.

# The School and Delinquency

## SOPHIA M. ROBISON

*Sophia M. Robison, who is Research Co-ordinator for the Adelphi College Institute of Health, Education and Welfare, received her A.B. degree from Wellesley College (1909) and her M.A. (1913) and Ph.D. (1936) degrees from Columbia University. She also has a diploma from the New York School of Social Work, granted in 1928. She is a member of the American Association for the Advancement of Science, the American Sociological Society, the American Statistical Association, and the American Association of Social Workers. Dr. Robison's publications include the following two books:* Can Delinquency Be Measured? *(1936), and* Juvenile Delinquency, Its Nature and Control *(1960). Dr. Robison served as a special technical advisor on delinquency for the 1950 White House Conference on Children and Youth. In her long and distinguished professional career, she has taught at various municipal colleges, at Yeshiva University and at Columbia University in New York City, at Smith College in Northampton, Mass., and at Howard University in Washington, D.C.*

This paper addresses itself (1) to the major complaints against the school as a precipitating factor in delinquent behavior and (2) to a consideration of some of the major attempts to explain or to deal with delinquency in a school setting.

## COMPLAINTS AGAINST THE SCHOOL

It is no doubt general knowledge that our public school system was designed to counteract ignorance and illiteracy which were assumed to be generators of crime and delinquency. Today we expect the school to perform many functions which in simple societies were the province of the family or the church. It was not recognized then, however, and it is not always remembered today, by the proponents of reading and writing as a cure for crime and delinquency, that these tools of learning do not have built-in devices to assure their proper use. Unfortunately, knowing right does not always mean doing it.

The use to which any tool is put depends not only upon the skill, but upon the will and the needs of the user. In sociological terms, as MacIver (1947, p. 6) says, technological factors do not explain *why* something occurs, but *only the form* which it assumes. The pen may be used to write a slanderous letter or an "Ode to the Skylark." The instrument is indifferent to the aim of the user; or, as the German proverb puts it, "Paper is patient"; it does not protest against what is written upon it.

Not only is there no guarantee that education is an automatic corrective for either crime or delinquency but it may, as a matter of fact, suggest to the individual or child contemplating antisocial action a way in which he can carry out his intention. Hewitt and Jenkins (1946) remind us that confidence men make expert use of their knowledge, without guilt feelings, for objectives of which society disapproves.

There are three major complaints against the schools as a factor in delinquency, which are the following: (1) discipline is lax; (2) the children do not make appropriate progress in their studies: i.e., the pedagogical methods are at fault; and (3) the age requirements in compulsory education laws contribute to the delinquency of "reluctant scholars."

*Lax Discipline.* Progressive educational methods have been blamed for delinquency. Persons who firmly believe the biblical injunction, "He that spareth the rod hateth his son," often quote their own beneficial experience of sessions in the woodshed or with a razor strop. They fail to remember, however, that frequently this type of punishment was accompanied by an underlying acceptance of them by their parents, which may have served as a cushion in more ways than one.

While a painful experience is usually avoided, we know that many factors, not all of them immediately obvious, play some part in decisions to desist from or to avoid antisocial behavior. Punishment may follow so rarely in comparison with the number of occasions for which it was "deserved" that the culprit may be willing to take the chance that his misdeeds will escape punishment. Psychiatric studies disclose that for some persons punishment provides relief for a sense of guilt, and so reactivates the cycle: delinquency—punishment—relief—delinquency. In other cases, punishment slides off the back literally, as something to be tolerated, because the antisocial act had its own rewards.

Refusing to recognize the operation of these different meanings and values attached to punishment by the miscreant, the advocates of the "get tough" policy still insist that the stricter the discipline, the less the revolt. These adherents of extreme disciplinary measures, however, do not ask whether automatic obedience to law or to custom is always a healthy manifestation.

Although they are often assumed to be clear-cut, the alternatives of freedom and restraint are not black and white. The need is to find, in the school and out of it, a clear balance in the setting of limits which will permit reasonable freedom of action for the component parts of a democratic society in the light of the general welfare.

*School Retardation.* The second general complaint against the public school as an ineffective bulwark against delinquency is that its pedagogical methods are ineffective. A very large proportion of the children in the New York City public schools cannot read, write, or figure adequately even after they have been in school for some years. According to an official report used as a guide for supervisors and teachers:

> It can be expected that at least one-half of the entering class of the junior high school will score at reading grade levels below the seventh (with norms adjusted for age). Nearly one out of five entering students scores at fourth grade or below. . . . Nearly half of these elementary grade readers may be considered retarded readers—that is, they have the capacity to read better. . . . Practically all of the 10,000 to 15,000 children scoring below grade 5 are also retarded readers, many of them severely so, although most of them are of normal or near-normal intelligence (New York City Board of Education, Bureau of Educational Research, 1955, p. 9).

According to the Presiding Justice of the Domestic Relations Court:

> It has been shown conclusively that there is a definite link between reading retardation and delinquency. Reading difficulties were reported for 75 percent of the delinquents in the non-school part of the Children's Court; and 85 percent of the boys in detention at Youth House are handicapped by being unable to read books appropriate to their grade in school" (New York City, Presiding Justice of Domestic Relations Court, 1955, p. 18; Peck, 1955).

Whether or not this statement implies a *causal* connection between delinquency and reading disability, it is clear that reading disabilities, as likely barriers to social and emotional adjustment, are apt to impede the rehabilitation of the delinquent. Reading was not so important a skill in the days when there were plenty of jobs which did not call for reading facility. Today, however, the child who is unable to read is definitely handicapped. Some such children may try to compensate by indulging in undesirable behavior.

Before a causal connection between reading disability and delinquency could be established, however, we would need to know more than we do today. For example, we have no evidence of how many retarded readers are *not* delinquent. Furthermore, there are indications that, of the children who attend school regularly today, there are proportionately no more non-readers than there were formerly. Teaching methods are as good as, or perhaps better, today than they were formerly. Educational research directed at discovering the advantage of various methods of teaching reading has not shown that any one method is decidedly superior to another. Because more parents of our day have themselves gone relatively far in school, however, they are more critical than their parents were. Perhaps, too, the personal element of the interest of the teacher or the boy's identification of reading with the female role in certain classes of society and among certain cultural groups not formerly on the school rolls may be deciding factors in learning how to read regardless of the method employed.

*Compulsory Education Laws.* Apart from these complaints about discipline and pedagogy, the school is occasionally blamed for the "willful truancy" of children. Most cities or states have regulations about the age at which children must enter and may leave school as well as about permissible absence.

In striking contrast to American, the European delinquency statistics do not include truancy. Part of the explanation may be that European school systems often select students in their early adolescence for continued training of various types. Furthermore, the age at which one is permitted to leave school is lower; in England, for example, school attendance is not compulsory beyond the fifteenth birthday. There are those who claim that our insistence on school attendance for youths who are apparently not progressing normally, contributes to delinquency. The appropriate solution is complicated, not only by work opportunities in an increasingly automated world, but by understandable labor union resistance to increasing the labor pool. Our laws regarding youth employment partially reflect supply and demand.

Although the New York "City Fathers" in 1852 deplored the indifference for education of the numerous poor families, there was no legislation until 1870. The 1855 Report of the Superintendent of Schools notes that less than 8 percent of the city's children attended school regularly. Cincinnati and Boston had twice as good a record with approximately 17 percent regular school attendance and Philadelphia claimed 13 percent.

We are reminded that 1854 was a peak year for Irish and German immigrants who crowded into the already overcrowded living facilities of New York City. At that time about half of the city's inhabitants lived in tenement houses without central heating, or indoor toilets. Water was available usually only at a faucet in the rear court or at a public hydrant. Reminiscent of today's "slum lords," landlords made as much as 30 to 40 percent profit. Above 30th Street, Irish and German immigrants lived in board or mud shanties with their dogs, goats and pigs. The men got what work they could in the nearby quarries and "the German women, especially, lived on the bones and rags which they and their children gathered all day long throughout the streets of the City" (Jansen, 1954, p. 24).

We can claim vast improvement in general sanitary conditions under which most of the descendants of those German and Irish immigrants of a century ago now live as predominately middle or upper middle class persons. Today the explanation of irregular school attendance and lack of school progress of immigrants from Puerto Rico or the South intrigues the student of delinquency.

The familiar slogan, "Truancy is the first step in delinquency," has initiated several studies.

*Truancy Studies.* Truancy was the focal point of several studies of the New York State Crime Commission in the late 1920's. The first study proclaimed that delinquents begin as school truants and come from slum areas (New York State Crime Commission, 1928a). The second study, of an institution known as the Parental School, established especially to deal with the persistent truant in New York City, reported also that chronic truancy, in a disquieting number of cases, was the first step in a criminal career (New York State Crime Commission, 1928b). More than half the boys committed to an institution came to the attention of the police and the courts in the six- to eight-year-period following their release from the institution. It may be legitimate to ask whether the subsequent delinquent behavior was a reaction to the experience of the boys in the institution, which was closed because of disclosures of the abusive measures employed by the head of the school.

Furthermore, as a basis for findings on the relation between treatment provided by the correctional field and subsequent behavior, the boys who were committed to the school represent a highly selected group of truants. Boys from "broken homes" who had given evidence of not being amenable to the family's control, many of them children of immigrant Italians, predominated. To assume that this sample represents the "universe" of truants is another illustration of circular reasoning: putting into a situation unconsciously the very factors which one later pulls out and labels as causes.

Subsequent studies of truancy in New York City raise further questions about the implications of findings of these Crime Commission Studies. In 1930, the Bureau of Attendance of the Board of Education of the City of New York made available 25,000 records, which were subsequently analyzed: (a) to clarify the basis of the official label of "Truant" in the delinquency count (a very small proportion of New York City truants were referred to the court); (b) to estimate the size of the problem in New York City; (c) to discover whether or not there were any special characteristics such as age, sex, color, ethnic group or progress in school which distinguished truants from other delinquents known to the juvenile court (Robison, 1936, Ch. 8).

In 1930, truancy was defined by the Board of Education of the City of New York as absence for *three consecutive days* without a satisfactory explanation. About one third of the 25,000 hearings in 1930 represented cases of willful truants—children whose parents were unaware of the fact that they were not in school; the remaining two-thirds were children who were unlawfully detained at home by their parents, children who wished to leave school to go to work, some who were industry. We talk about building close family relationships and send children to nursery schools at three and to summer schools, recreational programs and summer camps for the remainder of their childhood years. We advocate respect for authority while we disparage the public officials we helped to elect. We tell the adolescent he must respect the law while we bribe policemen. We tell him to be decent and honest and, above all, upright while we cheat on our income tax. We try to teach him the value of money while plunging ourselves more heavily into debt. We deny him an advance on next week's allowance while we use carte-blanche and apply for ready credit. We insist that he obtain the best education possible and we cooperate by voting down school budgets. We tell him about the dignity of an honest day's work and formulate plans for the twenty-hour week. We stress the importance of scientific and academic achievement while we make millionaires of our entertainers and paupers of our professors and arrange things in such a way that many teachers need outside employment to survive.

Is it any wonder that the adolescent is confused, that he is disillusioned, that he is rebellious and that he feels cheated? For how has he been helped toward resolving his conflict in favor of independence when the ideals we have held up to him are empty and the values are false?

## ADULT AMBIVALENCE TOWARD ADOLESCENT INDEPENDENCE

The ambivalence of adults toward children caught in the struggle between their dependency needs and their striving for independence is astonishing. We literally push our children out of infancy by weaning them, toilet training them and sending them off to school before they are really ready for any of these events. We rob them of their childhood by organizing their games and structuring their society according to adult rules and standards. We even try to make something productive out of their play activity as evidenced by a teacher's comment on an elementary report card which stated paradoxically, "This child does not use his recess time constructively."

There appears then a tendency to propel the child toward maturity and independence and to make him aware of responsibility sometime before he is ready for it. And in this way we frustrate his dependency needs when they should be indulged. Having done this during childhood, the ambivalence of adults becomes apparent when they reverse the process during adolescence. At least it seems that the weight of adult pressure during adolescence is in the direction of retarding growth. And in this way we frustrate the striving for independence which should now be strengthened. This ambivalence is reflected in our very lack of agreement as to when adolescents can do what. How much more confusion do we add to that which I have already outlined when we tell the adolescent that he is old enough to serve his country but he is too young to vote; old enough to drive but not old enough to avoid the penalty of increased insurance premiums and, in this connection, we suggest to the boy of twenty that he is not yet as old as his sister of eighteen. We tell him that he may use alcohol in New York but not in Connecticut, he may marry in Maryland but not in New Jersey, he may work in Kentucky but not in California. We tell him in short, that he is a man physically and morally at about sixteen but that he is an infant legally until twenty-one. We pass laws to compel his attendance at school until he is seventeen and we pass other laws to prevent him from working before that time and then we berate him because he is not earning his own way as was his father at thirteen. And we tell him all of these contradictory things at a time when he is unconsciously struggling with a monumental decision whether to remain a child with all of the protection, comfort and security signified by that state or whether to frustrate his own unconscious inclination and decide in favor of maturity which means sacrifice, courage and responsibility.

Certainly our way of life has done much to intensify this struggle. Educational requirements, being what they are today, tend to keep adolescents and young adults in a state of complete dependence on their parents for a much longer period than formerly. The harsh economic realities of life have also contributed in this regard. Even in marriage there is the tendency for families to remain together and three generations in one home is becoming more usual. And the new parents seem to begin raising their children without in any way altering their relationship to the new grandparents. All of these considerations seem to have the net effect of prolonging the dependence-independence conflict and our adolescents become more and more reluctant to give up the pleasures of dependence in favor of assuming responsibility. It hurts more than a little to grow up and to become independent and the freedom and privilege of adult life is purchased only by the assumption of responsibility. But a good many of our young people are managing to avoid that expense and having been skinned Puerto Ricans, from low-standard rural communities, to New York City life. In the conflict with their children, the parents carried over from their own childhood the pattern of going to work as soon as possible, at the expense of continuing school, in order to supplement meager family incomes.

The fact that practically none of these children had been truants before their transfer from the six-year elementary schools to the junior high school suggests that the impersonal relationship with the half dozen teachers of the specialized subjects in the junior high school, compared with the one classroom teacher of the elementary school, plus the breaking of friendships in the small neighborhood school and the pressures of adolescence, brought the difficulties of these boys into sharper focus. As a result, they became more insecure and retreated from the unaccustomed new school experiences. From the point of view of the speaker, the junior high school system has created more problems than it was designed to solve.

However, even in this sordid background there were some positive factors. Although they were not always consistent in setting limits of permissible behavior the mothers showed affection for their children. The boys were of normal intelligence, not aggressively delinquent, and they appeared to be seeking an adequate manhood. Despite their potential capacities, there was unusual fluctuation in school performance. The stammering and the exhibitionism of some boys, and the withdrawal of others, seemed to be symptomatic responses to their deprivations. There was no evidence, however, that *any* of them were engaging in antisocial activity in the community. In not a single one of these cases was the persistent truancy the first step to delinquency. Instead, it seemed to be a signal of their need for help.

*Truancy as School Phobia.* A similar emphasis on truancy as a signal for help, rather than as a self-explanatory legal entity calling for strict enforcement of school attendance regulations, is disclosed in a study of truants made by Dr. Emanuel Klein (1945). In examining children referred to him at the Bureau of Child Guidance of the New York City Board of Education, Dr. Klein found that actually many of them were afraid to go to school. This finding has important implications for treatment. To force these children to return to school without understanding the basis for their fear would not only fail to cure the symptom, but would undoubtedly result in much more serious disturbances.

A study of 53 cases of school phobia referred to the Judge Baker

Guidance Center in Boston, Massachusetts, and reported by Wald-fogel, Coolidge & Hahn (1957), concludes that school phobia can become one of the most disabling disorders of childhood. Almost invariably accompanying school phobia, there were psychosomatic symptoms. The most typical picture was a child who vomited his breakfast and used this device to be able to remain at home. The explanation usually given is that the child is fearful of being separated from his mother. The ways in which these children may be helped are the subject of current research at the Judge Baker Guidance Center (Waldfogel, Hahn & Teasman, 1958).

*A Proposal to Redefine Truancy as Neglect.* A reconsideration of the meaning of truancy is proposed by a committee of juvenile court judges who were assigned the responsibility in 1955 for revising the 1949 edition of the Standard Juvenile Court Act. In commenting on whether or not truancy should be included in the description of behavior classified as "delinquency" and within the jurisdiction of the Juvenile Court they say:

> Truancy as juvenile court jurisdiction is better defined as neglect than delinquency. The *Standard Juvenile Court Act* gives truancy jurisdiction in the following words—'any child who is neglected as to proper or necessary support or education as required by law' (Rubin, 1952, p. 431).

On the evidence of the studies quoted above we may reasonably conclude that retardation in school and truancy are often indices of the ineffectiveness of the school in its role of controlling and socializing some children of the most economically deprived segments of our multi-ethnic urban populations.

Since many persons credit the school with considerable responsibility both for causing and for controlling delinquency, in general or in specific form of truancy, it is no surprise to find that the school is the locale of services to prevent delinquency. The programs described below include some evaluation of the results. In each, the school plays a central but *different* role in the program for delinquency prevention.

SCHOOL PROGRAMS FOR TREATING DELINQUENCY

*Passaic, New Jersey Program.* The Passaic, New Jersey Children's Bureau was modeled after the bureau initiated originally by Mayor Hague of Jersey City in the early 1930's to forestall the referral of children to Juvenile Court. The Passaic Bureau still investigates all

Without the conviction of masculinity or of femininity it is impossible for any growing boy or girl to achieve adequate self-identity. Whenever a young boy feels that he is "different" or that he is "effeminate," he finds it extremely difficult to believe in his own self-identity. Similarly, the girl who is flat-chested, and looks very much like the proverbial beanpole, with no seductive curves to lure the unsuspecting male into some kind of relationship, finds it hard to think of herself as a woman, and feels that the search for identity leads into endless blind alleys.

In this search for identity, there must of course be more than a healthy body-image, or sex identity. The child grows up within a context of interpersonal relationships that have a great deal to do with his search for and achievement of identity. Normally, the growing boy tends to identify with his father, and the girl with her mother, and this process of external identification is very helpful in establishing the conviction of masculinity or femininity, and therefore of both sexual and self-identity. The youngster also identifies with other important facets of his daily life, such as his family, his nationality, his religion, his community, and his school; from all of these identifications he derives some measure of self-identity. Later on in adulthood, some of these identifications will have to be broken up, as when the individual leaves the community, graduates from school, or establishes a home of his own. But in the normal course of events this does not happen until after the individual has forged his own personal self-identity out of the many identifications he has formed during the process of growing up.

These are some of the factors that enter into the adolescent's search for identity. To the parent, growing up physically may mean nothing more than that the adolescent is getting taller and heavier, is developing a voracious and sometimes peculiar appetite, and is always growing out of recently purchased clothes. But to the teenager, growing up is much more than this, and he finds himself involved in a continuous search for himself. Too often this search is fruitless.

# Problems of Dependence
# and Independence

## FRANCIS C. BAUER

*Francis C. Bauer, M.D., is Director of the Student Adjustment Center of the Third Supervisory School District of Suffolk County on Long Island. His undergraduate degree is from St. John's University, and his medical degree from Georgetown University. Dr. Bauer is a member of the American Psychiatric Association, the New York State Medical Society, and the Suffolk County Medical Society. He is a lecturer at St. John's University, a consultant to the Marriage Tribunal in the Diocese of Brooklyn, and a member of the Executive Board of the New York State Welfare Conference.*

I would like to begin our discussion by calling attention to the obvious and stating, at the risk of redundance, that the dependence-independence conflict is by no means limited to the period of adolescence. It is rather a conflict which is basic to human existence, which begins for all at birth and which for some continues to manifest itself in one way or another until, as with most conflicts, it is conveniently resolved in death. Stated in its simplest terms, it is a conflict between man's strong emotional need always to avoid the frustration essential to progress and to maintain a perpetual status quo on the one hand and, on the other, his equally strong but opposite need, symbolically to sever the recreational program might, they argued, offset some of the handicaps of living in a rapidly deteriorating area. Psychiatric and medical services as well as remedial tutoring and vocational guidance were provided.

In the course of the two-year program of service, it could not be claimed that the clinical services in this school were to any large degree effective in changing either the boys' behavior or the attitudes of the teachers to the boys. Considerable evidence however was accumulated on the needs of the boys and the skills of the teaching staff.

The boys who were referred to the school clinic talked about their school life without rancor. They said they preferred the departmental system of the junior high school because in an elementary school, if you get mad at the teacher and stay in her class all day, you stay mad. When you change classes, you may "get pleased" by the time you move to the next teacher.

Apparently the boys neither questioned nor strongly resented this kind of treatment. What happened at school may possibly have been similar to what happened at home. The clinic staff was, in fact, surprised by the boys' passive acceptance of many of their school experiences. Apparently no boy considered discussing his experience with any member of the school faculty.

The study revealed *startling gaps* between the boys' capacities, as measured by their I.Q.'s, and their accomplishments. Although the median I.Q. was 99 for the group studied, only one-tenth of the boys read at their grade level, and *all* of them were retarded in arithmetic.

The boys saw no relation between their school accomplishments and job opportunities. None of them had discussed their vocational ambitions with anyone at the school, and few of their parents had ever come to the school to discuss their boys' progress.

In order to appraise any effect which the presence of the project might have on the atmosphere in the classroom, arrangements were made to observe the teachers both in the first and in the second year of the project. The observers were members of the Department of Education of New York City's Municipal Colleges. In the opinion of these observers, 40 percent of the lessons they observed had been inadequately planned. The teaching methods of 20 percent of the teachers were described as formal and routine. The approach of the teachers to the pupils was described as "poor," "patronizing," or "listless" in one-fifth, and "authoritative" or "scolding" in another fifth, of the observations. The pupils' response to the teaching was categorized as "uninterested" in more than one-third of the classes. And there was no appreciable difference between the observations at the end of the first and second year with respect to the quality of classroom instruction or the nature of the boys' response.

The overall appraisal of the teachers in this school by persons responsible for training teachers in the city system rated about one-quarter (23 percent) below the city's average. Explanations for the low rating of the teachers include: the number of teachers assigned to the school who were unsympathetic or even hostile to Negroes; the excessively high proportion of substitute teachers and the consequent shifting of teacher personnel; the lack of training or preparation of teachers to meet the problems of an underprivileged community; and the failure of the school to provide in-service training. An additional handicap is that the principal of the school is allowed little choice in the selection of teachers.

The Sponsoring Committee of the project concluded that no school could be expected to meet and handle the problems of so many disturbed adolescents. Too many of these children had been so repeatedly knocked about, rejected and punished, that their rebellion and aggression seemed a reasonable response.

*The Maximum Benefits Program in Wash., D. C.* The Maximum Benefits Project is a research and service activity under the auspices of the Washington, D. C. Youth Council designed to forestall delinquency through preventive measures in the elementary schools (Hodges, Tait & Trevett, 1959). The program has three aims: (1) to offer service, including clinical services, if necessary, to individual children with severe behavior problems; (2) to identify the predelinquent; and (3) to demonstrate how increased services can help the elementary school to prevent delinquency.

The area selected as "The Wickedest Precinct," i.e., Washington's Second Police Precinct, has witnessed, in common with other cities, a recent rapid shift of its economically priviledged residents to the suburbs. Services were set up in the Taylor School where pupils, both white and negro, have moved more frequently than Washington school children in general. The records for attendance and for scholastic readiness are well below the average.

To help these children and these families, more than service to the individual child in the school and traditional methods of working with hard core families was needed. Almost all of the 179 families had had contact with many of the agencies offering financial or other identity knows the answers to such questions as "What am I?," "Who am I?," "What am I supposed to be or to become?," and "Where am I going?" The person lacking self-identity, on the other hand, is confused and uncertain as to what he is supposed to be and where he is going. This state of affairs is clearly exemplified in the deeply neurotic person and in the homosexual, neither one of whom has a clear picture of what he is supposed to be.

Adolescents often manifest lack of self-identity, which is one of the reasons why they are at times uncertain, confused, and extremely vacillating in their opinions, behavior, or goals. We see this clearly exemplified in the high school senior who cannot decide whether he should go on to college, go into the army, or get a job; and in the college student who cannot decide on a definite curriculum. We see it also in young adults who, having left college, flounder from one position to another. We see it exemplified in the extremely large number of boys and girls who, after a period of one or several years, leave the convent or seminary because of a "lack of vocation," often bitterly disappointed, disillusioned, and more confused than they were before. There are countless instances of such vocational disorientation that has its roots in the failure to achieve self-identity.

### THE DETERMINANTS OF SELF-IDENTITY

What is it that determines or facilitates the gradual emergence of self-identity? From the practical standpoint, in our dealing with adolescents, this is one of the most crucial issues since we should do whatever we can to promote conditions favorable to the growth of self-identity. Needless to say, this is a complex process that has its roots not only in the earliest experiences of childhood but in the very being of the person himself. It is not something that occurs during adolescence in the birth of a "new self" but it is true that the achievement of self-identity is not fully realized until the conflicts and problems of the adolescent period have been lived through.

In early childhood, we can discern a number of events that contribute at least in a small way to the development of self-identity. For example, the child is given what the parents hope is a distinctive name, and in some instances he is even given a distinctive number, as when he is called John J. Asteroid, III. He may also have a nursery devoted exclusively to his needs, clothes that not only belong to him but set him off clearly from his younger sister, playthings alloted for his pleasure, and so on. All these little things help to lay the groundwork for the gradual development of selfhood.

But there are more basic developmental factors at work that contribute much more to personal selfhood. Important among these is the growing individuality of the physical organism. It is the physical body that enhances the realization of sex differences, even though these differences may not be apparent or known to the child in the early years of growth. There are of course many factors that contribute to the distinction between maleness and femaleness, but there is none that outranks in importance the structure of the body. In any single case, it may be that the child is brought to an awareness of these differences before he is aware of structural characteristics. The attitudes of parents, relatives, and playmates; methods of segregation that are used to prohibit familiarity; differences in toys and dress; injunctions with respect to privacy in dressing and matters of toilet; the use of boy names and girl names—all serve to enforce the distinction between the sexes almost from infancy. However, cultural practices regarding names, toys, or clothes bear no *intrinsic* relation to the actual fact of maleness or femaleness. To treat a boy like a girl will not make a girl out of him, although it may make him "girlish" in his attitudes and reactions. But it is definitely known that physical structure can have a decided effect on sex status. The awareness of basic sex differences may come as a shock, as a pleasant surprise, or with little feeling; but whatever the reaction, we can be sure that the fact itself profoundly affects the development of the self-concept. The reason is that the self-concept hinges to an important extent on sexual identity; and sexual identity in its turn is dependent upon adequate physical development and a clear realization of physical maleness or femaleness. In this way the self-concept, sex identity, and self-identity become closely interwoven and interdependent, and form a solid groundwork for later maturity.

SEX DIFFERENCES AND SEX IDENTITY

There is perhaps no surer way to stifle self-concept development than by masking or obscuring the differences between the sexes. This is true of the childhood period, and even more true of adolescence. A knowledge of this difference is essential for the adequate growth of the child's idea of what he is and what he should be. Thus the child should be allowed to discover sexual differences early in life, and in a

Rubin, S. Protecting the child in the juvenile court. *J. crim. Law, Criminology, Police Sci.,* 1952, *43,* 425-440.

Waldfogel, S., Coolidge, J. C., & Hahn, Pauline B. The development, meaning and management of school phobia. *Amer. J. Orthopsychiat.,* 1957, 27, 754-780.

Waldfogel, S., Hahn, Pauline B., & Teasman, Ellen. Evaluation of a program for early intervention in school phobia. Paper read at 35th annual meeting of American Orthopsychiatric Association, New York, March 6-8, 1958.

# The Role of the Courts
# in Delinquency Control

## FLORENCE M. KELLEY

*Honorable Florence M. Kelley, Presiding Justice of the Domestic Relations Court of the City of New York, received her B.A. degree from Smith College in 1934, and her LL.B. degree from Yale University in 1937. She received the honorary degree of Doctor of Laws from her alma mater, Smith College, in 1960. Prior to her appointment to the bench, Justice Kelley was Assistant District Attorney for New York County, and in private legal practice. She has been the Attorney-in-Charge, Criminal Branch, Legal Aid Society from 1947 to 1960. She has been a frequent contributor to Legal Aid periodicals for the past fifteen years. Effective September 1, 1962, Justice Kelley assumed her new post as Administrative Judge, Family Court of the State of New York, New York City.*

I am extremely happy to have the opportunity to discuss with this group the role of the courts in delinquency control. There has been in the recent past, and will of necessity be in the future, a good deal of very serious thinking done as to the most productive role for courts in their dealings with young people.

orientation seem to me to be the principal areas within which these conflicts rage.

## REFERENCES

Blaine, G. B., Jr. and McArthur, C. C. (with collaborators). *Emotional problems of the student.* New York: Appleton-Century-Crofts, 1961.

Erikson, E. H. Identity and the life cycle; selected papers. *Psychol. Issues,* 1959, *1,* No. 1 (Monograph 1).

Gallagher, J. R. and Harris, H. I. *Emotional problems of adolescents.* New York: Oxford Univer. Press, 1958.

# The Adolescent's Search for Identity

## ALEXANDER A. SCHNEIDERS

*Alexander A. Schneiders has been a key figure in the Fordham University Pastoral Psychology Institutes from the time of their inauguration. He served as the Chairman of the Institute Committee for the four Institutes held to date, beginning in 1955 and continuing in alternate years through 1961. His own undergraduate degree is from Creighton University in Omaha, and his master's and doctoral degrees are from Georgetown University. From 1939 to 1944, Dr. Schneiders was Director of Student Personnel at Loyola University in Chicago, and from 1945 to 1953 he was Chairman of the Department of Psychology at the University of Detroit. He served as professor of psychology and Director of Psychological Services at Fordham University from 1953 to 1961. He is the author of numerous journal articles and the following books (among others):* Introductory Psychology (*1951*), Personal Adjustment and Mental Health (*1955*), *and* Personality Development and Adjustment in Adolescence (*1960*). *Currently, Dr. Schneiders is professor of psychology in the School of Education at Boston College.*

### THE PRINCIPAL TASKS OF ADOLESCENCE

There are many ways of looking at adolescent development and behavior—from the physiological viewpoint, the moral viewpoint, the perspective of the spiritual counselor, or from the standpoint of sociol-

137

numbers of facilities and the lack of diversity among them will always serve to limit the role that it is possible for the Children's Court to play in delinquency control. The full services of the Court are always available and stand ready to be brought into play for the task of identification of a child and identification of the needs of that child. If one assumes that the probation department does an excellent professional job and that the diagnostic psychiatric clinic also does an excellent professional job and, furthermore, that the Judge sitting on a case is a dedicated, interested and knowledgeable person ready to exercise warm, human discretion, still none of this professional staff work and judicial talent can benefit a child if the help the Judge and staff determine that child must have is not available. If, in the opinion of the Judge, the psychiatrist and the probation officer, a specific child should be removed from its home and put in an institution which would give the child certain specified help and there is no such institution or, if the institution exists, it is full, what indeed has been the value of the processes of the Children's Court?

If the institutions needed, whether public or private, whether in the community of the child's home or out of it, are not available to the Court, then only in cases where the probation report and the diagnostic report provide a proper basis for a judicial determination that a child should be returned to the community and to its own home in the community have these reports served any useful function. But as long as the lack of variegated facilities must necessarily dictate judicial determination it will be impossible to evaluate the entire process of the Court in terms of its effectiveness in individual cases.

*Utilization of potentials in the home.* The picture is, of course, not entirely negative. The very fact that the Court lacks all the institutions it would like to use has forced the Court to scrutinize more carefully the potentials of a home community of an individual child to see whether or not the child could be returned home. The Judge is often faced with the choice of committing a child to an unsuitable institution or taking the risk of returning the child to an unsuitable home environment. I think it fair to say that one thing we have learned is that a child in trouble must somehow learn to cope with himself in his own community. It is true that he may be strengthened by being extricated from a bad home surrounding for a limited time and placed in an institution where his life is regularized and he is under the care and protection of people dedicated to strengthening his inner being as well as his general health, the better to cope with the problems of day-to-day living. But in many cases where the Court has been forced to return a child to his own home because of lack of available space in a suitable institution, great success has been achieved even where the home was not considered suitable, if a resource of strength to work with the child and the home was found. Such a resource of strength at times may be found in an organization working in the community. It may also be found in the probation staff of the Children's Court. To this end we have been fortunate in being able to enlarge our Children's Court probation department considerably in the last year. Hopefully, more and more probation officers will have available time to provide this service to children returned to the community and their families. In addition, in such cases the traumatic shock of being extricated from what the child knows as "home," which is unsuitable through no fault of his, and the even greater traumatic shock of being returned to that same unchanged "home" is avoided.

### ROLE OF FAMILY COURT IN DELINQUENCY

We are now led to what I consider the part of the Court that may very well be used to much better advantage in strengthening the role of the Domestic Relations Court in delinquency control. I address myself to the Family Court division of the Domestic Relations Court. This Court, unfortunately, over the years, has developed into a collection agency concerning itself almost exclusively with obtaining monetary support for wives and children from those upon whom the law places the financial responsibility. In the last year and a half real efforts have been made to strengthen services in family rebuilding in the Family Court. The strengthening of families must certainly appear to everyone as the first and most effective attack on delinquency. The child in trouble is a signpost and warning of a family in trouble. The amount of money made available for support to that family cannot be the full answer to the family's trouble although no one can live without money for rent, food and clothing.

The New York State constitutional amendment, which has now passed two consecutive State legislative sessions and will appear on the ballot in November providing for Court reorganization, specifically provides that the projected new State-wide Family Court will offer family counseling to those persons who seek the help of the Court.

come out close to the bottom of the heap. This feeling may be unconscious but nevertheless operates to prevent a student from making a total effort and presenting himself prepared to the best of his ability to be judged at an examination or a test. He is basically too afraid that he will show up badly and needs the excuse that he did not try.

Another unconscious deterrent to conscientious studying is a fear of aggression. It has been found that often the first area to be affected in an illness involving guilt and fear concerning aggressive impulses may be in the area of studying. People who have feelings of resentment and antagonism against individuals or the world at large often develop an unconscious fear of what they will do to other people if these resentful and antagonistic impulses get loose. This leads to a feeling that one must repress emotion and lead an isolated and withdrawn life. Often this choice of a way of life is not conscious, and all that is obvious is shyness and a passive outlook. People like this often cannot force themselves to study. They seem to have equated studying with being aggressive and have a fear that, if they commit themselves emotionally to a job of studying, they may be overwhelmed by the power of their own aggressiveness—that opening the dam a little will result in the release of uncontrollable forces.

A student was sent to me by his tutor. He came from a family where there was considerable lack of control. His mother was an alcoholic. His father, a man who lost his temper violently and frequently, was constantly at odds with the world and expressed his resentment against people at work, the government, his family, his wife, and his children, in angry terms much of the time. Because of this, the patient spent most of his childhood frightened to express himself in any way for fear that it would bring an explosion from his father. He remembers sitting at the table with his fists clenched and his eyes closed tightly, holding in his feelings while his father and mother were fighting. He did fairly well at college, until one day he became intoxicated at a cocktail party following a football game, and while in this state of intoxication was trying to fix a radiator with a screwdriver. Another boy came up behind him to give him some advice. The patient suddenly became furious and whirled around in such a way that his screwdriver pierced the boy's chest. The other boy was seriously ill, but recovered. My patient had to withdraw from college for a year because of this incident. When he returned, he began having difficulty doing his studying. As we worked in treatment, it became clear that he had always been afraid of exhibiting just the kind of powerful and uncontrollable anger which did show itself at the time of the screwdriver incident. Before that, his controls had always been good enough to keep him from exploding, but after this episode he had had to exert tighter and tighter control, and this had spread into the field of study. He had repressed himself so completely that he could not even throw himself into his work for fear that enthusiasm in this area would spread over into an expression of aggression in other ways.

Students affected in this way must learn to make friends with their aggressive impulses and discover that they are not as uncontrollable as they fear them to be. In this way they can learn to invest some of this repressed energy in constructive studying.

### CONFLICT OVER SEXUAL ORIENTATION

Finally, there is the problem of sexual orientation—the development of the capacity to give and receive love in a gratifying mutual relationship. In most adolescents the achievement of this requires resolution of some inner conflict between homosexual and heterosexual impulses.

No clear-cut conclusions have been reached about the origin or the causes of homosexuality. Most psychiatrists and psychoanalysts today feel that a combination of constitutional and environmental factors are involved. It seems to be fairly well accepted that everyone has some degree of homosexuality in his make-up and that there is a variation in amount from one person to another. This varies from the rare homosexual dream or a homosexual yearning all the way to the living of a homosexual life with the heterosexual desires non-existent. Although it is felt that some people are born with more homosexual instincts than others, it is also believed that certain factors in the growth and development of an individual are responsible for the re-enforcing or the repression of these instincts. Certainly the encouragement of a child to behave as though it had been born the opposite sex will have an effect on the sexual orientation of this child when it becomes older.

This is not the only environmental factor which is important, however. Ability to identify with the parent of the same sex is extremely important. If there is something about this parent which makes such identification difficult, then the child will tend to identify more with the parent of the opposite sex. Also, if there is a remoteness in the relationship between a child and its parent of the same sex, there may develop a need for a closer relationship with people of that sex. If a father and son do not have sufficient closeness in their relationship with each other and, on the contrary, there is misunderstanding and coldness, then a boy may grow up still needing this kind of intimacy

It was apparent, too, that any community faced with a problem as serious and complex as juvenile delinquency must be prepared to confront a wide field of strongly held opinions as to how the problem can be solved. Some community leaders may minimize the problem. Others may reach for any panacea which promises a quick and easy solution. Still others may admit that the problem is serious but disclaim community responsibility for reaching a solution and seek to rid themselves of the responsibility for dealing with it. On the other hand, there are leaders who will face up to the problem, recognize that answers can come only from a total community effort, and accept the demanding obligations, expense and work, in meeting the problem.

### ESTABLISHMENT OF THE YOUTH BOARD

The establishment of the New York City Youth Board as New York City's official agency for the prevention and control of juvenile delinquency under the New York State Youth Commission Act of 1945 by the New York City Board of Estimate is evidence that our community chose the final and most realistic alternative.

We all recognize that New York's problems are deep and widespread. As the nation's greatest metropolis, as a major port of entry, and as a city with a constantly shifting population, we have a correspondingly high number of delinquents. We experience delinquency in all its forms.

It is important to know, however, that there are other large cities with higher delinquency rates and that the vast majority of our young people are not delinquents. In fact, only a little over three percent come to the attention of the authorities.

But even one delinquent can be too many. In a city the size of New York, this three percent translates itself into approximately sixty thousand offenses annually by children and other young people.

In keeping with the recognition that the roots of this problem are many and varied, the Youth Board has been empowered to develop a many-sided program of attack. With the emphasis on a multiple approach, several basic principles have formed the foundation of the Youth Board's program from the very beginning. Among these are the following:

(1) An effective program must concentrate on the individuals, groups, and neighborhoods in which the problem is most severe.

(2) It is always better to use existing resources and facilities, both public and voluntary, than to establish new and duplicating systems. Only when there is no existing agency to do a particular job, should a new one be created.

(3) If the delinquent prevention programs of public and voluntary agencies are to achieve maximum impact, they must be united through planning and coordination.

Moving from these basic principles, the Youth Board, over the past thirteen years, has evolved a comprehensive program of service to the individual, the family, the group and the community. Increasingly, we have found that our efforts must be focused on the hard core of the problem, as exemplified in the multi-problem family, the teenage fighting gang and the depressed and deteriorated neighborhoods in which delinquency and so many other social ills abound.

Planning and coordinating this program of service, and welding it into a strong, unified and effective whole, has been the job of the Youth Board and the Office of the Commissioner of Youth Services. This function includes assuring that existing resources and facilities are utilized to best advantage in order to fill whatever gaps are found to exist. Planning and coordination of services has been conducted with the aid of committees of concerned citizens, professional social workers, public officials, businessmen, doctors, lawyers and clergymen representing a cross section of the entire city. Their accomplishments have had far-reaching influence and impact.

Procedures have been expedited in the courts serving youth, and additional probation officers assigned. Detention and correctional facilities for young offenders have been enlarged and improved. The rate of reimbursement for voluntary institutions serving young people has been increased.

The program of the New York City Youth Board, particularly its Street Club Project which works with fighting teenage gangs and their girl associates, has been greatly expanded. Altogether, New York City is spending almost seventy-five million dollars annually for the prevention and control of juvenile delinquency.

### MULTI-PROBLEM FAMILIES

Before effective planning and coordination could take place, however, it was necessary to view the field in which we had to work. A series of studies by our research department leads us to believe that through with it. He described the situation as being like trying to tune in on a radio, knowing that each program was good, but that if you chose one, you would not be able to listen to any of the others. He would spend time sitting and thinking about himself, first as a banker, then as a lawyer, then as a doctor, then as a research chemist; but each time after about five minutes he would throw up his hands in disgust saying that it was all an impossible fantasy.

These symptoms fit into the pattern of what is termed "role diffusion" and the causative influences appear clearly delineated in the family constellation described above.

The second alternative, that of negative identity, is an identification on the part of the child with everything that his parents least want him to be. This does not spring simply from rebellion against parental standards but rather seems to come often as a result of feelings of inferiority which are unconsciously instilled in the child by parents who are constantly warning him against being a certain kind of person. Thus a mother with a brother who is an alcoholic may talk to her child of her concern about this brother and how little she wants her son to be like him. This results in a feeling on the part of the child that the uncle who is an alcoholic is getting more attention because of his alcoholism than the child is getting for being just what the family does want. Also, if too-high standards are set, a child may feel that it is impossible to achieve what the parents expect, and rather than be just halfway good it may be more satisfying to be all bad. One receives more attention from parents if one is at the bottom of the class than in the middle. If one cannot get kudos for being the class leader, better be dunce than settle for the anonymity and the silent disapproval in barely passing.

### PROBLEMS IN ACADEMIC WORK

Emotional problems lying below the surface in this age group are often manifested by underachievement in school. This is something which is certainly self-defeating and frustrating both to the student and his parents but again does not fall into the category of psychiatric illness. However, exploration of the basic conflicts with an understanding teacher, priest or counselor can often bring gratifying results in terms of improved school performance. The types of underlying problems are varied.

The simplest of these is preoccupation with other matters. A relationship with a loved one, the death of a member of the family, or financial difficulties may be occupying a lot of the student's thinking and be such a strong source of worry that it intrudes itself constantly into his mind when he tries to pick up a book or sit down to write a paper. The treatment for this sort of thing consists in helping the student ventilate the amount of concern he feels about this problem and to effect some kind of resolution of this conflict if possible.

Another source of difficulty, which lies more below the surface than this first and is not quite so easily perceived, is a feeling, either conscious or unconscious, on the part of the student that he is working in a void—that no one around him cares whether he does well or badly. His parents may be a long way off physically, or it may be simply that they and others who are important to the student are psychologically remote and distant—cold and undemonstrative people, who do not give the student any feeling that his work is appreciated. If there is no reward for studying well, then often it becomes such a dry and sterile task that it is impossible to focus one's mind on the subject matter.

A rather dramatic example of this occurred a few years ago. A sophomore at college who had always done good work and never been a procrastinator came to the clinic one day in an acute panic, saying that he was exceedingly frightened. He had an overwhelming fear of impending disaster but could not pin it on any specific thing. He was restless, nervous, unable to sit in a chair to do his work. He was seen daily, in order to reassure him, and to keep him from doing something desperate.

In the course of his treatment, it was learned that his parents had been living in California and were moving to Florida. They were going to take a trip of eight weeks throughout the West and Midwest in the process so that they could see as much of the country as they could. During this time they were incommunicado, as they had no definite itinerary; because of this the boy could not write to them nor telephone them, and for eight weeks he was going to be cut off from them. He felt lost and lonely, but it was only after several interviews that he was able to see this himself and to admit it to his psychiatrist. As the days went by, he became progressively more upset, and because of our concern about him, we had his parents found by the state police, and they telephoned him. Immediately after speaking with them, he began to feel better and could settle down to do a little studying; they changed their plans and came immediately to Cambridge. As soon as they arrived, the boy became calm again and has been perfectly well since.

This case illustrates the great importance of support and communication in keeping many people stable and able to work efficiently and productively.

pressures are greatest, most of these young people do not remain in school and, upon leaving, join the group we call "dropouts." Having left school early, they find that in seeking employment they do not meet even the minimum requirements for unskilled jobs, not to mention those categories where additional training and education are required.

In New York City approximately ten thousand of these young people are currently seeking full-time employment. As each school term ends, they are joined by thousands of others, similarly unskilled, who seek part-time as well as full-time employment. It is needless to say that the majority of these young people do not obtain jobs. They join the other unemployed youngsters who hang out on the streets where their idleness can lead to many of the problems we all have come to know so well.

The Youth Board has attempted, and with some success, to make employment available for some of these young people. Until now, we have concentrated largely on summer employment and have received help from other city agencies as well as private industry. However, with the growing problem and changing national economic outlook, we have had to view the problem on a long-range basis.

Stemming from the collaboration of the Youth Board, the Board of Education, the Community Council of Greater New York and the Manpower Utilization Council, the mayor called a Conference on Youth and Work which was held June 1, 1961.

It was attended by leaders from business, industry, labor, education, government, employment and youth-serving agencies. Among the subjects discussed were how to keep more young people in school longer, how to equip them for employment by improving their training in job skills, how to improve the attitudes and motivations of those young people with special problems and how to help more young people achieve economic self-sufficiency.

It is expected that, from the conference will emerge a long-range, city-wide program which will make deep inroads into preparing school dropouts and other problem youth with minimum skills and training, so that they can take their places in a job market which, of necessity, must be geared to the challenges of tomorrow.

## NEIGHBORHOOD COOPERATION

In working with individuals and families in high delinquency areas, the Youth Board is deeply aware that the community must be creatively served. Therefore, it collaborates with civic groups, neighborhood associations and other combinations of citizens interested in developing plans, programs and resources to meet neighborhood needs.

We are aware that any community self-help program must have the interest and the cooperation of people living in that neighborhood. It is they who know the community and its resources best. In our work with such groups, we cooperate in the preparation of a program stemming from them. We offer support in the form of statistics, we expedite the contacting of individuals and organizations which can be of help and provide an advisor who is constantly on call.

## YOUTH BOARD ACHIEVEMENTS

We feel that we have made some tangible progress in preventing juvenile delinquency in New York City. Our Street Club Project, in working with fighting teenage gangs, has been successful in that from 65 to 75 percent of the gang membership has made an adjustment in the community. Further, the present membership is two years younger than ten years ago, and gang fights involving large numbers of young people have been curtailed to smaller numbers of gang members involved. This type of conflict is requiring a new approach on an individual basis. Also, in our work with girls associated with fighting gangs, we feel we are making some progress because of their constructive interest and participation in our program.

Although it is still early for evaluation, our employment program is receiving the active support of individuals, organizations and agencies in a broad and sweeping program to expand job opportunities for young people.

As testimony to its work as a vital service to a sorely deprived community, our pilot project, the Interdepartmental Neighborhood Service Center, will soon be able to announce additional support, from a foundation, for a special project.

The budget of the Youth Board in its service to young people and

## CONFLICT BETWEEN INDEPENDENCE AND DEPENDENCE

The conflict between independence and dependence is one which must be resolved in favor of independence if a healthy individual development is to take place. Adolescence is marked by extremes in both types of behavior. A teenager at one time will be defiant and rebellious, objecting to the slightest kind of parental control, and at another will act in a childish, immature way, demanding help and guidance from a parent who has been rudely criticized a few moments before for proffering just this kind of help. There seems to be a need on the part of growing children to create some kind of disturbance within the home—as though they had to make the family a place of conflict and unpleasantness in order to leave it more easily and become independent. Perhaps they can leave home only if they first make it such an unattractive and tumultuous environment that no one could comfortably live there. Unfortunately, much of this adolescent rebellion is treated by parents with such intolerance that the child who is trying to become an adult is overwhelmed by so much guilt and remorse over his behavior that his attempts to be independently aggressive are thwarted, and he is forced to mollify his parents by curbing his natural instinct to be free of them.

It is this overweening desire to be independent and to defy family standards that leads to a pattern of delinquency. We cannot find a common type of family background present in all delinquent children. It does appear, however, to be a matter of extremes. Parents who are overindulgent, as well as those who are overly rejecting, seem to produce children who get into trouble with the law.

For example, a boy came to our clinic who was a freshman in college. His problem on the surface was simply that he was not doing good work and had refused to hand in several assigned papers. He said that the deans were worried about him, and his religious counselor had told him that his problem was too deep for simple conversational talks. It became clear soon after treatment began that this boy was a sophisticated kind of delinquent. He was practicing numerous deceptions around college and in the surrounding city as well, stealing from the local stores, plagiarizing his papers, and cheating on his examinations. His family history revealed that his father was an itinerant painter, having been at home only for two- or three-month periods during the boy's entire life and never showing any interest in his two boys except to upbraid them for being sissies. The boy's mother had had to work and had been away from home almost all day ever since the boy was old enough to be on three meals. He had been left alone in an apartment in New York, so terrified that he had spent his time huddled close to the door listening for his mother's footsteps. She often found him asleep against the door. During his later school years, he lived with a grandfather and grandmother, who felt imposed upon, and punished him unmercifully for every small misdemeanor. He worked overconscientiously at school and did extremely well, but still his grandparents did not appreciate his work and continued to ridicule and punish him. He later returned to his mother, who had now become successful at selling real estate but preferred to spend her money on luxuries for herself, insisting that her son work his way through college as well as gain as much scholarship aid as possible. Meanwhile she lied about her income so that he would be able to obtain a scholarship.

It is no wonder, with such a severe and rejecting background, that this boy acted out against his parents by misbehaving and being dishonest, even as his mother was. His anger and fury at her was taken out against the college and against the forces of law and order by dishonest and illegal behavior.

Another boy was expelled from college because of two rebellious episodes, one involving pretending he was blind and soliciting money on the sidewalk and the other selling dance tickets for a freshman prom and pocketing the money for himself. He came from a very different sort of background. His parents were extremely affectionate and tried their best to give him everything he wanted. They went overboard in this respect, however, and the result was that the boy found that he could get away with anything, both within the home and within the community. His parents would bail him out whenever he got into any kind of trouble. Both his mother and father were completely permissive people and felt that the boy should be allowed to do whatever he pleased, whether it was to disappear for a week without telling them where he was or be given a Ford Thunderbird. When I worked with this student, it became clear that he was just as angry with his parents as the first boy was; it was not for their cruel and rejecting treatment of him but rather for their overindulgence. His feeling was that they could not really love him because they never seemed to care about what he did. He gave examples of times when he would purposely do things which he thought would annoy them and of how disappointed he was when they simply smiled and pretended that they didn't care. Of course, he thought they really did not care and that no one who really loved their child could allow him to do the things he did without becoming upset. Since he could not get a reaction out of his parents, he tried irritating the university.

In the adolescent's struggle for independence, he is bound to tread on some toes, and often the price of his freedom must be the kind of misunderstandings and disharmonies within a family which cannot but be distressing and upsetting.

# The Institutional Approach to Delinquency

## BROTHER AUGUSTINE, F.S.C.

*Brother Augustine, F.S.C., has two master's degrees, one in Latin from Fordham in 1945, the other in psychology from the Catholic University of America in 1955. He is Director of Lincoln Hall, Lincolndale, N. Y. This school, situated in upper Westchester County, about fifty miles from New York City, is conducted by the Christian (Teaching) Brothers, and is devoted to the rehabilitation of boys from delinquent backgrounds. The boys are sent to the school by the New York State Children's Court. Most of them come from New York City, and the rest from a few surrounding counties. The school has one Brother for each eight boys, plus a lay staff of approximately 150. The boys usually remain in the school between one and two years, and the average enrollment is 260.*

An institution is for the community a kind of last resort. When a boy or girl can no longer be contained in the community at large without serious risk to his or her own welfare or the general welfare of the community, the parents are informed of this by an official authority of the community and the child is "sent away" to an institution.

An effort is made by the community through its various officials to interpret this action in a benevolent light and assist the parents and the child to accept institutionalization in a voluntary spirit. The fact is, however, that the commitment is an exercise of a community's supreme judgment and authority over even the sacred rights of parents.

Such an action necessarily conditions the institutional approach to delinquency. The institution is given an authority over the child. It is, in effect, told, "We in the community at large can no longer get along peaceably with this child. Take him, you, and see to it that he does not bother us again. We hold you responsible for him."

This responsibility given to an institution is not simply to contain the child, although this is part of the approach that the community expects of an institution, but to deal with him in such a way that he may be returned to the community as soon as possible as a law-abiding, useful adolescent citizen.

### INSTITUTION'S AIM IS REHABILITATION

In a single word, then, the institutional approach to delinquency is rehabilitation. It is, perhaps, unnecessary to point out that this function, however important, is different from and really secondary to the job of preventing delinquency which should rightly occupy the first place in the attention and efforts of a community.

It should be clear, too, that the institutional approach is not so much to delinquency as it is to individual delinquents. Delinquency is a sociological problem as well as an individual problem, and this is, perhaps, beginning to get its proper place in community awareness (Cloward and Ohlin, 1960; Martin, 1961). The institution can, perhaps, give some help to the community on this problem through the research it can carry out on its institutional population and through the education of the community which it can carry out through its program of public relations. But while these two functions are part of the institutional approach to delinquency, the primary approach of the institution is the rehabilitation of the individual delinquent rather than the rehabilitation of society.

A further precision of the institutional approach to delinquency must be made by stating that it is *social* rehabilitation which is the aim of an institution. It is not sufficient that an institution succeed in teaching its boys or girls to read, write, and do arithmetic well enough to earn a high school diploma and pass the college entrance examina-

toward these children, especially when they return to the community. In this the people of the community can be of considerable help in the job of rehabilitation.

The members of the boy's own family, his teachers in the school to which he returns, or his employers, and the clergy in his parish are key persons in this aspect of an institution's total program. Some of the work that an institution carries on with these and other people are:

1. A program of visits for the boy to and from his family while he is at the institution;

2. Casework service with the boy's family while the boy is at the institution and after he has returned to his home;

3. Assistance given by the social worker to the administration and teaching staff of the school to which the boy returns in order to help them understand and work with the boy;

4. Assistance given by the social worker to the boy for obtaining employment and to the employer when questions or problems arise concerning the boy;

5. Alerting the parish priests to the help needed by the boy or his family while the boy is at the institution and after he returns to the parish again;

6. Giving the child experiences with the outside community while he is still at the institution through volunteer groups, through athletic contests, entertainment programs, occasional excursions, etc.

7. Foster homes and boarding homes as halfway houses are special, all-out methods of effecting a successful reintegration of the child into the community after institutional discharge.

So much for the principal members of the body of the institution.

### THE SOUL OF AN INSTITUTION—ITS STAFF

The soul of an institution is, of course, the people who are its staff, and specifically the experience which they personally provide the children in the institution. What the child in any institution needs more than anything else is an experience of a relationship with other people, adults and equals, that is true, good, consistent and enduring. Socialization may be described as the process whereby an individual develops the ability to sustain a relationship with persons in which the true values of persons are understood, esteemed and given appropriate honor in action. The attainment of this socialization by any individual is almost entirely dependent on an experience of such relationships during the formative periods of life.

This is why the rehabilitative strength of the school department in an institution is obviously to be found in its teachers, especially in the wisdom and the generosity of their relation to the pupils; this is why the heart of psychotherapy is the skill and disinterestedness shown by the therapist in his relationship with the client; this is even why the success of a religion program is measured for the most part by the success of all the members of the staff in allowing the wisdom and the goodness of God Himself to shine through in their dealings with the child; this is why when the professionals devise a treatment program for the guidance of the cottage parents, who provide more than ninety percent of the child's relationship in the institution, they always prescribe the same treatment. "This child," they say, "needs two things: first, a sense of his own worth through your interest and honest esteem for him and the way you treat him, your acceptance of him, your affection for him, your kindliness to him regardless of how he acts; and secondly, a sense of his responsibilities to other people and the strength acquired by the practice of these responsibilities through your wise guidance of him, your direction, control and punishment of him, given prudently, patiently, perseveringly, all within the framework of your personal relationship with him." This is a fairly accurate statement of the residential treatment plan applicable to every juvenile delinquent. There are always details specified for each child within this general formula, but all of them are expressive of these two basic recommendations.

In the final analysis the institutional approach to delinquency is an effort to provide an individual child with a prolonged experience of the specific relationship he particularly needs between himself and other persons who can represent the kind of truly wise and truly generous behavior that our society desires. Upon this experience is built the whole program of rehabilitation: self-knowledge, self-control, a sense of values, and the strength to act according to them.

### LIMITATIONS OF INSTITUTIONAL APPROACH

It must be added that this effort is carried out under many limitations which are largely inherent in the institutional approach to delinquency. Before concluding it seems that for the sake of being complete some of these limitations must be mentioned briefly.

The first of these is the fact that the institution is not the child's own home and the staff are not his parents. There is a role in every child's life that belongs to his parents and this role can be played by someone else only with extreme difficulty, if at all. And yet this role is crucial in the normal development of the child.

A second limitation is the fact that the children who are sent as delinquents to an institution are generally severely damaged in their basic capacity to relate to other people. This damage has resulted from the nature of their previous life's experiences. It is a damage that touches the very core of the human person. When a child's ability to relate to other people has been damaged there is no special magic, or even medical drugs, whereby it may be repaired. It is only through relationship, the very bridge which has been damaged, that the damage can be repaired.

The repairing of this bridge is a tremendous challenge to the staff of an institution. But here is another, and third, limitation almost inherent in the institutional approach to delinquency. A sufficient number of the necessary kind of staff is really hard to come by. And it is another very real human problem for such a staff to act at all times in conformity to its wisdom and its generosity, to meet the challenge.

A fourth limitation is that almost all institutions for delinquent children are overcrowded and under almost constant pressure from the communities they serve to become more overcrowded. And yet this overcrowding creates a gap between the child and the staff, an impersonalization which is the major obstacle to the achievement of an institution's purpose.

Lastly, since rehabilitation is effected in the community and not really in an institution, a serious obstacle to success is the prejudice of many members of the community against boys returning from an institution. Very often instead of a willingness to understand and help, such boys meet with a readiness to condemn on the slightest provocation or the smallest shred of evidence.

## REFERENCES

Breed, A. What is treatment? *Proceedings of the National Association of Training Schools and Juvenile Agencies,* 1960, *56,* 58-69.

Cloward, R. A. and Ohlin, L. E. *Delinquency and opportunity.* New York: Free Press, 1960.

Kahn, A. J. *For children in trouble.* New York: Citizens' Committee for Children of New York City, 1957.

MacIver, R. M. *The institutionalization of young delinquents.* (Interim Report No. XI) New York: New York City Juvenile Delinquency Evaluation Project, 1958.

Martin, J. M. Three approaches to delinquency prevention. *Crime and Delinquency,* 1961, *7,* 16-24.

Ohlin, L. E. and Lawrence, W. The role of the inmate system in the institutional treatment process. *Proceedings of the National Association of Training Schools and Juvenile Agencies,* 1958, *54,* 115-135.

Robison, Sophia M. *Juvenile delinquency, its nature and control.* New York: Holt, Rinehart & Winston, 1960.

# Range of Adjustments in Adolescence

## GRAHAM B. BLAINE, JR.

*Graham Burt Blaine, Jr., M.D., is psychiatrist to the University Health Service, Harvard University. His A.B. degree is from Harvard, and his M.D. degree from the College of Physicians and Surgeons of Columbia University. In addition to his post at Harvard, Dr. Blaine is also associate psychiatrist to the Adolescent Unit, Children's Medical Center, Boston, and assistant in psychiatry, Harvard Medical School. From 1951 to 1953 he was consultant psychiatrist to Williams College, Williamstown, Massachusetts, and from 1957 to 1958 he was Associate Director of the Harvard University project on Religion and Mental Health. He is a member of the American Psychiatric Association and of the American College Health Association. Dr. Blaine is the co-editor with Charles C. McArthur of the recent book:* The Emotional Problems of the Student *(1961). A review of this book in the NEWSLETTER of the American Catholic Psychological Association characterized it as ". . . the best book yet produced on the conduct of psychotherapeutic services in an academic setting."*

Actions and attitudes, which in an adult would be considered symptomatic of severe emotional disturbance, are now understood by professional people and parents alike as being a normal part of that tumultuous period of life, marking the transitional stage between childhood and adulthood, known as adolescence. Rebellious and provocative behavior, isolation and withdrawal, extreme lethargy and apathy, peculiar ways of dressing, a bizarre and unintelligible language, peculiar obsessions and fads; all these are characteristics which could scarcely be tolerated in an adult, but they are now accepted, somewhat reluctantly and woefully, by parents as growing pains in their teenage sons and daughters and not cause for alarm.

Despite the more recent trend toward stricter discipline and a more authoritarian approach to child rearing, there still remains a strong current of feeling among parents in favor of the permissive upbringing of children. This is to be regretted and has resulted, I feel, in making the conflicts and the turmoils of adolescence more difficult for the growing child as well as his parents. A healthy conscience developed as a result of good parental example and discipline is the most essential accessory for the growing child's trip through this trying stage of life.

It is sad, but true, that once a child has reached the age of about twelve or fourteen parents can have very little influence on the formation and development of his conscience. He now must go it alone and it is important for parents to realize that now there must be a subtle and gradual change in attitude toward their offspring. There must be a shift from an emphasis on explanation, direct advice, clearly set limits on behavior, and definite scheduling to one involving more freedom for the child in his own choices, expression of confidence in the ability of the child to succeed on his own, and particularly a willingness on the part of the parent to let the child learn his lessons by experience rather than from warnings and prohibitions from his mother and father.

No matter how skillfully the parents may adjust themselves to the beginnings of maturity in their children still there will remain some evidences of insecurity and unhappiness. No one steps from childhood into adulthood without experiencing some distress. In trying to classify the main conflicts which arise during this stormy period of development, there appear to be four main areas: first, the conflict between independence and dependence; second, the problem of the formation of identity; third, the problem of performing academic work; last, the conflict over sexual orientation.

### CONFLICT BETWEEN INDEPENDENCE AND DEPENDENCE

The conflict between independence and dependence is one which must be resolved in favor of independence if a healthy individual development is to take place. Adolescence is marked by extremes in both types of behavior. A teenager at one time will be defiant and rebellious, objecting to the slightest kind of parental control, and at another will act in a childish, immature way, demanding help and guidance from a parent who has been rudely criticized a few moments before for proffering just this kind of help. There seems to be a need on the part of growing children to create some kind of disturbance within the home—as though they had to make the family a place of conflict and unpleasantness in order to leave it more easily and become independent. Perhaps they can leave home only if they first make it such an unattractive and tumultuous environment that no one could comfortably live there. Unfortunately, much of this adolescent rebellion is treated by parents with such intolerance that the child who is trying to become an adult is overwhelmed by so much guilt and remorse over his behavior that his attempts to be independently aggressive are thwarted, and he is forced to mollify his parents by curbing his natural instinct to be free of them.

It is this overweening desire to be independent and to defy family standards that leads to a pattern of delinquency. We cannot find a common type of family background present in all delinquent children. It does appear, however, to be a matter of extremes. Parents who are overindulgent, as well as those who are overly rejecting, seem to produce children who get into trouble with the law.

For example, a boy came to our clinic who was a freshman in college. His problem on the surface was simply that he was not doing good work and had refused to hand in several assigned papers. He said that the deans were worried about him, and his religious counselor had told him that his problem was too deep for simple conversational talks. It became clear soon after treatment began that this boy was a sophisticated kind of delinquent. He was practicing numerous deceptions around college and in the surrounding city as well, stealing from the local stores, plagiarizing his papers, and cheating on his examinations. His family history revealed that his father was an itinerant painter, having been at home only for two- or three-month periods during the boy's entire life and never showing any interest in his two boys except to upbraid them for being sissies. The boy's mother had had to work and had been away from home almost all day ever since the boy was old enough to be on three meals. He had been left alone in an apartment in New York, so terrified that he had spent his time huddled close to the door listening for his mother's footsteps. She often found him asleep against the door. During his later school years, he lived with a grandfather and grandmother, who felt imposed upon, and punished him unmercifully for every small misdemeanor. He worked overconscientiously at school and did extremely well, but still his grandparents did not appreciate his work and continued to ridicule and punish him. He later returned to his mother, who had now become successful at selling real estate but preferred to spend her money on luxuries for herself, insisting that her son work his way through college as well as gain as much scholarship aid as possible. Meanwhile she lied about her income so that he would be able to obtain a scholarship.

It is no wonder, with such a severe and rejecting background, that this boy acted out against his parents by misbehaving and being dishonest, even as his mother was. His anger and fury at her was taken out against the college and against the forces of law and order by dishonest and illegal behavior.

Another boy was expelled from college because of two rebellious episodes, one involving pretending he was blind and soliciting money on the sidewalk and the other selling dance tickets for a freshman prom and pocketing the money for himself. He came from a very different sort of background. His parents were extremely affectionate and tried their best to give him everything he wanted. They went overboard in this respect, however, and the result was that the boy found that he could get away with anything, both within the home and within the community. His parents would bail him out whenever he got into any kind of trouble. Both his mother and father were completely permissive people and felt that the boy should be allowed to do whatever he pleased, whether it was to disappear for a week without telling them where he was or be given a Ford Thunderbird. When I worked with this student, it became clear that he was just as angry with his parents as the first boy was; it was not for their cruel and rejecting treatment of him but rather for their overindulgence. His feeling was that they could not really love him because they never seemed to care about what he did. He gave examples of times when he would purposely do things which he thought would annoy them and of how disappointed he was when they simply smiled and pretended that they didn't care. Of course, he thought they really did not care and that no one who really loved their child could allow him to do the things he did without becoming upset. Since he could not get a reaction out of his parents, he tried irritating the university.

In the adolescent's struggle for independence, he is bound to tread on some toes, and often the price of his freedom must be the kind of misunderstandings and disharmonies within a family which cannot but be distressing and upsetting.

## THE FORMATION OF IDENTITY

The second important conflict in need of resolution is that of the identity crisis. Suddenly the growing child begins to realize that he is an individual and not simply an extension of his parents. Sometimes he is shocked to find that there are people in the world who do not have the same standards and values which his parents have and that these people are respected and admired, both by his parents and by others. This often throws him into some degree of confusion. For many years he had looked up to his parents as the ones who had the final answer. It is a surprise to find that many well-respected people in the world believe that things which his parents said were wrong are quite all right; it makes him wonder whether the things which he had been afraid to do in the past were really so bad after all. It encourages him to find new criteria for behavior and to look within himself for a scale of values. Often when the adolescent comes to do this, he finds a blank wall, and no clear picture of what he is emerges. No immediate answer flashes directly to him as to whether he believes that a certain sort of behavior is good or bad. This is often frightening. It makes him think that perhaps there is no real substance to him and that up to then he had been borrowing opinions and ideas from others or simply following judgments and opinions which conform with those of whomever he happened to be speaking to at the moment. This contributes to a state of "adolescent turmoil," a condition which may paralyze an individual so that he cannot become interested in anything or make progress in any direction, or it may consist simply of an inner questioning which is not disturbing enough to show on the outside.

The achievement of a sense of identity, as described by Erikson, is "A feeling of being at home in one's body; a sense of knowing where one is going; and an inner assurance of anticipated recognition from those who count. We are most aware of our identity when we have just gained it, and we are somewhat surprised to make its acquaintance" (Erikson, 1959, p. 118). In more detail he describes it as follows: "Man, to take his place in society, must acquire a conflict-free, habitual use of a dominant faculty to be elaborated in an occupation; a limitless resource, a feed-back as it were, from the immediate exercise of this occupation from the companionship it provides; and finally, an intelligible theory of the process of life" (Erikson, 1959, p. 110). On the surface, this does not sound very difficult or complicated. Actually all it means is that he gain a sense of inner security and enough self-knowledge to feel like an individual who, though different in some ways from his fellowman, is nonetheless capable in certain areas, that he find a job to do which is interesting and pays back something in the way of satisfaction and gratification, and, lastly, that he have a religion or some theory about what life is all about which is thoroughly satisfying to him. This may seem routine, but adolescents find problems here and take these problems very seriously. Much of their conflict centers around them.

It is important in the development of identity to incorporate into it various identifications which result from an assimilation of characteristics from people who have been important in one's life. These may be parents or teachers or even actors and movie stars. These imitations do not apply to the whole personality, as hero worship does, but simply to portions of the personalities of many people, which are modified and coalesced finally into one individual identity. In order to achieve a solidified personality, certain factors seem to be important. One is that there is no loss of an identity figure at a crucial stage of life, such as in the early teens. This loss may occur through death or through sudden disillusionment in a person who was formerly respected and admired. Another inhibiting factor is the overly intrusive parent, one who is constantly prodding, questioning, probing, in this way preventing his children from accomplishing anything on their own and by themselves. Also, an overly dependent parent, one who cannot be independent either of his wife or of his own parents, tends to have a weakening influence on the formation of identity in his child.

When a number of these factors are present, two things may happen instead of the formation of a solid identity. One is "role diffusion," and the other "negative identity." In the first, the person finds himself torn between a number of possible roles in life, and unable to settle on any one for more than a short time.

A boy consulted a guidance clinic who had been brought up in a poverty-stricken community. His mother was a dominating, overriding kind of person who hovered around him constantly, always concerned about how he was eating, what kind of clothes he was wearing, how much homework he was doing, whether he was going around with the right kind of people, and so forth. His father was a harassed, weak, gentle man, who was left out of the picture completely, and finally took to drinking because of his loneliness. When this boy came to describe what he was going to do after high school, he found himself completely at a loss. He felt tempted by a number of different things but never by one enough to actually follow through with it. He described the situation as being like trying to tune in on a radio, knowing that each program was good, but that if you chose one, you would not be able to listen to any of the others. He would spend time sitting and thinking about himself, first as a banker, then as a lawyer, then as a doctor, then as a research chemist; but each time after about five minutes he would throw up his hands in disgust saying that it was all an impossible fantasy.

These symptoms fit into the pattern of what is termed "role diffusion" and the causative influences appear clearly delineated in the family constellation described above.

The second alternative, that of negative identity, is an identification on the part of the child with everything that his parents least want him to be. This does not spring simply from rebellion against parental standards but rather seems to come often as a result of feelings of inferiority which are unconsciously instilled in the child by parents who are constantly warning him against being a certain kind of person. Thus a mother with a brother who is an alcoholic may talk to her child of her concern about this brother and how little she wants her son to be like him. This results in a feeling on the part of the child that the uncle who is an alcoholic is getting more attention because of his alcoholism than the child is getting for being just what the family does want. Also, if too-high standards are set, a child may feel that it is impossible to achieve what the parents expect, and rather than be just halfway good it may be more satisfying to be all bad. One receives more attention from parents if one is at the bottom of the class than in the middle. If one cannot get kudos for being the class leader, better be dunce than settle for the anonymity and the silent disapproval in barely passing.

### PROBLEMS IN ACADEMIC WORK

Emotional problems lying below the surface in this age group are often manifested by underachievement in school. This is something which is certainly self-defeating and frustrating both to the student and his parents but again does not fall into the category of psychiatric illness. However, exploration of the basic conflicts with an understanding teacher, priest or counselor can often bring gratifying results in terms of improved school performance. The types of underlying problems are varied.

The simplest of these is preoccupation with other matters. A relationship with a loved one, the death of a member of the family, or financial difficulties may be occupying a lot of the student's thinking and be such a strong source of worry that it intrudes itself constantly into his mind when he tries to pick up a book or sit down to write a paper. The treatment for this sort of thing consists in helping the student ventilate the amount of concern he feels about this problem and to effect some kind of resolution of this conflict if possible.

Another source of difficulty, which lies more below the surface than this first and is not quite so easily perceived, is a feeling, either conscious or unconscious, on the part of the student that he is working in a void—that no one around him cares whether he does well or badly. His parents may be a long way off physically, or it may be simply that they and others who are important to the student are psychologically remote and distant—cold and undemonstrative people, who do not give the student any feeling that his work is appreciated. If there is no reward for studying well, then often it becomes such a dry and sterile task that it is impossible to focus one's mind on the subject matter.

A rather dramatic example of this occurred a few years ago. A sophomore at college who had always done good work and never been a procrastinator came to the clinic one day in an acute panic, saying that he was exceedingly frightened. He had an overwhelming fear of impending disaster but could not pin it on any specific thing. He was restless, nervous, unable to sit in a chair to do his work. He was seen daily, in order to reassure him, and to keep him from doing something desperate.

In the course of his treatment, it was learned that his parents had been living in California and were moving to Florida. They were going to take a trip of eight weeks throughout the West and Midwest in the process so that they could see as much of the country as they could. During this time they were incommunicado, as they had no definite itinerary; because of this the boy could not write to them nor telephone them, and for eight weeks he was going to be cut off from them. He felt lost and lonely, but it was only after several interviews that he was able to see this himself and to admit it to his psychiatrist. As the days went by, he became progressively more upset, and because of our concern about him, we had his parents found by the state police, and they telephoned him. Immediately after speaking with them, he began to feel better and could settle down to do a little studying; they changed their plans and came immediately to Cambridge. As soon as they arrived, the boy became calm again and has been perfectly well since.

This case illustrates the great importance of support and communication in keeping many people stable and able to work efficiently and productively.

Another cause for study block is the need to fail. This is a more complicated mechanism and is related to the exploitation of children by their parents. When very high goals are set for children, they often are made to feel that no matter what they do, it is not quite enough. The reward for achievement is like the carrot that is held in front of the nose of the donkey to keep it going but can never be reached and enjoyed. Many students are repeatedly having the standard of success set higher. Each time they do well, the goal is pushed up a notch or two, and they never can achieve complete approval, no matter how well they do. However, when they do very badly, a great deal of fuss is made, and even though it is negative in nature, it still is flattering and pleasurable.

A freshman who was in academic trouble was referred to me by his faculty adviser. His father was a writer for a well-known magazine, and his mother was an executive secretary for a publisher in New York. They had their boy's life all planned for him in the field of writing, but also, since he was a good mathematician, they had several other careers lined up for him as alternatives which were almost as satisfactory. He told me that anything which he did was hailed by his parents as being evidence that he was doing just what they had always expected that he would do and that there was nothing which he could do and feel was his alone. Everything had been pre-empted from him by his parents and immediately became part of what they had planned for him. The only thing which he could do and feel was his own private performance was to fail miserably, and this he succeeded in doing despite all my efforts.

He was an unusual boy, in that he gathered around him a coterie of people who were interested in him because he seemed to be so brilliant and to have such great promise. He would encourage each of them to think that this person alone understood him and could help him out of his despondent, paralyzed state; but the more they did, the less he did. He had learned how to bring attention to himself by disappointing people rather than pleasing them.

Another unconscious mechanism which operates to keep students from doing well despite the fact that they want to, and think they are trying their best to succeed, is rebellion against authority. For many, there is an unconscious desire to rebel against parents by flunking out of school and thus bringing disgrace to the family name. Of course, this is irrational and therefore cannot be accepted into consciousness. Clearly it is not sensible to rebel in a way that hurts oneself more than the person in the position of authority. Nonetheless, in therapy with students caught in this strange paradox, where, despite wanting to do good work, they cannot force themselves to, we find strong hostility against a parent.

A boy came to the guidance service at a small college complaining of a sudden inability to do assigned work—a problem he had never been troubled with in high school. He had been brought up in the Middle West in a very strict religious home. His father insisted that there be no smoking, drinking, or card-playing in the household. He was a man who felt that any kind of fun was wicked. He believed in hard work, both physical and mental, and insisted that his son live up to the kind of standards which he set for himself. The boy, a freshman, thrown into the comparative gaiety and relaxed living of a college environment, was at a loss to know what to do. When he first came to see me, he talked with high praise about his father and his father's ideals, describing him as "the most perfect father a boy could have." As he came back for further interviews, however, he gradually became aware of feelings which he had previously kept locked up in his unconscious, feelings of antagonism and resentment against his father for insisting that he continue to live according to these fixed standards, even though he was away at a college where no one else had ever heard of such self-denial, much less practiced it. He spoke with considerable anger about his father, and as he was able to get this off his chest, he began studying much more efficiently and to get passing grades. He never spoke angrily to his father, but only to me in describing his father. This was enough, however, to free up his powers of concentration and prevent him from working off his antagonism against his father by doing badly at college.

Another problem in the unconscious which often works as a deterrent to study is a feeling of basic inferiority, which leads to a fear of actually trying hard to do well, because of the need to have an excuse for failure. It is often necessary to think to oneself and to have it obvious to others that one did not get good grades because one had not studied hard enough rather than to fail despite having tried as hard as one could. These basic feelings of inferiority can remain buried in the unconscious and work effectively to sabotage good performance even though there is external evidence of excellent intellectual endowment. Many boys who have high intelligence quotients and have been told so are still haunted by deep feelings of inferiority. These are often based on parental attitudes which may have been appropriate during childhood but not at the present. Children who were unreasonably punished or who were constantly compared unfavorably with brothers and sisters often grow up with a feeling that they are basically different from other people and that they are doomed always to come out close to the bottom of the heap. This feeling may be unconscious but nevertheless operates to prevent a student from making a total effort and presenting himself prepared to the best of his ability to be judged at an examination or a test. He is basically too afraid that he will show up badly and needs the excuse that he did not try.

Another unconscious deterrent to conscientious studying is a fear of aggression. It has been found that often the first area to be affected in an illness involving guilt and fear concerning aggressive impulses may be in the area of studying. People who have feelings of resentment and antagonism against individuals or the world at large often develop an unconscious fear of what they will do to other people if these resentful and antagonistic impulses get loose. This leads to a feeling that one must repress emotion and lead an isolated and withdrawn life. Often this choice of a way of life is not conscious, and all that is obvious is shyness and a passive outlook. People like this often cannot force themselves to study. They seem to have equated studying with being aggressive and have a fear that, if they commit themselves emotionally to a job of studying, they may be overwhelmed by the power of their own aggressiveness—that opening the dam a little will result in the release of uncontrollable forces.

A student was sent to me by his tutor. He came from a family where there was considerable lack of control. His mother was an alcoholic. His father, a man who lost his temper violently and frequently, was constantly at odds with the world and expressed his resentment against people at work, the government, his family, his wife, and his children, in angry terms much of the time. Because of this, the patient spent most of his childhood frightened to express himself in any way for fear that it would bring an explosion from his father. He remembers sitting at the table with his fists clenched and his eyes closed tightly, holding in his feelings while his father and mother were fighting. He did fairly well at college, until one day he became intoxicated at a cocktail party following a football game, and while in this state of intoxication was trying to fix a radiator with a screwdriver. Another boy came up behind him to give him some advice. The patient suddenly became furious and whirled around in such a way that his screwdriver pierced the boy's chest. The other boy was seriously ill, but recovered. My patient had to withdraw from college for a year because of this incident. When he returned, he began having difficulty doing his studying. As we worked in treatment, it became clear that he had always been afraid of exhibiting just the kind of powerful and uncontrollable anger which did show itself at the time of the screwdriver incident. Before that, his controls had always been good enough to keep him from exploding, but after this episode he had had to exert tighter and tighter control, and this had spread into the field of study. He had repressed himself so completely that he could not even throw himself into his work for fear that enthusiasm in this area would spread over into an expression of aggression in other ways.

Students affected in this way must learn to make friends with their aggressive impulses and discover that they are not as uncontrollable as they fear them to be. In this way they can learn to invest some of this repressed energy in constructive studying.

### CONFLICT OVER SEXUAL ORIENTATION

Finally, there is the problem of sexual orientation—the development of the capacity to give and receive love in a gratifying mutual relationship. In most adolescents the achievement of this requires resolution of some inner conflict between homosexual and heterosexual impulses.

No clear-cut conclusions have been reached about the origin or the causes of homosexuality. Most psychiatrists and psychoanalysts today feel that a combination of constitutional and environmental factors are involved. It seems to be fairly well accepted that everyone has some degree of homosexuality in his make-up and that there is a variation in amount from one person to another. This varies from the rare homosexual dream or a homosexual yearning all the way to the living of a homosexual life with the heterosexual desires nonexistent. Although it is felt that some people are born with more homosexual instincts than others, it is also believed that certain factors in the growth and development of an individual are responsible for the re-enforcing or the repression of these instincts. Certainly the encouragement of a child to behave as though it had been born the opposite sex will have an effect on the sexual orientation of this child when it becomes older.

This is not the only environmental factor which is important, however. Ability to identify with the parent of the same sex is extremely important. If there is something about this parent which makes such identification difficult, then the child will tend to identify more with the parent of the opposite sex. Also, if there is a remoteness in the relationship between a child and its parent of the same sex, there may develop a need for a closer relationship with people of that sex. If a father and son do not have sufficient closeness in their relationship with each other and, on the contrary, there is misunderstanding and coldness, then a boy may grow up still needing this kind of intimacy and look for it in relationships with other men. Since he never can create the ideal father-son relationship as an adult, he will be constantly disappointed. Attempts to deepen and intensify these relationships often lead to sexual involvement. Sometimes, on the other hand, the parent of the opposite sex plays a part in predetermining sexual orientation. A boy may be extremely frightened by his mother, particularly if she is a strong, aggressive, dominating, overpowering person, who runs the household and is quick-tempered and punitive. She serves as a prototype for the female sex in the child's early development, and if a boy is frightened in this way by his own mother, he may well steer clear of women in later life and seek closer associations with men, who seem to him to be safer.

Adolescence is a time when there is confusion about sex, probably because the first strong sexual impulses are felt at this time and seem to some degree frightening and mysterious. At any rate, homosexual feelings and homosexual behavior are much more common at this age. Many people feel and do things at this time which are never repeated during their adult life. During late adolescence boys and girls pass through a critical period of choice. How much of this is voluntary and how much is predetermined by constitution and upbringing is hard to say. Each year priests and counselors see boys who have been frightened by a homosexual dream or a transient homosexual yearning toward another boy. These boys interpret this as an indication that they are truly homosexual themselves and fear that at any moment they may be overpowered by the force of these latent impulses. Actually they are experiencing what almost everyone has felt at some time in his life, and these sensations simply represent a confirmation of the fact that there is homosexuality in everyone. Occasionally this homosexuality shows itself dramatically in a dream or fantasy untempered by the heterosexual impulses which are also present. These transient homosexual feelings are among the commonest presenting complaints in the sexual area. They often occur at a time when a student has been sexually frustrated in his experiences with women or has been rejected by a girl.

Another concern commonly expressed is anxiety over a "crush" on someone of the same sex. This seems to serve as an outlet for relatively strong adolescent homosexual yearnings and also to be a way of finding closeness and understanding during periods of uncertainty and turmoil. Some deep "crushes" occur as late as college, but this tendency disappears with the coming of maturity.

These are students whose homosexual orientation is such that apparently a complete heterosexual life cannot be achieved.

A divinity student came to see me, stating that he was worried about himself because he would rather take boy scouts on a camping trip than go out on a date with a girl. He was disappointed in himself because of this, but as we talked further, it became clear that he really had no sexual desire for girls, and had never had. He came to see that while he had no sexual interest in the work he was doing with boys, still it was somehow satisfying to him, and as long as he could do it he had no sexual feelings toward other men.

By associating with members of the male sex in a helpful and altruistic manner this student was gaining gratification through companionship rather than sexual relationships. His worrying about it was not true anxiety but simply an intellectual curiosity. He needed help in reconciling himself to the fact that, although he probably would not ever have a fully satisfying heterosexual life, he had found a resolution of his problem through his work, which was socially well accepted and should not cause him to feel ashamed.

Exactly how each student will make his permanent adjustment is hard to prophesy, but in the long run it is safe to say that concern about homosexuality, like identity and the struggle for independence, is another one of the hurdles which must be taken by most adolescents before achieving the emotional maturity of adulthood.

Because there is so close a resemblance between what might be termed normal adolescent behavior and emotionally disturbed, truly symptomatic behavior, it is important for physicians and parents to have as clear a picture as possible of what adolescence is like. I have tried to sketch in the part of this picture which I see while working as a psychiatrist; some of those I see are troubled by the normal adjustment problems faced by most older boys and girls on the brink of adulthood. Others have experienced severe pathological reactions to the stresses accompanying the achievement of maturity, and these will be discussed later.

The physician, the psychiatrist, and the counselor at times working independently and at other times in direct conjunction with one another can help children and parents through this transitional period with a minimum of turmoil if they themselves can offer help based on an understanding of the kinds of conflicts, conscious and unconscious, which seem to be present at this time. Relationships with parents, identity problems, school and college productivity, and sexual orientation seem to me to be the principal areas within which these conflicts rage.

## REFERENCES

Blaine, G. B., Jr. and McArthur, C. C. (with collaborators). *Emotional problems of the student.* New York: Appleton-Century-Crofts, 1961.

Erikson, E. H. Identity and the life cycle; selected papers. *Psychol. Issues,* 1959, *1,* No. 1 (Monograph 1).

Gallagher, J. R. and Harris, H. I. *Emotional problems of adolescents.* New York: Oxford Univer. Press, 1958.

# The Adolescent's Search for Identity

## ALEXANDER A. SCHNEIDERS

*Alexander A. Schneiders has been a key figure in the Fordham University Pastoral Psychology Institutes from the time of their inauguration. He served as the Chairman of the Institute Committee for the four Institutes held to date, beginning in 1955 and continuing in alternate years through 1961. His own undergraduate degree is from Creighton University in Omaha, and his master's and doctoral degrees are from Georgetown University. From 1939 to 1944, Dr. Schneiders was Director of Student Personnel at Loyola University in Chicago, and from 1945 to 1953 he was Chairman of the Department of Psychology at the University of Detroit. He served as professor of psychology and Director of Psychological Services at Fordham University from 1953 to 1961. He is the author of numerous journal articles and the following books (among others):* Introductory Psychology *(1951),* Personal Adjustment and Mental Health *(1955), and* Personality Development and Adjustment in Adolescence *(1960). Currently, Dr. Schneiders is professor of psychology in the School of Education at Boston College.*

### THE PRINCIPAL TASKS OF ADOLESCENCE

There are many ways of looking at adolescent development and behavior—from the physiological viewpoint, the moral viewpoint, the perspective of the spiritual counselor, or from the standpoint of sociology and psychology. All of the persons represented by these different disciplines are interested in finding out what the adolescent is like, and in understanding his basic needs and drives, his goals and his aspirations. Regardless of viewpoint, there is no disputing the fact that the adolescent is confronted with certain fundamental tasks—tasks that he must fulfill if he is to reach the goal of maturity or adulthood. Sometimes we refer to these tasks in other terms, as when we speak of adolescent goals, or desires, or ideals. But the simple fact is that in traversing the distance between childhood and adulthood, the adolescent must confront certain tasks, just as the adult must confront the tasks of earning a living, providing for his family, or changing jobs when it becomes necessary. These are tasks in the strict sense of the term. They are demanding, often arduous, and always require a certain amount of skill, know-how, and capacity for continuing adjustment.

There are several prominent tasks for adolescents, each one of which is inextricably bound up with the others. Probably the foremost task is that of *growing up*. If the adolescent is to make the transition from childhood to adulthood successfully, he has no alternative but to grow up in the literal sense of the term. If he is to face the responsibilities and demands of adulthood living, he must grow up physically, physiologically, emotionally, socially, and psychologically. He must, in other words, *become a man* (or a woman) in the best sense of the term. He must achieve not only manhood, but also manliness and masculinity. And the adolescent girl must achieve not only womanhood, but also femininity. In our society this is not always easy to do, and that is why the term "task" is particularly appropriate in describing this goal of adolescent striving.

A second fundamental task which confronts the adolescent is the *achievement of independence,* which also bears directly on the adolescent's search for identity. In a very real sense this task cannot be clearly differentiated from that of growing up, since to grow up means in part to become independent. The adolescent must learn to think for himself; he must achieve independence of decision and of action; he must sever the umbilical cord of emotional dependence that has fettered his striving for individuality. The adolescent must, in brief, *actualize the individuality* that lies at the root of personal existence. As long as he yearns for, or requires, the warm milk of emotional succorance from the maternal breast, he cannot achieve independence of thought, of emotion, or of volition; and therefore he cannot grow up. He cannot become a man until he disengages his psychic being from the tentacles of "smother" love.

From the very beginning of adolescence, and even before, the young-ster manifests a strong tendency toward this goal of independence. If he is normal, he shows every indication of wanting to "be on his own," of choosing his own friends, of deciding which school he will attend, of thinking for himself. At fourteen and fifteen, he is not ready for these serious decisions, but he does indicate a readiness to try them out. Gradually, throughout the span of the adolescent period, he shows an increasing desire and willingness to stand on his own feet, to accept responsibility for himself, and to reach out for the added responsibili-ties of adult living. Without this development, he remains a dependent, passive, clinging person who has no idea of, and little inclination to accept, the status of adulthood.

The third great task of adolescence is the *achievement of self-iden-tity*. This is, in a real sense, the crowning achievement of adolescent striving. Without self-identity, the adolescent does not know how to work toward independence. Without self-identity, he finds it difficult to grow up, and to continue moving toward the goal of adult respon-sibility. It could be said just as easily that without growing up, and without the achievement of independence, it is impossible to achieve self-identity. This fact indicates very clearly the basic interrelation-ships among these fundamental tasks of the adolescent period.

### THE NATURE OF SELF-IDENTITY

As we have seen in other presentations of this Institute, a leading feature of human development is the gradual emergence of that part of the psychic structure, the ego, which mediates between self and reality. The emergence of the ego, plus the development of the self-concept and the self-ideal, are closely correlated in adolescence with the development of self-identity. This process begins in childhood, is continued throughout adolescence, and normally is achieved with the realization of maturity. Self-identity is a quality of personal experience and of existence that is linked to the growth of the self-concept and the self-ideal, and thus profoundly influences mental stability and adjust-ment. In simple terms, it means a clear awareness of one's role and status in life, one's goals and purposes, and one's relationships to reality, to society, and to a Supreme Being. The person with self-identity knows the answers to such questions as "What am I?," "Who am I?," "What am I supposed to be or to become?," and "Where am I going?" The person lacking self-identity, on the other hand, is confused and uncertain as to what he is supposed to be and where he is going. This state of affairs is clearly exemplified in the deeply neurotic person and in the homosexual, neither one of whom has a clear picture of what he is supposed to be.

Adolescents often manifest lack of self-identity, which is one of the reasons why they are at times uncertain, confused, and extremely vacillating in their opinions, behavior, or goals. We see this clearly exemplified in the high school senior who cannot decide whether he should go on to college, go into the army, or get a job; and in the college student who cannot decide on a definite curriculum. We see it also in young adults who, having left college, flounder from one position to another. We see it exemplified in the extremely large number of boys and girls who, after a period of one or several years, leave the convent or seminary because of a "lack of vocation," often bitterly disappointed, disillusioned, and more confused than they were before. There are countless instances of such vocational disorientation that has its roots in the failure to achieve self-identity.

#### THE DETERMINANTS OF SELF-IDENTITY

What is it that determines or facilitates the gradual emergence of self-identity? From the practical standpoint, in our dealing with adolescents, this is one of the most crucial issues since we should do whatever we can to promote conditions favorable to the growth of self-identity. Needless to say, this is a complex process that has its roots not only in the earliest experiences of childhood but in the very being of the person himself. It is not something that occurs during adolescence in the birth of a "new self" but it is true that the achievement of self-identity is not fully realized until the conflicts and problems of the adolescent period have been lived through.

In early childhood, we can discern a number of events that contribute at least in a small way to the development of self-identity. For example, the child is given what the parents hope is a distinctive name, and in some instances he is even given a distinctive number, as when he is called John J. Asteroid, III. He may also have a nursery devoted exclusively to his needs, clothes that not only belong to him but set him off clearly from his younger sister, playthings alloted for his pleasure, and so on. All these little things help to lay the groundwork for the gradual development of selfhood.

But there are more basic developmental factors at work that contribute much more to personal selfhood. Important among these is the growing individuality of the physical organism. It is the physical body that enhances the realization of sex differences, even though these differences may not be apparent or known to the child in the early years of growth. There are of course many factors that contribute to the distinction between maleness and femaleness, but there is none that outranks in importance the structure of the body. In any single case, it may be that the child is brought to an awareness of these differences before he is aware of structural characteristics. The attitudes of parents, relatives, and playmates; methods of segregation that are used to prohibit familiarity; differences in toys and dress; injunctions with respect to privacy in dressing and matters of toilet; the use of boy names and girl names—all serve to enforce the distinction between the sexes almost from infancy. However, cultural practices regarding names, toys, or clothes bear no *intrinsic* relation to the actual fact of maleness or femaleness. To treat a boy like a girl will not make a girl out of him, although it may make him "girlish" in his attitudes and reactions. But it is definitely known that physical structure can have a decided effect on sex status. The awareness of basic sex differences may come as a shock, as a pleasant surprise, or with little feeling; but whatever the reaction, we can be sure that the fact itself profoundly affects the development of the self-concept. The reason is that the self-concept hinges to an important extent on sexual identity; and sexual identity in its turn is dependent upon adequate physical development and a clear realization of physical maleness or femaleness. In this way the self-concept, sex identity, and self-identity become closely interwoven and interdependent, and form a solid groundwork for later maturity.

#### SEX DIFFERENCES AND SEX IDENTITY

There is perhaps no surer way to stifle self-concept development than by masking or obscuring the differences between the sexes. This is true of the childhood period, and even more true of adolescence. A knowledge of this difference is essential for the adequate growth of the child's idea of what he is and what he should be. Thus the child should be allowed to discover sexual differences early in life, and in a wholly natural manner, so that later confusion and the development of unhealthy attitudes can be avoided. Knowledge correctly imparted is the only secure antidote to the uncertainty often bred by ignorance of these facts. The conviction of maleness is a prerogative of every man; the conviction of femaleness the prerogative of every woman. And the sooner this conviction comes the more likely will the development of the self-concept progress in a normal and healthy manner, free of distortions caused by ignorance and half-truths.

With this realization the life style of the individual takes on a different aspect. The future role of the boy or girl as an adult, what he or she wants to be when grown up, is thoroughly conditioned by this awareness. The boy wants to be an aviator or a garage mechanic, the girl a nurse or a teacher. That this is not mere imagination or child's play, but is actually based upon a realization of physical differences, is evidenced by the fact that physical differences are often mentioned by children as reasons why they chose a certain role. In adolescence, the future roles of male and female are more clearly envisioned. Terms such as father, mother, wife, husband, and sweetheart take on new meanings. Perhaps for the first time the youngster becomes aware of what these terms really mean.

These projections of self into adult roles are, to an important extent, predicated on the physical differences that distinguish men and women. They extend to many other goals which involve physical differences. A boy of good physical condition may dream of college sports, and a career in professional football. The anemic youngster tends to drift into the more sedentary occupations. The attractive girl dreams occasionally of a career in motion pictures or on the stage. Gracefulness, precision of movement, beauty, physical charm, athletic prowess and strength suggest to adolescents the roles that they ought to assume. Whether or not they ever actually realize such aspirations is not important. The important thing is that these physical factors play a significant part in determining the character of their thinking and in the development of their self-concept.

### SELF-IDENTITY AND BODY-IMAGE

In the graduai emergence of this male and female identification, the body-image plays a distinctive role. This psychic reality, which is the core of the self-concept, is the adolescent's mental picture of his physical self. It is what the adolescent pictures himself to be along physical dimensions, including height, weight, posture, gestures, smile, etc. These factors are organized into the body image, and this image constitutes the center of the self-concept. The concept of self as distinct from the body-image naturally embraces psychological as well as physical qualities of personality, and the one is no less important than the other. But, in the early stages of development the body is much more real than the mind. It is something tangible, something that can be seen and felt, perceived as well as imagined, something that casts a reflection when the child stands in front of a mirror. This realism of the body is reflected in the inviolability with which it is regarded by its owner. Children and adolescents, and even adults, will readily submit to the influence of ideas, opinions, and values that may threaten their personal integrity, but it is the rare individual who will not rebel violently against physical attack or punishment. Mental integrity is more important than physical inviolability, but physical attack is often much more real to the experiencing person.

These facts enable us to understand why physical deficiencies and physical excellencies can be so important to the healthy growth of the child and adolescent. The body image can lead to self-confidence, self-assurance, and to the realization of important goals; or it can lead to self-rejection, inferiority and inadequacy. The social implications of physical characteristics, whether good or bad, are most clearly exemplified in the relationship between these characteristics and sex roles. In this area physical deficiency and advantages can be of the utmost significance. The young girl who fails to develop a bustline and other typical feminine contours finds it difficult to establish a clear-cut sex role. Her body image prevents her from feeling attractive to the opposite sex, even though she may have a pleasing personality and a high moral character. Similarly, the boy who is physically puny, lacking in muscular development, shallow chested, or effeminate in facial features and voice, finds it difficult to feel strongly masculine. What is worse, this lack of self-identification will be projected into relationships with the opposite sex and obstruct the development of healthy interpersonal relationships. A girl must learn gradually to feel that she is a woman in the full sense of the term, and the boy that he is a man; only then will personal and sexual identity be assured.

Thus, in the growth of the self-concept and of self-identity the body-image plays a leading role, and this factor in turn is closely related to and dependent upon sexual identity. The body-image and sexual identity taken together may be regarded as the *hard core of self-identity*.

Without the conviction of masculinity or of femininity it is impossible for any growing boy or girl to achieve adequate self-identity. Whenever a young boy feels that he is "different" or that he is "effeminate," he finds it extremely difficult to believe in his own self-identity. Similarly, the girl who is flat-chested, and looks very much like the proverbial beanpole, with no seductive curves to lure the unsuspecting male into some kind of relationship, finds it hard to think of herself as a woman, and feels that the search for identity leads into endless blind alleys.

In this search for identity, there must of course be more than a healthy body-image, or sex identity. The child grows up within a context of interpersonal relationships that have a great deal to do with his search for and achievement of identity. Normally, the growing boy tends to identify with his father, and the girl with her mother, and this process of external identification is very helpful in establishing the conviction of masculinity or femininity, and therefore of both sexual and self-identity. The youngster also identifies with other important facets of his daily life, such as his family, his nationality, his religion, his community, and his school; from all of these identifications he derives some measure of self-identity. Later on in adulthood, some of these identifications will have to be broken up, as when the individual leaves the community, graduates from school, or establishes a home of his own. But in the normal course of events this does not happen until after the individual has forged his own personal self-identity out of the many identifications he has formed during the process of growing up.

These are some of the factors that enter into the adolescent's search for identity. To the parent, growing up physically may mean nothing more than that the adolescent is getting taller and heavier, is developing a voracious and sometimes peculiar appetite, and is always growing out of recently purchased clothes. But to the teenager, growing up is much more than this, and he finds himself involved in a continuous search for himself. Too often this search is fruitless.

# Problems of Dependence
and Independence

## FRANCIS C. BAUER

*Francis C. Bauer, M.D., is Director of the
Student Adjustment Center of the Third Supervisory School District of Suffolk County on
Long Island. His undergraduate degree is from
St. John's University, and his medical degree
from Georgetown University. Dr. Bauer is a
member of the American Psychiatric Association, the New York State Medical Society, and
the Suffolk County Medical Society. He is a
lecturer at St. John's University, a consultant
to the Marriage Tribunal in the Diocese of
Brooklyn, and a member of the Executive
Board of the New York State Welfare Conference.*

I would like to begin our discussion by calling attention to the obvious
and stating, at the risk of redundance, that the dependence-independence conflict is by no means limited to the period of adolescence. It is
rather a conflict which is basic to human existence, which begins for
all at birth and which for some continues to manifest itself in one way
or another until, as with most conflicts, it is conveniently resolved in
death. Stated in its simplest terms, it is a conflict between man's strong
emotional need always to avoid the frustration essential to progress
and to maintain a perpetual status quo on the one hand and, on the
other, his equally strong but opposite need, symbolically to sever the

145

umbilical cord and whatever other attachments might limit his freedom of action. It is a conflict in which the will seeking good and the intellect seeking truth demand acceptance of and adaptation to reality while the pleasure principle of the primitive, infantile, chaotic unconscious demands with equal strength a rejection of reality in favor of a state of irresponsible ease and comfort.

During the formative years, the dependence-independence conflict gives rise to a number of problems but these rarely assume serious proportions since they can so conveniently be rationalized on the basis of immaturity or parental overprotection. It is often during adolescence then that problems surrounding this conflict first emerge as significant.

### DEPENDENCE-INDEPENDENCE CONFLICT CENTRAL TO ADOLESCENCE

There is a tendency to define adolescence in terms of chronological age or physical growth and development. These efforts at definition result in such meaningless phrases as: the time of life between puberty and maturity and the adolescent accordingly becomes a child between puberty and adulthood or simply, a person in his teens. More accurately, I would like to suggest that adolescence is a phenomenon which is primarily emotional and has very little to do with either puberty or chronology. An adolescent might properly be defined as a person whose behavior indicates that he has come to grips with the conflict between his dependency needs and his conscious desire to become independent.

In primitive cultures, problems in this area did not arise or were at least less pronounced since the conflict was resolved for the child through rigidly prescribed customs and taboos. A child in primitive society remains a child until he achieves orgastic potency at which time, regardless of chronological age, he becomes an adult and thereafter is treated as such. The transition from childhood to adult life is not gradual but abrupt and is often only symbolized by some sort of puberty rite or trial by ordeal. Be it as simple as wearing a bone necklace or as painful as circumcision, the pubescent child is thereafter regarded as an adult with both the privilege and responsibility of that state. This may be an extreme and even a traumatic way to resolve a conflict but the sudden and unequivocal conferring of status delivers the adolescent from what otherwise can become an interminable sojourn in the limbo of teenage indecision where he ponders the question, "Shall I remain a child or become a man?"

In our own culture the events most often compared to puberty rites are the Bar Mitzvah of the Hebrews and the Christian Confirmation. I will not discuss the spiritual significance of either of these events nor have I the intention to demean their sacramental character but at present these events have little social significance except in terms of a much diluted symbolism. For which youngster who publicly professes his manhood is taken seriously by his elders and which newly confirmed heir of heaven finds his position in the family or his daily activities in any way altered?

### ADULT BEHAVIOR INTENSIFIES ADOLESCENT CONFLICT

The problems of dependence and independence are essentially problems of status, problems of relating to authority and, most important, problems of assuming responsibility. And I am very much afraid that these problems of adolescents are largely the result of the way in which they are treated by adults. The interaction between the adult world and the adolescent world is an area of much confusion to both and sometimes results in a contest between parent and child. Instead of recognizing the struggle of the adolescent and helping him to resolve the conflict of dependency needs, it seems to me that the behavior of adults serves often to intensify the conflict and to multiply the problems. Consider how confusing, to say the very least, must appear the behavior of adults to children who observe the following. For the first thirteen years of his life we regulate the behavior of the child by exposing him to the pressure of the peer group. Being like all the other kids on the block or in the class is offered as the compelling reason for the child to do everything from eating spinach to taking baths. But at thirteen, when the children have become thoroughly homogenized and now attempt to make decisions at the group level, we arbitrarily change the ground rules and tell them that we do not care what all the other kids do— "You do what I say."

And we do other equally confusing things. We belabor the concept of togetherness which feeds dependency needs and at the same time work ceaselessly for a house large enough to afford each member of the family a room of his own. We speak reverently about the concept of family unity while we build baby-sitting into a substantial national industry. We talk about building close family relationships and send children to nursery schools at three and to summer schools, recreational programs and summer camps for the remainder of their childhood years. We advocate respect for authority while we disparage the public officials we helped to elect. We tell the adolescent he must respect the law while we bribe policemen. We tell him to be decent and honest and, above all, upright while we cheat on our income tax. We try to teach him the value of money while plunging ourselves more heavily into debt. We deny him an advance on next week's allowance while we use carte-blanche and apply for ready credit. We insist that he obtain the best education possible and we cooperate by voting down school budgets. We tell him about the dignity of an honest day's work and formulate plans for the twenty-hour week. We stress the importance of scientific and academic achievement while we make millionaires of our entertainers and paupers of our professors and arrange things in such a way that many teachers need outside employment to survive.

Is it any wonder that the adolescent is confused, that he is disillusioned, that he is rebellious and that he feels cheated? For how has he been helped toward resolving his conflict in favor of independence when the ideals we have held up to him are empty and the values are false?

### ADULT AMBIVALENCE TOWARD ADOLESCENT INDEPENDENCE

The ambivalence of adults toward children caught in the struggle between their dependency needs and their striving for independence is astonishing. We literally push our children out of infancy by weaning them, toilet training them and sending them off to school before they are really ready for any of these events. We rob them of their childhood by organizing their games and structuring their society according to adult rules and standards. We even try to make something productive out of their play activity as evidenced by a teacher's comment on an elementary report card which stated paradoxically, "This child does not use his recess time constructively."

There appears then a tendency to propel the child toward maturity and independence and to make him aware of responsibility sometime before he is ready for it. And in this way we frustrate his dependency needs when they should be indulged. Having done this during childhood, the ambivalence of adults becomes apparent when they reverse the process during adolescence. At least it seems that the weight of adult pressure during adolescence is in the direction of retarding growth. And in this way we frustrate the striving for independence which should now be strengthened. This ambivalence is reflected in our very lack of agreement as to when adolescents can do what. How much more confusion do we add to that which I have already outlined when we tell the adolescent that he is old enough to serve his country but he is too young to vote; old enough to drive but not old enough to avoid the penalty of increased insurance premiums and, in this connection, we suggest to the boy of twenty that he is not yet as old as his sister of eighteen. We tell him that he may use alcohol in New York but not in Connecticut, he may marry in Maryland but not in New Jersey, he may work in Kentucky but not in California. We tell him in short, that he is a man physically and morally at about sixteen but that he is an infant legally until twenty-one. We pass laws to compel his attendance at school until he is seventeen and we pass other laws to prevent him from working before that time and then we berate him because he is not earning his own way as was his father at thirteen. And we tell him all of these contradictory things at a time when he is unconsciously struggling with a monumental decision whether to remain a child with all of the protection, comfort and security signified by that state or whether to frustrate his own unconscious inclination and decide in favor of maturity which means sacrifice, courage and responsibility.

Certainly our way of life has done much to intensify this struggle. Educational requirements, being what they are today, tend to keep adolescents and young adults in a state of complete dependence on their parents for a much longer period than formerly. The harsh economic realities of life have also contributed in this regard. Even in marriage there is the tendency for families to remain together and three generations in one home is becoming more usual. And the new parents seem to begin raising their children without in any way altering their relationship to the new grandparents. All of these considerations seem to have the net effect of prolonging the dependence-independence conflict and our adolescents become more and more reluctant to give up the pleasures of dependence in favor of assuming responsibility. It hurts more than a little to grow up and to become independent and the freedom and privilege of adult life is purchased only by the assumption of responsibility. But a good many of our young people are managing to avoid that expense and having been overprotected and overindulged during most of their lives, they couldn't care less about freedom and independence. And why should they care when our society seems dedicated to the cultivation of dependency needs? Through the creation of numerous institutions and practices during the last thirty years, we seem to have made it easy to transfer satisfaction of dependency needs from the parents to the employer, the corporation, the agency, the school or to the local, state or federal government. And every time we allow the responsibility of the individual or of the family to be shifted and to be absorbed by any other agency, we are catering to and reinforcing dependency needs. This is the inherent danger in much social legislation which has been very much ignored. The institution of any service in which a shift of responsibility becomes possible always permits a revitalization of dependency needs and, in this connection, our efforts to help others may often do them harm.

## OUR CULTURE FAVORS CONTINUING DEPENDENCE IN ADOLESCENCE

The principle of inertia states that a body in motion tends to remain in motion and in the same direction unless acted upon by some external force. The tendency of the human organism to preserve the comfortable state of dependence into which it was born is simply an example of emotional inertia. It is reasonable then to expect that if the individual is to move in the direction of maturity, some external force must be applied and in our example, it would be the force of frustration, without which no progress is possible. However, if the goal of a mature independence is not made desirable and the force applied is made even weaker, there remains little hope and less purpose in changing direction at all. And this is precisely the situation as a result of which we are creating a society of extremely dependent individuals. It appears that we have taken the proposition that, "I am responsible for what happens in the world" and reversed it to read, "The world is responsible for what happens to me."

Although we deny the intent, our efforts toward the creation of a welfare state have progressed further than one might imagine. And the philosophy that only goods should be purchased and services should be provided, which is largely responsible for this situation, is more prevalent than we think. Personnel managers meet it every day when they interview youngsters in their late teens who are more concerned with pension plans, retirement funds and hospitalization benefits than with the kind of work being offered. There is something emotionally unhealthy about this preoccupation of youth with security.

In too many instances the struggle toward independence is being abandoned during adolescence and our youth join the army of soft Americans recently described by our President. Perhaps we are traveling the path of Greece and Rome whose civilizations fell not from external aggressors but from an internal sapping of their moral and spiritual strength. Both Greece and Rome became soft and traded their freedom for an easy, comfortable life.

My task has been an easy one. I was asked to discuss the problems of dependence and independence in the adolescent, and fortunately I was not requested to offer a solution.

# The Emotionally Ill Adolescent

## GRAHAM B. BLAINE, JR.

*Graham Burt Blaine, Jr., M.D., is psychiatrist to the University Health Service, Harvard University. His A.B. degree is from Harvard, and his M.D. degree from the College of Physicians and Surgeons of Columbia University. In addition to his post at Harvard, Dr. Blaine is also associate psychiatrist to the Adolescent Unit, Children's Medical Center, Boston, and assistant in psychiatry, Harvard Medical School. From 1951 to 1953 he was consultant psychiatrist to Williams College, Williamstown, Massachusetts, and from 1957 to 1958 he was Associate Director of the Harvard University Project on Religion and Mental Health. He is a member of the American Psychiatric Association and of the American College Health Association. Dr. Blaine is the co-editor with Charles C. McArthur of the recent book:* The Emotional Problems of the Student *(1961). A review of this book in the NEWSLETTER of the American Catholic Psychological Association characterized it as ". . . the best book yet produced on the conduct of psychotherapeutic services in an academic setting."*

In my earlier paper I spoke about the range of normal reactions in adolescence. Now I want to describe some of the serious pathological illnesses which can occur. In essence they are similar in every respect to those psychiatric illnesses which affect adults and the treatment of them is no different. Diagnosis, however, is more difficult because of the marked similarity between the symptoms of normal adolescence and those of severe psychosis.

### SCHIZOPHRENIA

The most malignant psychotic illness is schizophrenia. It is often incurable by present methods and worst of all there is no way of predicting for whom it is to be quickly curable, in whom it will be recurrent with intervals of normalcy and in whom it will be a chronic progressively deteriorating illness without remission at any time.

Originally schizophrenia was called dementia praecox, which is Latin for insanity of adolescence. Probably this was because so many schizophrenic symptoms are seen in adolescence and not because this illness was actually more common in this age group. Its onset may come at any age and it is thought by most to be precipitated by an acute stress occurring in an individual already predisposed to the illness by heredity or a congenital deficiency in basic personality.

Symptoms vary but the most consistent characteristic of the disease is a break with reality—a distortion in perception of the world around us. This may take the form of auditory or visual hallucinations, delusions of persecution, or misconceptions concerning oneself and one's purpose or mission in life. A child who has always seemed somewhat odd or secretive may gradually drift into schizophrenia but often a seemingly healthy sometimes even an unusually good, model youngster may develop extraordinarily bizarre symptoms almost overnight. It is important to recognize schizophrenic symptoms early and to arrange for immediate psychiatric evaluation. The reason for this is that a patient suffering from this illness often shifts his orientation rapidly to those around him. His conscious thoughts are completely irrational and he is at the mercy of his unconscious with all its primitive and violent impulses. A patient with this illness may at one moment feel that those around him are filled with affection for him and at the next moment believe that one individual is plotting against him and must be destroyed at once for self-defense. Also suicidal impulses without reason may become irresistible to them despite the fact that no depressive feelings are present.

A sixteen-year-old high school senior was sent to the school guidance counselor by his mother because of his poor showing on College Board examinations. He had been one of the top students in his class and had not shown any symptoms of emotional instability while in high school or during his childhood except for one period of insomnia at the time of the College Board examinations in his junior year from which he rapidly recovered with the aid of tranquilizers. His father was a rabbi and a graduate of Princeton. His mother was a musician and somewhat temperamental. She seemed overly concerned about discrimination but otherwise appeared stable.

In his initial interview the boy seemed calm but did express some resentment against his father for the high expectations he held out for him. In his second interview ten days later no change was noted. He was somewhat uncertain about which college to apply to and was given some direct advice about this. Two weeks later he was interviewed at Princeton and given assurance that he would be accepted. That same day his mother called to say that he seemed well but was spending all his time skating at the municipal rink and refused to come home. The following day she called to say that her son had gone crazy. An immediate interview was arranged and the boy presented a totally different picture. He said that he felt inferior, that his classmates were laughing at him and that the Russian Olympic hockey team were all spies. He wanted to leave immediately for Washington to report them to the FBI. He was dressed sloppily and explained that this was to show his school friends that it was more important to be a good guy than to study well. He was clearly psychotic and was hospitalized that same day.

## DEPRESSION

Depression of psychotic proportion is rare among adolescents but it is something which must always be watched, for the irrevocable resolution of this illness—suicide—is a terrible tragedy. It seems paradoxical that young men and women who write in prose and poetry so often about death do not often develop serious depressions. In a study made of 34 suicides at Harvard over a twenty-five year period none was found to have been profoundly depressed before killing himself. Most adolescents who commit suicide do so impulsively and give little or no warning of their intention. The act seems to be a manifestation of distorted thinking similar to that already described in schizophrenia. Still in dealing with depressed adolescents one must always be on the alert for the signs of a psychotic type of thinking as opposed to the milder and more easily dealt with neurotic depressive expressions of sadness and discouragement. Expressions of utter despair and hopelessness are warning signals, of course, as are statements about being trapped in a situation in which there is no exit—no possible way out. The most important clue of all, however, is the appearance of irrational self-recrimination. When one hears talk of being a basically evil person who is a disgrace to his family and a burden to society then is the time to become seriously concerned about the depth and nature of the depressive process.

## ANOREXIA NERVOSA

Another serious emotional illness seen in adolescents, usually girls, is anorexia nervosa. It is characterized by a disturbance of appetite. The patient often has started a strenuous program of dieting to reduce weight which then gets out of control. All food becomes repugnant and the weight falls to dangerous levels threatening the patient's life. Sometimes this inability to eat alternates with eating binges followed by vomiting. This is a very serious illness and has led to death. Treatment is complicated and prolonged. Its chances of success are much greater if begun in the early stages of the disease.

A thirteen-year-old girl from Montreal was brought to the Children's Hospital by her parents because of severe weight loss over a period of six months which had been resistant to treatment by the family doctor. At the onset of her illness she had weighed ninety-two pounds and at the time of examination her weight was fifty-four pounds. She was emaciated, weak and obviously depressed. She registered no concern about her appearance nor did she seem in the least aware of the seriousness of her condition.

This girl had a normal childhood and her parents and siblings appeared to be stable, well-adjusted individuals. Her symptoms began when she noticed fuller breast development in herself than her classmates. She was embarrassed by this and also was self-conscious because of earlier menstruation. Dieting began as an attempt to decrease her breast size but soon became so obsessional that she could not eat at all. She prepared meals for her younger sisters and did her best to fatten them up. She became rapidly weaker and more depressed. Her periods ceased as is usual in anorexia and despite her obviously deteriorating condition she was not concerned enough about it to want treatment. In her later interviews she admitted feeling reluctant to grow up and after a period of hospital care and later psychiatric treatment made a good recovery.

## OBSESSIVE BEHAVIOR

Phobias and obsessive-compulsive neuroses are sometimes seen during adolescence. Ritualistic behavior or transient fears of a non-pathologic kind are often seen and should not be cause for alarm. Wearing a certain article of clothing to bring luck in examinations, walking a certain route on the way to or from school, arranging the bedroom in a very special way, or reciting magical lines of gibberish at certain moments are common examples of the sort of harmless rituals which often appear at this age. Sometimes however this obsessive behavior becomes so extreme that performance is seriously interfered with and the resultant distress and anxiety cause the patient to become upset and panicky.

A twelve-year-old girl was very attracted to her father who was a moderately successful business man. Her mother was an outgoing person who was civic-minded and active socially. The girl herself was conscientious and meticulous. She had high ideals and was quite ambitious, feeling that some day she would be a confidential secretary to a business executive. On the day after her father's unexpected promotion to president of his company he dropped dead of a heart attack. Shortly after the funeral this girl began walking very slowly and within a few weeks was only able to walk ahead by taking one step back for every two she took forward. This progressed to the point where she could only walk facing backwards and then only at a snail's pace. She could never finish a job of any sort whether it was a school assignment or a household task. Obviously this behavior was incapacitating as she fell further behind in her school work, lost her friends and became nervous and tense as well. Help from school counselors and her family physician were to no avail. It was not until she had been in psychiatric treatment for many months that her unconscious fear that death would come to her as it had to her father if she moved ahead and achieved success was brought to the surface and she was able to return to normal activities.

## DISTINCTION BETWEEN EMOTIONAL ILLNESS
## AND NORMAL ADOLESCENT CRISIS

In previous days you have heard extensive discussions about delinquency and sexual perversion which are also serious illnesses with some emotional component. Here also the distinction between normal and pathological behavior is not easy to make. Some lying and stealing, some exploratory sex play, and transvestitism is to be expected, but when this behavior persists, is extreme, or unaccompanied by feelings of guilt or shame then it becomes the concern of the court and the psychiatrist. We can offer something of value in the way of treatment in some of these illnesses but for the most part therapy has to be accomplished with help of the legal structure of the community.

I do not mean to frighten you with these descriptions of real illness in the adolescent but merely to give you a glimpse of what the extremes are. The incidence of serious illness in the adolescent group is low. At Harvard we hospitalize only 15 to 20 students per year out of a population of 10,000. A large majority of these young men return after a brief hospital stay and go on to graduate without further trouble.

Making the distinction between the emotionally ill adolescent and one going through a normal crisis is important for all of you doing counseling work of any kind, and I feel it deserves some attention at this point. While it is hard to lay down hard and fast rules as to the specific moment when referral to a trained clinical psychologist or psychiatrist is indicated still there are certain indicators which are helpful. The most important of these is the emotional reaction of the counselor. If he feels uncomfortable, frightened or mystified by the attitudes or behavior of the individual he is counseling, then the chances are strong that he will not be able to be of much help in the first place and furthermore, his own discomfort and concern about it will interfere with his ability to understand what is going on in his counselee.

While it is true that many adolescents with problems have to get worse before they get better there is a limit to how much worse and for how long. A troubled youth who shows no improvement after three to four months of interviews should be referred for consultation. It may be that no one else can accomplish more than has already been done but in most cases it is best to get confirmation of this from a consultant.

When a boy or girl is obviously withholding information about his activities or his feelings and the counselor has reason to believe that this is being done out of fear or guilt then it may be best to ask the individual to talk with someone else as well. Bizarre behavior, grimacing, and preoccupation during interviews are often signs of psychosis and suggest that referral would be a wise course. Persistent delinquent behavior or practice of sexual perversion also are symptoms which can be better handled, as a rule, by psychologists and psychiatrists. Usually they are in a better position than a counselor to gain appropriate help from the law agencies when this is necessary.

I am often asked about methods of referral. Actually those who are ill are usually not reluctant to be referred but occasionally there are recalcitrant individuals who do not recognize their need for help or who are afraid or suspicious of psychiatrists. It is helpful in such cases to know a psychiatrist in the community yourself so that you may make a recommendation based on personal knowledge. Then too it is reassuring to discuss possible referrals first in order to confirm your impression of the necessity. Finally, I would suggest that the counselee be told that a consultation would be in order rather than that a transfer for further or different treatment is being made. The idea of going for one visit to find out whether treatment is necessary or not is much easier to accept than to believe that a diagnosis has already been made and long-term treatment with a stranger about to begin.

# The School Counselor

## LAWRENCE R. MALNIG

*Lawrence R. Malnig is Director of the Office of Guidance and Testing at St. Peter's College, a post which he has held since 1948. His A.B. degree is from Brooklyn College (1938), his M.A. from Columbia University (1940), and his Ph.D. from New York University (1959). Dr. Malnig is a member of the American Psychological Association, American Catholic Psychological Association, the American Personnel and Guidance Association, and the National Vocational Guidance Association. He has contributed to professional journals, especially in the area of the vocational guidance of college students.*

The title school counselor is rather vague and does not imply any particular viewpoint or philosophy. For this reason I would like to consider him as a counseling psychologist and take a few moments to trace his unique function, which is often blurred due to the interest he shares with the psychotherapist.

### DEVELOPMENT OF COUNSELING PSYCHOLOGY

Shortly after the turn of the century, the Vocational Guidance movement originated in order to help people entering the world of work. Soon this movement was joined by psychologists who were developing new instruments in psychometrics. Finally, with the publication of Carl Rogers' *Counseling and psychotherapy* (1942) a great interest was aroused in therapeutic techniques. As these three streams of interest blended we saw the birth of counseling psychology.

This was more than a new title; it involved a new outlook. Since the individual was considered as needing assistance not only in changing attitudes but also in handling daily situations, the counseling psychologist made use of tests, occupational information, school activities and other environmental influences.

Unlike the clinical psychologist who traditionally has been concerned with the diagnosis of psychopathology and the modification of negative tendencies, the counseling psychologist is primarily concerned with the integration and development of the normal person. Super enlarges this distinction by saying that counseling psychology ". . . concerns itself with *hygiology;* with the normalities even of abnormal persons, with locating and developing personal and social resources and adaptive tendencies so that the individual can be assisted in making more effective use of them" (1955, p. 5).

Rogers also found that people in distress basically had a positive direction and states that, "I have come to feel that the more freely any person is understood and accepted the more he tends to drop the false fronts with which he has been meeting life, and the more he tends to move in a forward direction" (1959, p. 26).

The counseling psychologist who works in a school setting, therefore, concerns himself with all the resources at his disposal to further normal growth and development. But to do this he must understand himself as well as the needs of the adolescent.

The caution Pearson extends to psychiatrists applies equally well to counselors. He says, ". . . the therapist treating an adolescent always has to be aware of his own reactions. If he has difficulties with his own rebelliousness, he may side too much with the adolescent against the adults in the youth's life; or he may try to strengthen his own reaction formation by trying to combat the adolescent's rebellion" (1958, p. 181).

Only by being constantly alert to our own feelings and reactions can we improve our effectiveness in dealing with the client.

### NEEDS OF THE ADOLESCENT

The needs of the adolescent must also be understood, especially at this stage of development. Among the more basic ones we would all recognize are the following:

1. The need for self-acceptance
2. The need for acceptance and love from others
3. The need for recognition and achievement
4. The need for independence
5. The ability to face reality.

Time does not permit the elaboration of these points, but they all add up to a sense of competence and assurance in finding one's direction in a world surrounded by uncertainties.

Previously we mentioned the façades one uses in facing reality. These façades are also encountered by the psychiatrist, but perhaps not to the same degree. The adolescent who comes to the psychiatrist's office has accepted the fact that he needs help and is actively seeking it. Often when he comes to the counselor's office there is only an unconscious hope that his problem will be uncovered in spite of the smoke screen with which he surrounds it. He uses many approaches, all of them aimed at testing how safe he can feel in the situation. These approaches may be labeled as follows:

1. The comparative shopper
2. The backdoor entrance
3. The gift bearer
4. The debunker
5. The dictator

Perhaps some explanations are in order.

1. The *Comparative Shopper* will use the same gambit with a number of people on campus until he finds someone who will accept him as he is. An example of this is the student who would meet me periodically in the outer-office to ask for an opinion regarding psychology. As soon as he got one, he would launch into a caustic refutation and wait for a reaction. After repeatedly hearing that he was entitled to his opinion—thereby testing the limits of acceptance—he felt safe enough to make an appointment to the inner-office.

2. The *Backdoor* approach refers to the adolescent who comes to the counselor to seek help for a friend or for a member of his family. If the counselor shows the proper understanding and provides the necessary leads, he will open up and reveal his own difficulties.

3. The *Gift Bearer* is the one who, with a gleam in his eye, blurts out his dark secret—usually some moral transgression. His attitude is "here is a meaty problem for you to work on!" If you dwell on this

false lead, you either delay coming to grips with the real problem or you completely close off all meaningful communication.

4. The *Debunker* will come in loudly protesting that the tests he took are worthless and that no one can tell him anything about himself that he doesn't already know. Should you take the bait and try to prove him wrong, he will feel his victory is complete and you will have seen the last of him.

5. The *Dictator* will come to the counselor and resist making an appointment to review his test performance. He will imperiously declare that all he wants are the scores and the scores alone. The sudden change that takes place after the interview begins and he has recognized that the counselor cannot be bullied is often quite dramatic.

To the extent that we can recognize and cope with these characteristic defenses, we open up deeper channels of communication, which permit the client to come closer to self-understanding and maturity. Should our own feelings and vulnerabilities get in the way, causing us to repeat the pattern the client has so often encountered in approaching adult relationships, we shall have failed in providing the bridge he urgently needs.

## SCHOOL ACTIVITIES AS INSTRUMENTS FOR GROWTH

We also have many opportunities for using school activities as instruments for growth and development. I shall cite only one example, but I am sure you can find many similar to it in your own situation. In our Freshman Orientation Program we have our upperclassmen plan, execute, and evaluate most of the activities. By carefully delegating to the leaders the kinds of responsibilities that will challenge but not overpower them, we can see them grow in self-confidence almost day by day. In addition, we can see how students in subordinate positions manage themselves. And, above all, in the eyes of the much impressed freshman, we can see how he is already beginning to incorporate this image of the upperclassman in his own self-concept. It is interesting to note that frequently, when Orientation is over, many of the leaders have come for counseling in order to evaluate their own progress and plans for the future—something they unaccountably had postponed prior to this experience.

There is also the matter of social skills and their relationship to intellectual achievement. Too often we fail to recognize the sacrifice, the stress, and the loneliness the student must endure in pursuing his studies. If the acceptable social outlets are denied him due to timidity, shyness, or lack of social skills, he either falls into a meaningless, sterile routine or begins to show active signs of regressive behavior. However, in our school we found that through the influence of a warm and approachable social director many students who felt too threatened to seek counseling, appeared at Sunday socials where they learned to dance and to enjoy the companionship of members of the opposite sex. As this new avenue for social growth expanded, the signs of fresh interest in studies, and feelings of renewed purpose were unmistakable. Viewed in this light we can see the wisdom in the growing tendency to refer to student activities as co- rather than extra-curricular.

### CONTRIBUTION OF THE FACULTY

Finally, we must consider the great importance of the faculty in this developmental process. By consciously giving of themselves in contacts outside the classroom they can provide the adult model that will help students establish their own identity. In discussing the help faculty members can give to students Dalrymple says:

> The nonpsychiatric help they receive may be the most important event in improvement—and perhaps it will be the only significant event. For many students, the opportunity to talk to an older person who gives them understanding and acceptance is effective therapy. It can help the immature, the shy, the rebellious or the insecure to grow into more effective, comfortable human beings (1961, p. 19).

While many faculty members naturally lend themselves to such relationships, others resist—mainly out of fear and feelings of inadequacy. I recall a faculty meeting at which student conferences were discussed in terms of personality development, and how some professors were apprehensive about anything that had to do with personality. Their area of competence was in the intellectual realm, and there they wished to remain. Even when they were shown the influence they exerted in spite of themselves, they preferred not to strive consciously in this direction.

On the other hand those who were receptive, developed considerable anxiety because they did not have ready answers and solutions to the problems raised, as they did in class. In such instances we tried to show that specific solutions could well serve as a barrier to further communication, if the student found himself incapable of putting them into action. We also tried to convey what it meant to be accepting and to allow for the expression of feelings. Those who succeeded in achieving this were quite enthused by the results. Their relationship became much more comfortable and they were surprised by the manner in which students were able to arrive at their own solutions.

## SUMMARY

To summarize, the school counselor or counseling psychologist is primarily concerned with the growth and development of all students, and he will seek to develop whatever positive resources are present in the individual. To do this he will utilize—

1. Relationships with the faculty and counselors to provide an adult model for the development of self-concept.
2. Meaningful activities, such as Freshman Orientation, in which the more mature student leaders can contribute to the development of confidence and self-reliance in others.
3. Specific programs for the development of social skills to meet the needs that are characteristic at this stage of adolescent development.
4. The school society or culture to promote attitudes consistent with good mental health practices.

These then are but a few of the avenues open to the counselor who makes positive use of personal and environmental influences to develop the inner resources of all students. Many more are available if we will but seek them. The challenge to counselors to find new ways of meeting the changing needs of adolescents will require constant study and creative effort. In the words of Wechsler, "Wisdom and experience are necessary to make the world go round; creative ability to make it go forward!" (1958, p. 296).

I believe that to the extent that we strive to clarify our objectives and show a willingness to modify our techniques, we shall indeed contribute to the forward motion of our counseling universe.

## REFERENCES

Dalrymple, W. Faculty counseling and referral. In G. B. Blaine, Jr. and C. C. McArthur (Eds.). *Emotional problems of the student.* New York: Appleton-Century-Crofts, 1961. Pp. 17-28.

Pearson, G. H. J. *Adolescence and the conflict of generations.* New York: Norton, 1958.

Rogers, C. R. *Counseling and psychotherapy.* Boston: Houghton Mifflin, 1942.

Rogers, C. R. Lessons I have learned in counseling with individuals. In W. E. Dugan (Ed.) *Counseling points of view.* Minneapolis: Univer. Minn. Press, 1959. Pp. 14-26.

Super, D. E. Transition: from vocational guidance to counseling psychology. *J. counsel. Psychol.,* 1955, *2,* 3-9.

Wechsler, D. *The measurement and appraisal of adult intelligence.* Baltimore: Williams & Wilkins, 1958.

# The Pastoral Counselor

## GEORGE HAGMAIER, C.S.P.

*Father George Hagmaier, C.S.P., is Associate Director of the Paulist Institute for Religious Research in New York, and Instructor in Pastoral Psychology at the Paulist House of Graduate Study in Boston. His A.B. degree is from Santa Clara University, California, his M.A. from St. Paul's College, Washington, D. C., and his Ed.D. from Teachers College, Columbia University. He is the first priest to have been awarded the doctorate by the Department of Marriage and Family Life at Teachers College, Columbia. Fr. Hagmaier has contributed numerous magazine and journal articles, particularly in the area of marriage counseling and of religion and mental health. He is the author, jointly with Father Robert W. Gleason, S.J., of* Counselling the Catholic *(1959). Fr. Hagmaier is a member of the American Catholic Psychological Association, and an advisor to the Family Life Bureau of the National Catholic Welfare Conference.*

These remarks are not addressed to the professional psychotherapist or counselor who is presumed to have a wide background of study, reading and experience in dealing with the complex dynamics involved in the psychology of adolescence. I speak, rather, to the regular parochial clergy who confront the problems of the adolescent as sacerdotal counselors, in the classroom, in their youth groups, among the neighborhood families, in the confessional, in their retreat work, and in their occasional one-to-one relationships in the rectory parlor. Rather than list a series of detailed solutions to specific and individual adolescent problems, I propose to outline some of the principles underlying these problems, and some of the attitudes which the counselor should bring to their solution.

### COMPLEXITIES OF COUNSELING THE ADOLESCENT

Every priest should be deeply convinced that counseling the adolescent is a complex undertaking, because the adolescent himself is highly complex. Indeed, there are any number of variables which must be taken into account before the counselor can embark upon the solution of a concern which in a very real sense is unique to *this* adolescent before him.

The *age* of the adolescent has, for example, much to do with the approach the counselor will choose. The thirteen-or-fourteen-year-older is inclined to be uncommunicative, timid, and somewhat withdrawn. The presenting problem that he brings is very often not the real problem, and it requires considerable patience and careful listening to discover what is really on his mind. The seventeen-year-older, on the other hand, might be quite open, chatty, and even outspoken.

The relationship of the teenager to his community and his group can also be quite varied. In large urban parishes, for example, there is usually the difficult factor of sheer numbers. The individual teenager is lost in the crowd, and, for this very reason, is often more dependent on the group than he is on any other single individual. It takes much patience and talent to dislodge him from his peers and help him to examine his difficulties in terms of his private conflicts and inner life.

Socioeconomic factors play a vital role in the approach to the counseling of the adolescent. The pressures faced by the teenager from the more educated, ambitious, college-minded families are quite different from the earthy, more immediate challenges confronting the youngsters in, let us say, a low-income housing development.

Individual family backgrounds and attitudes are strikingly diverse and must be carefully appraised before the adolescent can be clearly understood. Finally, there are the galaxies of individual adolescent personalities, each quite different little worlds unto themselves, which must be studied.

Needless to say, the priest's *own* relationship, past and present, to all of these factors—his family background, the socioeconomic stratum from which he comes, his own upbringing, and his personal attitudes towards authority, individuality, sex, growth to maturity, and so on—will have much to do with his effective or short-sighted relationship to the adolescent and his world.

Then, of course, there is the very nature of *adolescence itself*. It's a time of puzzle, a time of flux, a time of change. There are new physical and emotional awakenings. And, most important in terms of counseling, there are three value systems with which the adolescent must deal, and which impinge upon his psychological, ethical and spiritual spheres.

There are first of all the values of childhood which the teenager is now re-examining and, to some extent, rejecting. For many of his early values are bound up with once-necessary yet arbitrary beliefs and practices, unquestioning submission to authority, blind obedience to untested principles, and a reasonable amount of compulsive behavior and magical thinking. The adolescent re-examines, picks and chooses, and is certain to revolt against a certain number of these past influences. This is part of normal human development. What will eventually emerge is a value system which he, happily, will be able to devise for himself. It will be largely a product of his own thinking and his own choice, but will, of course, be irrevocably linked to people and patterns important to his past. In addition to the evolution of understandably subjective, self-reliant standards and beliefs, there are the objective *moral* and *dogmatic* credos to which we fervently hope the youngster will commit himself as a mature and active Catholic.

The interplay of these three value systems—an interweaving, ever-changing, overlapping process—explains best of all why adolescence is a time of fluidity, confusion and unpredictability. Arthur Jersild (1957) has called this odyssey of the adolescent a search for selfhood, for self-identity. "Who am I?" is the most important question the adolescent asks himself. The emergence of his self-image, irretrievably colored by the views others have of him, in the past and in the present, is the essential experience of the teenage youngster.

## SOME GENERAL GUIDE LINES

Can we isolate certain general guide lines, which the perceptive counselor needs to keep in mind when he deals with a teenager? I think so. Here are a few.

1. The counselor may be inclined to over-rate the importance of emerging sexuality in the adolescent. It is true that the search for sexual maturity is high on the list of every adolescent's objectives. However, we must not view sexuality in isolation, and we must urge him not to do so either. So often, the management of inner drives and a growing readiness for mature heterosexual relationships are inextricably bound up with other immediate adolescent concerns— the need for independence, separation from past authority figures and institutions, loneliness, nameless anxieties, needless guilts, unvoiced ambitions. It is safe to say that the counselor should hardly ever deal with sexuality per se, but relate sexual difficulties and growth to problems of authority and rebellion, self-reliance and dependence, fears and hostility.

2. The adolescent is on the move. He is going somewhere—he's not sure where, but he is in motion. One thing is almost certain— he will not be *pushed* from behind, especially by elders whose authority he is seeking to outstrip. He can, however, be *led*. To lead effectively, the counselor must be able in some way to identify with the youngster. This is very difficult, because the adult, unlike the adolescent, is no longer himself searching for identity. He has arrived. It is hard for us to fly backwards, like the bird in the old vaudeville gag who likes to see where he's been rather than where he's going. Many adults would like to forget their childhood and their adolescent years, especially if they were somewhat painful or chaotic, or guilt-ridden. But in varying ways, and in keeping with our individual talents, we must be able to put ourselves back into the past. By no means should we become an adolescent again, a hail-fellow-well-met, a backslapper, a pal or buddy. The naive "boyologist" or thirty-year-old campfire girl are generally nauseating and unsettling companions who force themselves onto the younger set, but who hardly ever achieve positive and lasting relationships with them. The adolescent does not want an adult who sees himself or herself as an equal of the adolescent. The teenager wants a guide who does not share the turmoil

and confusion of adolescence, but who does reflect stability, who communicates empathy, compassion, interest—all those qualities which tell the teenager: "I *understand.*"

3. One of the mistakes too often made by the unperceptive adult is to see the adolescent's dissatisfaction and impatience with outside authorities only in terms of rebellion. Too often we fail to see the *idealism* that so often underlies revolt. This idealism is often naive and distorted, but it is essentially good. The teenager, more often than not, has a keen sense of principle, and a capacity for committing himself to a code of values. We see this even in the dedication of the delinquent to a weird set of amoral ethics to which he nevertheless rigidly adheres. The adolescent wants a value system, he wants to set *limits* for himself, he wants in some way to bring control to the new and chaotic drives and passions which he feels may overwhelm him.

Implicit in this idealism so characteristic of the adolescent is his capacity for responsibility. And here again, we are too often inclined to fall short in our ability to show him the confidence he deserves. The adult world, along with the adolescent, is understandably confused as to what is to be expected of today's young people. We often make adult demands far beyond the capacity of the youngsters to achieve, and at the same time we are reluctant to sever the silver cords which bind them in a needlessly dependent relationship upon their elders. The major complaint voiced by teenagers today concerns the inconsistency of adult demands—being asked to live up to adult standards on one hand, but being treated like a child at the same time.

Involved in the solution of this difficulty is a dangerous trap. The adolescent who has been prevented for too long a time from exercising responsibility may have a hard time when it is first given. His first stumbling efforts to manage a job by himself may meet with failure. It is a great temptation for the interfering and skeptical adult to be confirmed in his misgivings, and to declare, often with a feeling of vindication: "I told you so! You really were not ready." If we are to encourage responsibility in our young people—especially in those who have a reputation for irresponsibility—we must be patient, we must remain involved without interfering, and we must, above all, give absolute, wholehearted evidence that we have *confidence* in youth's ability to learn, even if it is through mistakes.

4. An important need for every adolescent is an heroic example— a model, a pathfinder, an unwavering guide who will not force compli-

ance, but whom the youngster will be moved to admire and imitate with spontaneity and enthusiasm. It is in this role that the priest-counselor can be particularly effective. He has the advantage of not being identified with the family circle. Ideally speaking, of course, every boy will come to admire his mother and want to imitate his father. But he has been living in a most intimate way with his parents for many years. He knows their weakness as well as their strength. When the drive for independence becomes acute, it often happens that his violent rejection of the less perfect qualities of his parents cloud his perception as to their good points. The relationship of the priest to his young people, insofar as emotional ties are concerned, are happily more remote. Therefore the good things for which he stands, his priesthood, his dedication, and his worthy qualities as a man, stand out with greater clarity. This is true, of course, not only of the priest, but the good teacher, the friend, and the leaders within the peer group.

## THE PRIEST-COUNSELOR

The priest as a *model* for admiration and imitation gives meaning to the words "permissiveness" and "non-judgmental." The priest-counselor need not be afraid of these words. There is little likelihood that his basic views will be misunderstood. Most teenagers know the Church and her teachings, and they know that every priest is in a special way the guardian and exemplar of these moral and dogmatic truths. The ideal priest-counselor then, is one who gives every adolescent credit for hoping that he will in some way be able to live up to the expectations of his God and his church, and at the same time makes clear allowances for the varying degrees of success achieved by the young people he knows. Struggle and failure do not dismay him; he is not easily shocked by the shortcomings and weaknesses of his counselees. He responds with patience and encouragement, rather than with censure and an immediate demand for change. He does not value sharp, absolute and legalistic compliance to a moral code above the slow, stumbling, yet certain emergence of *attitudes* towards morality which will, later on, make it possible for the mature adolescent to bring a meaningful and joyous obedience to God's laws.

In conclusion, may I mention this observation. It is my impression that a very large amount of counseling with teenagers can be done through group contact, rather than by becoming involved in a great number of individual interviews. As I indicated earlier, the impact of sheer numbers is an obstacle that individual counseling cannot overcome. Secondly, the average adolescent is naturally reluctant to discuss his problems in a one-to-one relationship. His own timidity and self-consciousness make it difficult for him to listen to even excellent advice in a private conversation with a priest. On the other hand, the priest who really understands the adolescent and is interested in helping young people to achieve healthy and holy maturity, can "tune in on" a tremendous number of adolescent questions, concerns, temptations, in his general dealings with them. From the pulpit, in the high school classroom, in neighborhood gatherings and CCD programs, through recreational activities, and in retreats the perceptive priest can speak in general terms about critical problems which the adolescent will recognize immediately as his own. These communications, involving both words and attitudes, will often encourage this or that youngster to seek a private conversation with a priest. The more remote and anonymous relationship to the group which he has heretofore enjoyed often paves the way and provides the courage for this more intimate discussion.

The interaction of the counselor-confessor role is a particularly difficult one for many priests to manage. Each priest must solve it in his own fashion according to his own inclinations. Some might prefer to deal with the teenager both inside and outside confession. This is often very advantageous with boys who are able to make a simple and untroubled confession at the end of a counseling session. Others may wish to keep the roles separate, and will encourage the youngster to go to confession to some other understanding priest. This is important where the individual is not yet ready to speak as frankly and openly as he might wish, which he feels obliged to do when he goes to confession.

Finally, we must not forget the possibility of priests working with professional lay people in a counseling liaison. We are fortunate today, especially those of us working in big cities, to have at our disposal a considerable battery of agencies and individual experts who are often far more capable than we are of dealing with the troubled teenager. Every priest should be able to call upon the advice of a judge, a social worker, a psychiatrist, a youth-board representative, a school counselor, and many other community experts and agencies. Sometimes the priest, better than any one else, can supply vital information about the family and background of the problem person.

He can also reassure the timorous counselee that he will be getting expert help from understanding laymen, and he can encourage him to seek such help. And, perhaps most important of all, he can be a kindly and informed confessor who has some understanding of what the professional agencies and individuals are trying to do, and can reinforce, through his sacramental office, the suggestions and procedures they feel are important.

Adolescence is a difficult time, and counseling the adolescent is a difficult undertaking. It is, however, psychologically speaking, nature's second chance, encouraging the well-adjusted child to grow majestically into manhood, and enabling the emotionally deprived and psychically stunted youngster to resolve those conflicts, deeply rooted in the past, which stand in the way of his full development. It is an awesome opportunity we face when these hopeful, troubled children of God look to us for help. Please God we will be able to respond with love, understanding, encouragement, and grace.

## REFERENCE

Jersild, A. T. The psychology of adolescence. (4th ed.) New York: Macmillan, 1957.

# The Professional Psychotherapist

## ALFRED R. JOYCE

*Alfred Robert Joyce, M.D., is Associate Professor of Psychiatry at the Fordham University School of Social Service. In addition to filling this post, he is also Director of the Mental Hygiene and Child Guidance Clinic of the New York Foundling Hospital, Director of the Iona Institute for Pastoral Counseling, and psychiatric consultant at several other educational institutions. His own B.S. degree was earned at St. Peter's College, Jersey City, and his M.D. degree at Marquette University. Dr. Joyce also has a certificate in Psychoanalysis granted by the New York Medical College and is a fellow of the American Psychiatric Association, as well as a fellow of the Academy of Psychoanalysis. Dr. Joyce is a contributor to professional journals, the titles of some of his articles being the following: "The Role of the Psychiatrist in a College Mental Health Program," "Psychiatric Consultation in a Child Welfare Agency," and "Psychiatric Concepts of Emotional Maturity."*

The understanding and treatment of the adolescent poses a most perplexing problem for the psychoanalyst. Many therapists regard the overall mood experienced during adolescence as a transitional state of being, intensified by the stresses of our times. Perhaps the member of our society who is least known is the adolescent. A great deal has been learned about the dynamics of children as well as adults, but only recently have psychoanalysts begun to focus their attention on the vital period of life known as adolescence.

Beyond childhood but not yet adults, adolescents move in a society of their own where invaders are not welcome unless they are invited in. Recently, considerable interest has been focused on the formulation of the dynamics of the normal adolescent, and for very good reasons. Neurosis or psychosis studied in an adult yield scant information or none at all about the period of adolescence. At the same time we are faced with an increasing rate of suicides, drug addiction and delinquency among adolescents. Consequently, it is imperative that more be learned about this particular segment of the human population.

Like the little child, the teenager has often been called the neglected child. By some it is considered simply a period of change during which the adolescent is neither child nor adult. But this in itself affords us no clue because all of life is a transition between birth and death. However, there are physical, psychological, and social factors appearing during adolescence which are not found in childhood or adulthood. All of the adjustments that were accomplished during childhood now have to be reorganized under the influence of these factors. It is this process which gives the impression that the adolescent's personality is changing.

### CHANGES OF ADOLESCENCE

There are two courses during the human life span which are similar. The first cycle starts with conception and ends at birth. The second cycle begins with puberty and ends on leaving the parental home. After birth, the baby intrudes into the parental environment and becomes entirely dependent upon them. These surroundings may be likened to a protective womb which has to be broken out of when the youngster, driven by the forces of adolescence, invades the world of adults. Dynamically, then, adolescence is a kind of second birth.

During childhood, the parents protect, feed and give unconditional love to their children. At the beginning of adolescence, however, this familiar scheme of things is disrupted. Physical changes occur rapidly. The general mechanism of puberty is fairly well known: the hormones from the anterior pituitary stimulate the secretion of sex hormones by the cells of the testes and the ovarian follicles. At the same time the production of seventeen keto steroids by the adrenal glands is increased to play a part in the development of the secondary sexual characteristics. Still unknown is the question of what mechanism causes the release of this gonadotrophic hormone from the pituitary gland.

The hands, feet, arms, legs are apt to grow disproportionately during puberty, giving the youngster the comical appearance of an ungainly spider. Also common is a rapid growth of nose and chin, throwing familiar features out of kilter. The development of secondary sexual characteristics clearly depends on the circulation of hormones, but curiously there seems to be no such spurt of androgen hormones to coincide with the onset of puberty. One theory has it that puberty is set in motion not by an increase in androgen hormones but by some still unexplained factor which makes tissues more responsive.

Psychological changes accompany the bodily ones, with unconscious fears, conflicts and hostilities suddenly rising to the surface. At such times the adolescent feels all alone and tries to hide these feelings. He has a sense of being banished both from the world of adults and from the world of children. He is like a foreigner in a new land who cannot communicate because of a language barrier. His one cry is "Nobody understands me!"

If the adolescent is able to leave the protection of his parents, he can find his place in society. His concern will now extend beyond the family circle. But this is when the parents might feel threatened by his sudden change of attitude. So we have the primary rebellion of the parents against a healthy maturing of the adolescent. The parents rebel against a biological, psychological and social phenomenon they do not understand.

The so-called normal individual is one who is balanced within himself and in his relations with society. One of the most important principles for helping mature individuals maintain this balance is a concept of moderation. Here we come to a major aspect of personality development—that of the ego. The ego is the balancing mechanism which keeps the individual within healthy and normal limits. The ego has the ability to develop a sense of reality and a sense of the right measure, the latter being derived from Greek philosophy. Dynamically, moderation is the basis for normality and maturity.

However, some adolescents try prematurely to take on the role of being mature and deny even to themselves the turmoil of conflicts going on inside. As a result they create a conflict with their parents.

In other words, they want to be mature but they are not mature, so they react with aggression toward the parents. In some instances, adolescents who have been getting good grades in school suddenly drop off in their marks and lose their rank in class. They cannot study or concentrate because they are perpetually trying to work out their conflicts in daydreams. The daydream of the adolescent has a special quality. In it physical senses are so sharpened that the youngster becomes extremely sensitive to the world about him. Colors, textures, sounds, odors are far more acute than at any other time in life, and he is almost overwhelmed by their onslaught and his own receptivity.

### FUNCTION OF ADOLESCENT DAY DREAMS

What are some of the problems that the adolescent has to work out in his daydreams? He tries to resolve many of his old childhood conflicts with his parents, plus the new problems brought on by his sudden awareness of his maturing body, his future role in society and his newfound sexual drives. He pictures the world as he would like it to be, not as it is. At the very center of the daydream we find the adolescent's image of himself. The world's pressures and conflicts bombard this inner picture. Therefore the adolescent withdraws from the outside world and tries to reform it so it will conform to his own ideas.

The image of oneself is related to the growth of the body, and now the adolescent becomes more than ever aware of his body. Gradually, there are fragmentations of his old inner image and a slow replacing of it with a more mature adult image. This is a period of reorganization which requires the formation of a new picture of the self. There are two important dynamics involved; the one having to do with the breaking up of the old image, and the other activating a slow reorganization of the new picture of the self in relation to the real world. In between these two dynamic processes there is a void where the adolescent feels alone, aloof and often moody and depressed.

In childhood, we know that the child identifies with his parents and we find parts of his parents in his self-image. This process of identification is an unconscious mechanism whereby the person is able to take unto himself the personality of those he loves or hates. We must realize that the child identifies with his parents because they are the first and most important people in the world to him. However, he can identify with others about him, such as siblings, friends, teachers and the like.

During adolescence, his sexual drives are extremely strong and as the body changes rapidly, so too do the emotions. The adolescent has to cope with these feelings and his ego has to be able to control them. He can neither repress these sexual drives nor express them openly, so he directs them into daydreams to be resolved in a safe way. He compensates for his aggressiveness and his sexuality by looking for idealized absolute values in the outer world. When he cannot find them he suffers a blow to his inner world and his image of himself and must then revamp his inner world to conform with the outer one.

Inevitably, he will find reality in the outer world which will bring him into conflicts with the image of himself. Then he must be able to accept the outer world and modify the inner image of himself. He must reach a compromise with the outer world. He must give up the absolute unrealistic perfectionistic drives of the image of himself.

When the adolescent is thrown into the world, his ego has to accept life and effect a compromise between perfection and nothingness. If he persists in clinging neurotically to his perfectionistic values, he will be driven back to nothingness, depression and, maybe, suicide. If the adolescent has not been able to identify with strong parental figures, his image will be weak, shapeless and confused. Such a youngster will feel threatened by inner danger or by any demands of the world outside which induce him to conform to adult standards.

These adolescents are found among juvenile delinquents who come from broken homes and parents who have a character disorder or are neurotic or psychotic. These young people are fixated at an infantile level and need mothering, fathering and identification on an oral level of development. Normally, the adolescent gradually develops a sense of reality and will overcome his daydreams as reality slowly modifies the elements in his personality, consciously and unconsciously.

We can readily see that the daydream is a necessary dynamic for reorganizing the personality. Daydreaming in adolescence is said by many authors to be the bridge leading the individual to maturity. Examination of the daydreams of the adolescent reveals that they are composed of a mixture of erotic and ambitious drives. Underlying this reorganization of the image of oneself is a weakening of the ego. What is more, the psychological weakening is accompanied by a physical weakening. The sexual hormones possess elements of both sexes. The adolescent is bombarded by both male and female sexual hormones. Consequently, he may present indefinite sexual tendencies which some people may take to be homosexual.

This weakening of the ego with an introduction of bisexual hormones accounts for the bisexuality observed for a short time in most teenagers. This stage of their sexuality may sometimes lead to a state of confusion but it is regarded as natural, varying in degree according to the individual's personality, background, and present environment. It is at this time that the adolescent is most susceptible to homosexuality and the parents can do a great deal to protect the adolescent while he is in this confused and weakened state.

### THE ADOLESCENT'S CONCERN ABOUT HIS FUTURE

Another problem which the adolescent is concerned about is the question of his future and the kind of work he will do or the profession he will pursue. Some adolescents decide early in childhood what they want to do and actively follow their chosen course. The act of leaving the home is accompanied by a minimum of anxiety on the part of some adolescents. They seem to know what they want and understand their potentiality, while their goals seem to be justifiable.

By contrast, there are many adolescents who are constantly questioning what they want to do and we find that they have a rather poor image of themselves. They tend to overestimate their potentiality and their goals are projected unrealistically from their daydreams into reality. There is a confusion between their egos and their image of themselves. Many of these adolescents suffer breakdowns because they are looking for infantile satisfactions in the real world.

The adolescent has to decide what kind of life he will lead, what work he will do. He has to assert himself at this particular time. He has to choose the goal and the path toward that goal. When he has selected a goal he builds up an image around it and tends to identify with that image. If he fails, then he has to destroy the goal, kill off a part of his own ego and re-establish a new goal, a new image and a new identity. When one image is gone, a void is left. Depression sets in and it is for this reason that we find many college students who have failed in obtaining their goals attempting suicide. Many failing students react with hostility toward the world and blame it for their failures. Others react with a healthy hyperactivity to overcome defeat and hurt, and immediately start out on some new project toward some new goal.

What about the attitude of parents toward their adolescent children? Adults usually repress memories of their own adolescence and have little insight into this dynamic area of life. Parents usually feel ashamed or guilty about their own adolescence, therefore becoming defensive and hostile toward the normal dynamics of their adolescent children. Most parents, when confronted with adolescent behavior, react subjectively. "He acts so queerly," they'll say, "something must be wrong," or "a good adolescent doesn't act that way." These feelings prevent parents from looking at their own children objectively.

When the adolescent breaks away from family ties, the parents will react according to their own level of maturity. Parents who are mature will accept the breaking of ties and tactfully avoid interfering with the normal dynamics of this period. Such parents know full well that it is best to leave their children alone. A word of caution is in order, however. Some parents are only too happy to get rid of their responsibilities and are overly eager to push their children out of the home. Many adolescents are prematurely evicted because of their parents' wish to have their own freedom.

The fact is that adolescents still need the guidance and protection of their parents. A mature parent continues to love his children through all phases of development and surely adolescence is no exception. Parental diplomacy is a basic necessity for helping all children through every phase of growth. Yet many parents lack mature tact and they are the ones who will rebel against the biological-chemical aspects of normal growth in their children.

It has been found that classical rebellion is always a reaction provoked by initial primary rebellion on the part of the parents. Rebellion is defined as a basic non-acceptance. Parents who are immature will rebel against the normal dynamics of adolescence. Such parents interfere with the delicate process of adolescence and bungle their relationship with the child. To reiterate, the rebellion of adolescence is secondary to the primary rebellion of the parents. One cannot detect any such upheaval in those adolescents whose parents show tact and love during this period of crisis. One of the greatest dangers of adolescence, where parents lack tact, is on the sexual level. During a time when there is sexual confusion as well as tremendous sexual urges, lack of protection from the external world will upset the adolescent, and a great deal of damage may be done.

Parents have to accept the fact that children have a right to feel things and act within the limits and protection prescribed by a loving mature parent. It has been said that where there is not at least some feeling of possessiveness there can be no love. It follows that parents who are completely devoid of possessive feelings toward their children have no love for them. A combination of love and possessiveness in moderate degree is found in the mature parent. There are two types of adolescents who rebel: (1) those who do so against the primary rebellion of their parents; (2) those who submit to the primary rebellion of their parents and go along with the parents' desires.

The degree of maturity conditions the reaction of the adolescent to the parents' rebellion. When the adolescent reaches the stage where he is ready to break the emotional ties with his family, a reaction of anxiety usually develops. This anxiety is specific for this particular dynamic interaction and every normal adolescent experiences it for a brief period of time. (We are not alluding to the neurotic or psychotic anxiety of the adolescent.) The tendency to daydream fades away and he begins to perceive the world as it is. The anxiety gives him the impetus to go forward in meeting the struggles of the real adult world.

In summary, the child, psychologically, leaves the protection of his parents and enters the world of adolescence. Here he stands alone. He is neither a child nor an adult. His childhood conflicts and the surge of sexual drives find an outlet in the safety valve of a daydream. While he must withdraw temporarily from the world, he still needs the protection and love of his parents. When he breaks the emotional bonds with his parents, he will experience a specific anxiety which he has to master. He stands at the threshold of the adult world but now he is not alone.

### PSYCHOTHERAPY WITH ADOLESCENTS

The adolescent has a set of dynamics unique to this phase of development. These dynamics are not similar to the phases of childhood or adulthood, but are specific for this period. It is important that they be recognized and identified, and techniques of therapy devised to cope with the special problems involved.

Many parents have a misconception based on their own unconscious or conscious needs about the freedom or restriction to be given adolescents. In my professional experience, adolescents need more guidance, protection and maturing discipline than at any other time of life. Internally, their egos are being bombarded anew by all their childhood conflicts, and externally society is making demands on them to live up to adult standards. It is like fighting a battle on two major fronts. At times it proves too much for the adolescent and he has to protect himself. This is when the self-preservative drive takes over.

In treating adolescents it is important that this combination of dynamics be kept in mind. The adolescent cannot be expected to solve all his childhood problems, grapple with the problems of the future, cope with the physical bombardment of sexual hormones, struggle with psychological and social problems of this period all at the same time. The ego simply cannot handle all these crises at once. Therefore, in therapy a technique is employed of dealing with the ego problems of the present, rather than probing for childhood conflicts or bringing future problems to the fore, such as questions of profession, work and the like. I concentrate on building up the ego, pointing out the reality of everyday situations and encouraging the formation of a positive relationship. When the adolescent phase is completed, the individual will return and concentrate on his or her childhood problems.

It is vital from this viewpoint to understand how much harm can be done during this weakened period of life to the ego which has such a tenuous hold on reality. The therapist who does not take this into consideration is like a surgeon who operates on a patient who has lost a great deal of blood without first replenishing the lost amount by transfusion. The patient's chances for physical survival are pretty slim if he is not given a transfusion to build up his strength. Likewise, the adolescent needs a transfusion to repair his ego.

How does the psychoanalyst select his patients for treatment, especially among adolescents? Diagnosis is important, but it is felt that an evaluation of the ego is even more important. We evaluate the following components: (1) the individual's ability to form relationships; (2) his ability to form relationships with the opposite sex; (3) his motility towards a realistic goal; (4) his sense of reality; (5) his conception of himself; (6) his intellectual functioning.

The adolescent who does well in a majority of these areas seldom requires psychoanalysis. If he is disturbed in several of these areas, then intensive therapy is indicated. Should these disturbances be left untreated, the adolescent can crystallize into a character-disorder individual whom no amount of therapy will help later on. In the initial sessions, the therapist listens with a third ear to what the adolescent is saying, without making any comments or judgments. The adolescent has to recognize that the therapist is there to help him and he eventually has to become aware of his own difficulties.

For his part, the therapist has to be an extremely flexible person, able to swing with the alternation of moods in the adolescent. The negativism that is so prominent in the adolescent is usually a defense against underlying infantile aggressive and sexual feelings. A couch is hardly ever used with the adolescent because it could encourage excessive fantasy and regression. The therapist becomes a real person who understands, protects and serves as a healthy model for identification. Eventually, the adolescent's ego grows under this atmosphere of understanding and unconditional love. At this point the ego has become sufficiently healthy for the youngster to leave the analyst and fact the anxieties of the real world.

In most cases the families of disturbed adolescents also need treatment, but there is so much resistance that the best we can do is give them support and guidance. In my several years of experience in dealing with juvenile delinquents at Children's Village in Dobbs Ferry, New York, as a Consultant Training Analyst, I have found that these boys have had deep-seated emotional problems during early childhood. Since their primary needs were unmet, they were unconsciously acting out their primitive desires to have these needs satisfied. I found that before any ego growth could occur these needs had to be met in symbolic ways on a nonverbal level. After a trusting relationship had been formed and the need fulfilled, the boy usually developed a transference neurosis. From then on the therapist was able to give the boy a constructive and corrective emotional experience.

## ROLE OF THE PASTORAL COUNSELOR

It is my opinion that the pastoral counselor constitutes the first line of defense against mental illness and can be of tremendous help to the disturbed adolescent. He can provide the youngster with a mature healthy atmosphere, free from judgment or criticism. He can listen with the third ear and refrain from giving advice too quickly. He can serve as a model of identification and can motivate the youngster toward healthy growth, or motivate him for professional help. Moreover, the pastoral counselor can educate the parents to the conscious and unconscious needs of the adolescent, and provide sexual education and guidance to the adolescent as well as his parents. I believe that the pastoral counselor can do more with the adolescent, initially, than any other figure of authority. It is therefore imperative that the dynamics of this period of development be fully understood by every pastoral counselor.

## REFERENCES

Aichorn, A. *Wayward youth.* New York: Viking, 1935.

Ausubel, D. P. *Theory and problems of adolescent development.* New York: Grune & Stratton, 1954.

Bernard, H. W. *Adolescent development in American culture.* New York: World Book, 1957.

Bender, Laurette. Genesis of hostility in children. *Amer J. Psychiat.,* 1948, *105,* 241-245.

Bettelheim, B. *Love is not enough.* New York: Free Press, 1950.

Erikson, E. *Childhood and society.* New York: Norton, 1950.

Freud, Anna. *The ego and the mechanism of defense.* London: Hogarth, 1947. (First German edition, 1936.)

Freud, S. *Civilization and its discontents.* London: Hogarth, 1949. (First German edition, 1930.)

Greenberg, I. M. A comparison of the crosscultural adaptive process with adolescence. *Comprehensive Psychiat.,* 1961, *2,* 44-50.

Hacker, F. J., and Geleerd, E. R. Freedom and authority in adolescents. *Amer. J. Orthopsychiat.,* 1945, *15,* 621-630.

Hoch, P. H., & Zubin, J. *Psychosexual development in health and disease.* New York: Grune & Stratton, 1949.

Jocelyn, L. *The adolescent and his world.* New York: Family Service Ass., 1952.

Johnson, A. Sanctions for super ego lacunae of adolescents. In K. Eissler (Ed.) *Searchlights on delinquency.* New York: International Universities, 1949. Pp. 225-245.

Kris, H. The psychology of caricature. *Int. J. Psychoanal.*, 1936, *17*, 283-303.

Mohr, G. J., and Despres, Marian A. *The stormy decade: adolescence.* New York: Random House, 1958.

Pearson, C. *Adolescence and the conflict of generations.* New York: Norton, 1938.

Redl, F. Pre-adolescents—what makes them tick? *Child Stud.*, 1944, *21*, 44-48, 58-59.

Rubé, P. Adolescence: I. Is there a problem of adolescence? *Amer. J. Psychother.*, 1955, *9*, 503-509.

Rubé, P. Adolescence: II. The inner world of adolescence. *Amer. J. Psychother.*, 1955, *9*, 673-691.

Strang, Ruth. *The adolescent views himself: a psychology of adolescence.* New York: McGraw-Hill, 1957.

Wilkes, E. T. *Family guide to teenage health.* New York: Ronald, 1958.

Wheelis, A. *The quest for identity.* New York: Norton, 1958.

# Tri-Une Conference for Teenagers*

JOHN C. KNOTT

*Father John C. Knott is a priest of the Archdiocese of Hartford, Conn. He was ordained to the priesthood in 1939, served as a U.S. Navy Chaplain from 1943 to 1946, and spent a year in graduate study at the Catholic University of America from 1946 to 1947, receiving a master's degree in marriage and the family. In 1950, Fr. Knott was appointed full-time Director of the Marriage and Family Apostolate of the Archdiocese of Hartford. He has given several hundred Conferences throughout the United States and Canada, including Tri-Une Conferences for Teenagers (which he inaugurated in the Archdiocese of Hartford), Pre-Cana Conferences for engaged couples, and various types of Cana Conferences for married couples. At the invitation of the Chief of Air Force Chaplains, Fr. Knott has conducted similar Conferences for Air Force personnel and their families at Air Force Bases in Europe, North Africa, Hawaii, and Japan. Articles by Fr. Knott have appeared in* Marriage, The Homiletic and Pastoral Review, Columbia, *and other publications. He is the author of the weekly syndicated column entitled: "Everyman's Family." He has been the Director of the Family Life Bureau of the National Catholic Welfare Conference since October of 1961.*

The Tri-Une Conferences for teenagers have been operating in the Archdiocese of Hartford since 1952. These Conferences are an at-

* Reprinted, after appropriate up-dating, from the 1957 Fordham Pastoral Psychology Institute.

tempt to help the adolescent understand himself as he is now, with the particular gifts of love that God has given to him and in the particular vocation that is his at the moment. They also aim to prepare him for the particular vocation of love-service that will be his later, whether it be in the religious, the married, or the single state.

### PURPOSE OF THE TRI-UNE CONFERENCE

The name, Tri-Une, comes from the fact that in God there is a trinity of persons and a unity of nature. There is also in human beings a trinity of vocations—married, religious, or single—with a unity of purpose, which is the love of God and the love of neighbor. The teenagers are in a transitional state from childhood into adulthood. Their big problem is understanding themselves and giving their gifts of love as well as they can in their present transitional vocation as a preparation for a successful fulfillment of their future vocation.

The Tri-Une Conferences originally were restricted to boys and girls of the 11th and 12th grades in high school in joint session. Initially the presumption was that the major problem of these adolescents was the boy-girl relationship. The correct understanding and use of sex is, of course, a challenge for anyone, and especially the teenager. Surveys demonstrated, however, that a statistically more common problem was the teenager's lack of understanding of his parents.

Experience in parent-child Cana Conferences also indicated that parents of adolescents were equally at a loss in understanding their children. Part of the difficulty was due to semantics, but a deeper reason for the lack of mutual understanding on the part of both parents and children might be traced to a lack of awareness as to the nature and needs of the other.

Consequently, a combined Tri-Une—Cana Conference was developed, commonly called a Tri-Cana. A Tri-Une Conference is given one evening to the adolescents from 7:30 to 10 o'clock. It consists of a talk by a priest, discussion in small groups in which principles enunciated by him are applied by the participants, reports made, questions asked and answered, with comments and a closing summary by the Director. The evening concludes with Benediction of the Blessed Sacrament, a prayer for choice of vocation, and refreshments.

A few night later the parents of this group are invited to a Cana Conference during which many of the things discussed at the previous conference are repeated to the parents, but from their viewpoint. The third evening's meeting is a joint session of parents and teenagers in which the priest-director sets the stage for open discussion between the parents and the apprentice adults who are their teenage children.

Since 1960 the Tri-Cana Conferences have focused on the 9th and 10th grade children and their parents. A special conference has been given to the 11th and 12th grade students without the parents.

The big advantage of the Tri-Cana arrangement is that it restores or at least strengthens communication between parents and children and shifts responsibility back to the family where it belongs. In its desire to help solve the so-called teenage problem the Church, if it is not realistic, can, like any extra-familial agency, actually weaken further the structure of the basic society that is the family.

The difficulty the teenager has in understanding his parents, as well as the whole boy-girl relationship, can be traced to a basic ignorance as to his own nature as a human being. The first talk in the Tri-Une Conference is on the subject of understanding oneself. We draw our knowledge not inductively from the sciences of psychiatry, psychology and allied fields, but deductively from the revelation of God concerning the nature of the teenager. The Bible says nothing about teenagers. They seem to be a modern, largely American phenomenon. But the theology books, and particularly the basic theology book that is the Catechism, has mentioned the human being. What we have to recognize about teenagers is that they are human beings. We emphasize that fact in the Cana Conference for parents because many of them wonder whether teenagers really are human.

### TEENAGERS NEED TO BE LOVED

The Catechism defines the human being as a creature composed of body and soul and made to the image and likeness of God. There are two elements here, I think, that are of practical importance. One is that the teenager, as a human being, is a creature. Now every creature is the product of the gift of love of other persons—first, of God Who gives His gift of love that is the gift of life, and then of parents who give their love. With the continued gifts of love of God and of the parents, complemented by the gifts of love of other persons—brothers, sisters, relatives, teachers, and so forth—the basic creature-need of this human being—the need to be loved—is being satisfied.

In the child it is obvious that his basic hunger is a hunger for love. He is a beggar for love. He travels the neighborhood begging cookies here and soda there, but always, and especially at home, begging for the satisfaction of his creature-need to be loved.

A couple of years ago I read a news account of an experience in a foundling home in South America. The home took care of abandoned infants. It was heavily endowed, had a fine medical staff, gave excellent nursing care, had good physical facilities, but it also had a very high infant mortality rate. Exhaustive research eliminated the usual reasons for so many infants fading away and dying.

It was finally established that the high death rate among the babies was due to one rather simple cause. There were in the Foundling Home an average of one hundred infants and only ten nurses—one-tenth of a mother for each child. It was not sufficient to satisfy the basic creature-need to be loved that was part of the nature of the infant. Auxiliary mothers were brought in from the neighborhood to give more personal care to the babies and the mortality rate dropped to normal standards.

Now, this need in the infant—the need to be loved—is also present in the teenager. Because he wears size 12 shoes, or she uses lipstick, many parents think that their adolescents do not need attention. Certainly they do not need the same kind of attention that they did a few years ago. But they do need to be recognized as human beings with the basic creature-hunger to be loved, this hunger to be satisfied especially by the parents.

### TEENAGERS NEED TO LOVE

There is another aspect to their nature that is equally important. They are made to the image and likeness of God. As His image and likeness they share in the essential operation of God, which is the operation of love. These teenagers not only need *to be loved* as creatures, they also need *to love,* they need to give of themselves, they need to give this gift that is theirs, they need to be this image and likeness of God. Along with the gift of life the other great gift that parents make to a child is the gift of independence. They recognize his right and grant him the opportunity to be himself and to give his gift of love and be the image and likeness of God that he is.

These, then, are the two basic needs of the human being, and of the teenager particularly—the need to be loved, and the need to love. As an adolescent he is going over the hump from childhood into adulthood. The mark of the adult involves two things: one is the know-how of love; the other is the will-do of love. The one involves acquiring through the period of growth an increasing skilfullness in the art of loving. The second is concerned with accepting the challenge of the sacrifice of self which love demands.

Most parents are careful in answering the child's need of being loved as well as they can and to the extent that they understand. In some cases they go to the extreme of doing too much for their offspring. They empty their purse, break their backs and sometimes their hearts to see that every possible want of the child is taken care of.

They fail to recognize that every baby is born in a psychological membrane of self-centeredness, and that one of the great challenges of parenthood is to help the child to stretch and finally break through to the world of other-centeredness that is the world of love. This takes time and patience and, most of all, awareness that the child has this need to love and consequently must be given the opportunity to love. and be encouraged to use it. Perhaps the best encouragement is the realization on the part of the child that no matter how fumbling or inadequate his efforts may be, his parents are concerned not with the perfection of the act but with the spirit behind it.

As he gradually develops the facility of love through practice and the guidance of his parents, his willingness to pay the price of love increases. He then is able to face with more security the increasing demands of the world of apprentice adulthood that is adolescence and see it as the opportunity to prepare for maturity.

The other alternative is not to demand anything much from adolescents as they grow and let them face completely unprepared the demands which a harsh and unsympathetic world will certainly make of them. Here is one of the hidden reasons why some marriages go "haywire" despite surface indications of success. The man who has grown up with only one knowledge, that of being loved, will see in his marriage only another means of satisfying that hunger. He will not understand it as an adult relationship in which he must focus on loving another. The woman married to such a husband will be more of a mother than a wife.

### PROPER MANNER OF LOVING AND BEING LOVED

The important thing in regard to teenagers is to open up to them the reality of their life as God has created it. They are made to love and to be loved, but the dominant focus now that they are approaching adulthood is on the former. The next question is: how are they going to love and be loved *well?* The answer here is rather simple. They are going to love and be loved well, according to how they are made.

In the natural order of things the one thing that teenagers have in common with each other is their human nature with the common needs of loving and being loved working through this body-soul unity that is a human person. It is important for the teenager to see life as a matter of a love relationship between human persons with himself as the image and likeness of God giving a gift of love to a creature according to his need of being loved.

It is also necessary for him to see himself as a particular human being. God does not use an assembly line for the mass production of persons. Each human being is the product of the unique act of the creative will of God. When this adolescent was to be born, God in a sense chipped off part of Himself and made this person a unique image and likeness of Himself. To him He gave a unique gift of love, a gift that no one else has but this individual.

Not even the Blessed Virgin in all her dignity and glory as the Mother of God and the Immaculate One can love as this person can. She had her gift which she gave tremendously and for which we are thankful. But this person also has his gift, different from all others, and because of which he possesses a tremendous dignity.

He can love as no one else can, but also has his unique need of being loved. In a real sense every human being is born lonely, lives a lonely life, and certainly dies a lonely death; but each human being has his own unique loneliness, his particular ache, his very personal need of being loved. No other human being will ever be able to satisfy completely this hunger, no matter how perfect the rapport, for this is the part of man reserved for God. For the adolescent to begin to accept this reality of life is for him to begin to achieve peace of mind and ease of spirit.

The other reality of his existence is that now the big focus of his life must be on his main role of loving uniquely with his gifts and according to the needs of this other unique person with whom he is dealing. Again there is the value to him in seeing life as this love-relationship between unique persons. In a real sense he is called to be this particular image and likeness of God to a girl friend on a date, to a parent at home, to a kid brother or sister. Always there is the task of understanding himself with his gifts of love and of understanding the needs of the other. The challenge to love another realistically and unselfishly should appeal to the ideals of the adolescent.

## ATTITUDE TOWARD SEXUAL LOVE

There is another way the teenager is to love and be loved well. It is according to his sexual gifts and needs. The teenager, as a human being, has always had the gift of sex, but it is only in his recent experience that it has begun to make demands on him. He needs a realistic, total and Christian understanding of sex so that he may see it as another challenge of love.

Complicating his life in regard to sex are those attitudes he has inherited from past generations. Part of his national heritage as an American has been a certain Puritanism. Sex is something that is not discussed within the sanctity of the home because it is not quite respectable, is rather indecent, shameful, dirty. Nice people don't talk about it. The hope seems to be that if sex is ignored it will go away.

Complementing this attitude is a certain Jansenism more prevalent among Catholics of particular racial backgrounds. This Catholic form of Puritanism says that sex is evil, that the sexual parts of the body are dirty, and that the physical attraction between a man and a woman is a snare of the devil. The over-emphasis on the negative aspects of the sixth and ninth Commandments does much to solidify the impression of badness about sex. The natural stirrings of sex within the adolescent become identified with sin, with a consequent increase in fear, guilt, and unhappiness.

Complicating his life further is the fact that the adolescent is living in a sexualized age surrounded on all sides by the symbols of sex. Advertising uses the physical display of sex to sell everything from cigarettes to coffins. Commercial entertainment uses sex as the come on. Books become best sellers because of their anatomical description of sex. Cosmetics and women's apparel sell because of their emphasis on the physical aspects of womanliness. Family newspapers and popular magazines titillate the senses with their pictures and stories. Thus does the teenager easily gather the impression that sex is primarily a physical appetite with some emotional overtones.

Caught between the frozen Puritanism of the past and the modern freedom, it is no wonder that the Catholic teenager is liable to develop two codes of morality in regard to sex. He parrots back to his parents and teachers the letter of the law and lives with his peers according to an unwritten code of situational ethics which allows privileges within limits. In either case he is being denied his birthright which is a realistic, total, human and Christian understanding of sex, its nature and its purpose.

To the Christian, sex is good because it is made by God. It is sacred because it is concerned with either giving life or completing it in another, and as such it is a means of expressing love. Hence, the gift of sex is always meant for somebody else.

Sex is the quality of manliness or womanliness. It colors the total personality of the individual. A man is not a man because he has a certain type of physical reproductive system. That does not cause him to be a man. It merely indicates the fact that he is a man. He is also a man psychologically and spiritually. Equally, a woman is not a woman because she has a different kind of reproductive system. That does not cause her to be a woman. It merely indicates the fact that she is.

The sexual natures, too, are complementary. Man's gifts of love are meant to complement woman's needs and vice versa. This complementariness of the sexes has been emphasized enough in modern literature and movements not to need further explanation. However, in regard to the adolescent striving for adulthood, he needs to see his sexual gifts as something meant by God to perfect another and not just as an appetite demanding personal satisfaction. The challenge to love with the gift of sex is something that should be made to the adolescent but in a realistic way. It is not sufficient to condemn the aberrations of the present by an appeal to the blanket condemnation of the past.

The Alpha and Omega of sex is God. It is a gift that comes from Him. It is a gift meant to be given back to Him. The term of sex is not the mutual completion of human beings, but the extension of the Kingdom of God.

All manliness is meant for paternity as womanliness is meant for maternity. It is the human participation in the creative love of the First Person of the Blessed Trinity, whom Pope Pius XII recently called the Mother-Father God. He, as it were, gives part of His love to the man who in giving it to another achieves fatherhood, as a woman in giving her gift achieves motherhood. The obvious illustration is marriage where the husband and wife through a mutual exchange of gifts which is blessed by God bring a child into the world.

The same process of creative productivity through the proper use of sex is also found in the psychological and spiritual areas. The priest through his manliness achieves fatherhood as a nun, in her way, achieves motherhood. The renouncing of sex in the usual sense of the word on the part of the religious does not mean rejection of paternity and maternity. These can be achieved in a psychological and spiritual way for creation is a continuing process. There is the obligation incumbent on all to complete and perfect the image of God in human beings as there is an obligation specific to married people to bring the image of God into a new existence in the child.

It is important for the adolescent to achieve some of this vision of the Christian concept of sex and to see it as a challenge of love. It is equally important that the approach be realistic enough to satisfy his present needs. As an illustration of practical realism, here is a case history of a boy and girl on a date. Why do they date? Because there is a sexual attraction, which is good. They like each other. They go to a movie and spend two or three hours in each other's company. They stop and he buys her a hamburger and he's learning more about her—she has a good appetite, God bless her. Then they take the car and drive down to Long Island Sound and watch the moon rise over the water. They are sitting there in the car; they've been together three or four hours; that general sexual attraction has become more and more focalized; there's the proper atmosphere—they're well fed and contented; the moon is rising and the air is balmy, the radio is playing soft music and they begin to talk—about the inroads of Communism into western culture. They may talk in this way in the very beginning but they soon turn to each other, and before you know it they're kissing, and before you know it they've gone overboard and what started out to be a beautiful evening has now ended in sin.

From the adult viewpoint it is very easy to say that they should have known better, but who taught them that they were willing to listen to? For a better understanding of the progression of the sexual attraction and its connection with love I would recommend a book called—*The Human Venture—in Sex, Love, and Marriage* by Peter Bertocci (1949). It is an excellent treatment from a natural viewpoint and, except for a paragraph where he approves of contraceptives, can be recommended. Combined with Father Gerald Kelly's (1944) *Modern Youth and Chastity* it should be very useful to the priest or teacher dealing with the modern adolescent. Also recommended is Father Joseph McGloin's (1961) trilogy for teenagers published under the series title *Love—and Live.*

All these concepts of loving and being loved must be seen, of course, in the light of two historical realities—one is that of original sin and the other is the reality of the redemption. The first reality makes love difficult because it blinds us to an understanding of the needs of the other and makes us unwilling to pay the price of love. There is here the root cause of the constant struggle in love.

But there is the more than compensating reality of our redemption in and through Christ, and by our participation in His Life through grace the elevation of all of our gifts of love to a supernatural level. Life then becomes not just a matter of a love relationship between human persons, but an active participation in the love relationship of the Divine Persons on a human level and to a shared degree, but none the less real.

To give to an adolescent an awareness of his place in the universe and in God's plan in all aspects of life is to give him the sense of vocation so necessary for the choosing and the fulfillment of the vocation or way of love that will be God's choice for him in the near future. Having been given the gift of life adolescents have a right to know what to do with it.

## REFERENCES

Bertocci, P. *The human venture—in sex, love, and marriage.* New York: Association Press, 1949.

Kelly, G., S.J. *Modern youth and chastity.* St. Louis: Queen's Work, 1944.

McGloin, J. T., S.J. *Learn a little! or, what's LIFE all about?* Book One. Milwaukee: Bruce, 1961.

————. *Yearn a little! or, why did God come up with TWO sexes?* Book Two. Milwaukee: Bruce, 1961.

————. *Burn a little! or, what's LOVE all about?* Book Three. Milwaukee: Bruce, 1961.

# Educational Choices in Adolescence

## MARTIN J. MEADE

*Martin J. Meade is Director of Admissions at Fordham University. His B.S. degree is from St. Joseph's College in Philadelphia (1953), and his M.A. degree is from Fordham University (1955). He is currently a doctoral candidate at Fordham University, and his doctoral research is on the topic: "A Biographical Inventory as a Predictor of Essentially Non-Intellectual Criteria of College Success." Prior to assuming his present post as Director of Admissions, Mr. Meade served as staff psychologist and guidance officer in the Office of Psychological Services at Fordham University. Mr. Meade is a member of the American Psychological Association, the American Catholic Psychological Association, the American Personnel Guidance Association, the National Vocational Guidance Association, and the National Association of College Registrars and Officers of Admission.*

The topic I am to discuss is one about which much has been written, especially during the past five years. Almost all of the major newspapers and magazines have bombarded their readers with articles which emphasize the importance of a college education and the increasing difficulty which students will encounter in getting into college. A recent television commercial—ostensibly presented as a "public service"—was entitled "The Closing College Door," and depicted a young man and woman being shut out of an institution by two massive iron gates. Although the gates were more reminiscent of a state penitentiary than an educational institution, the commercial helped to increase the mass hysteria which seems to be characteristic of the general public's attitude toward college admission.

The American public is, to use the vernacular, "being sold a bill of goods." The mass media are being used to convince the public that *everyone* should be a college graduate. It is as if "happiness," which we all have an inalienable right to pursue, can only be attained through a college education, preferably at an "Ivy League" college. This is patent nonsense.

In the midst of this propaganda barrage about higher education, we frequently forget several basic facts. First, it is predicted that a total of 14,000,000 children will be of college age by 1970 (Thompson, 1961, p. 6). We are led to believe that all of them will be qualified for, and desirous of obtaining, a college education. We forget that 7,000,000 of these children, by definition, must be *below average* in intellectual ability. If a college is intended to be an institution where *superior* children can develop their *superior* intellectual abilities, then the great majority of our high school students should not be considering a four-year college education as one of their educational goals.

A second fact which is frequently ignored in this "college conscious" age is that *all* adolescents, regardless of their level of intellectual ability should make an educational choice. In many instances, the adolescent is unaware of the fact that a choice should be made because he does not realize that alternatives exist. It is to the educational choices available to the adolescent that this paper is directed.

Let us agree from the outset that, although all adolescents should make an educational choice, some—through force of circumstances—are not free to choose. We are all familiar with cases in which parental pressure is exerted to force the child into programs of study for which he has neither the ability nor the motivation essential to success. We are also familiar with instances in which adolescents from the lower socioeconomic groups are forced into a position in which they must drop out of secondary school in order to provide essential financial assistance to their families. It is obvious that in these and in similar cases, the adolescent is not free to make an educational choice.

Fortunately, however, the young men and women included in the groups cited above constitute a relatively small minority of all adolescents. The majority of adolescents are relatively free to make an educational choice, if they are aware that a choice should be made and if they are aware of the alternatives. It is the responsibility of the high school guidance counselor, teachers, and parents to make the adolescent aware of the educational alternatives open to him and of the consequences of selecting one of these alternatives.

Let us consider the educational alternatives which are available. For purpose of clarity, let us classify adolescents into two general categories. The first category would be composed of those who never complete secondary school; the second, of those who do graduate from high school.

### HIGH SCHOOL DROPOUTS

As we have already indicated, a certain percentage of adolescents drop out of school in order to contribute to the support of their families. As such, they should be considered as involuntary dropouts. However, a large percentage of those who never complete secondary school are voluntary dropouts. For a variety of reasons, they choose to discontinue their education. These reasons include a lack of ability to cope with their studies, loss of interest and motivation for school, and social pressures within the adolescent group.

Whether or not they realize it, those who drop out of school are choosing to discontinue almost all forms of education, both formal and informal. Occupations open to the dropout must be categorized as "unskilled" or, at most, "semi-skilled." These occupations would include laborers, bus boys, elevator operators, garbage collectors, waitresses, and some clerical and sales positions. Obviously, such occupations offer little opportunity for new learning or for advancement.

A number of communities, aware of the social, cultural, and economic loss which these drop-outs represent, have taken steps to "reclaim" them. Generally, these "reclamation" efforts take one of several directions. Some communities have developed "co-op" programs, which enable the youngster to work as much as 20 hours per week while attending school. Other communities have instituted *evening* high schools, which permit a student to complete his secondary school education while holding a full-time position. Finally, many states award "equivalency" diplomas to adults who pass a series of examinations, attesting to their knowledge of material which they ordinarily would have learned in secondary school.

No effort should be spared to make adolescents aware of the tragic consequences of dropping out of high school. If, in spite of these efforts, they do leave school, programs should be available through which they can rectify their mistake.

Turning to the large group of adolescents who do complete their secondary education, we find that they are faced with a series of educational choices. Obviously, the most basic choice is whether or not to continue their education. If they choose not to continue their education in any form, they are little better off than those who drop out of high school. Fortunately, the great majority of high school graduates continue their education on either a formal or informal basis.

### TRAINING OPPORTUNITIES FOR HIGH SCHOOL GRADUATES

The adolescents who choose to discontinue their classroom education upon completion of secondary school, frequently continue to acquire new skills and knowledge through "on-the-job" training period. A recent issue of *Changing Times* (1961), indicates that there are at least ninety trades with apprentice programs. Included among them are butchers, automotive mechanics, printers, and jewelers. Entry into these apprentice programs is usually competitive and requires a high school diploma, in addition to specific aptitudes for the trade. Mention should also be made of the "on-the-job" training programs available through some of the larger companies. International Business Machines, and Pitney-Bowes, are only two of the business organizations which sponsor training programs for high school graduates in the fields of machine design, electronics, customer engineering, and others.

Although many educators would challenge the statement that "on-the-job" training programs constitute a form of education, it is apparent that these programs provide an opportunity for the high school graduate to grasp new relationships and to increase his knowledge. Not all adolescents have either the ability or the motivation to continue their post-secondary school education in a formal classroom setting. "On-the-job" training programs provide a sensible alternative for those adolescents who are interested and qualified. Guidance counselors should be familiar with these programs and their entrance requirements. Since many apprentice programs require specific aptitudes, psychological tests of aptitudes should be employed in attempting to direct the adolescent into the right vocational area. The General Aptitude Test Battery, developed by the United States Employment Service, is considered to be among the best of such batteries currently available (Super, 1957).

Many adolescents possess a specific aptitude of which they are unaware. In order to utilize this potential, it must first be identified and developed. In developing the aptitude, the adolescent is educating himself. It is through "on-the-job" training programs that many of these aptitudes can be developed. However, without an awareness of the existence of these programs, they cannot be selected by the adolescent. It is unfortunate, but true, that a relatively large group of young men and women drift into occupations below their true level of ability because they are unaware of the fact that they can develop their specific abilities in an *informal* educational setting.

Another educational program frequently ignored in this "college conscious" age is that provided by the technical institutes and vocational schools. Although dissimilar to the aforementioned training program in that they follow a more formal approach to education, technical or vocational institutes offer another alternative to the high school graduate who wishes to continue his education, but not in a college degree program.

At the present time there are more than four thousand vocational schools throughout the country. These schools, which are operated by a variety of organizations, offer programs of study and training in preparation for a career in almost any vocational area. Among the more common courses available are those in mortuary science, secretarial science, modelling, dress designing, automobile repair, and welding. The duration and cost of these programs vary with the nature of the training desired and the type of sponsoring institution. Programs offered by private schools can cost as much as $1,000.00. On the other hand, many vocational programs are sponsored by non-profit organizations, such as hospitals. An example of the latter type is the training in the field of X-ray technology. Naturally, care should be taken to ascertain that the sponsor of the program is a reputable organization.

It is evident that there is a certain degree of overlap between the type of training available through vocational schools and that which can be obtained through "on-the-job" training programs. This overlap of function is also evident when one compares the programs of vocational schools with those of technical institutes. However, technical institutes usually specialize in the various branches of engineering technology.

During the past decade, a serious shortage of qualified scientists and engineers has arisen. As a result, much of the routine work previously done by these highly educated and highly paid personnel is now handled by engineering technicians. Examples of engineering technicians include those in aeronautics, electronics, refrigeration and air-conditioning, civil engineering, instrumentation, metallurgy, and computer technology. Almost every field of endeavor in which engineers are employed has positions available for less highly trained, but essential, technicians.

The schools which offer technical training range from those which are privately owned to those which are government supported. We again find that the duration of the course of studies and the cost to the student varies widely. However, almost all technical institutes issue a certificate of completion to their graduates. Entrance into a technical institute is frequently selective, in a sense that certain aptitudes and preparation are usually essential to success. Almost all of these programs require that the applicant be a high school graduate with above average grades in mathematics and science, although requirements vary.

Guidance counselors should be aware of the educational programs available through vocational schools and technical institutes and bring these programs to the attention of their counselees. They are frequently the ideal educational choice for the adolescent with at least average intellectual ability who wishes to continue his education beyond the secondary school level in a practically oriented program of studies.

## SELECTION OF A COLLEGE

Finally, let us turn our attention to the vast number of adolescents whose ambition it is to earn a college degree. The educational alternatives available to these young men and women are almost limitless. Fortunately, much has been written already about these alternatives and it is not our intention to reiterate them here. However, several points are important enough to deserve mention.

Assuming that an adolescent has decided to attend college, his next decisions must center around the nature of the college which he will attend and the program of study which he will follow. One of the most important factors affecting the choice of a college is financial. The cost of a year in college, including living expenses, can range from several hundred dollars to more than $3,500 depending upon the institution selected (Irwin, 1960; Lovejoy, 1959). The student who enrolls in a publicly supported institution to which he can commute can frequently obtain a college education for little more than was spent in completing his secondary school education. On the other hand, a number of private colleges charge more than $1,500 per year for tuition alone. Some of the best institutions are the least expensive, and vice versa. In addition, the wide range of cost in attending various colleges is almost matched by the variety of scholarships, loans, and work programs available.

Although financial considerations are frequently of great importance in selecting a college, they should not be the *sole* determining factor. Of greater importance, is the selection of a college best calculated to develop the intellectual and personal potential of the student. Just as there are no two people alike in all characteristics, so too, there are probably no two colleges exactly alike. One of the most difficult tasks of the guidance counselor and the parent is to attempt to guide the student in selecting a college in which the opportunity is available for the adolescent to grow intellectually, morally, and socially. Naturally, any guidance must be based on a thorough knowledge of both the adolescent and the college.

Assuming that we are all familiar with the formal and informal techniques available for the assessment of the individual, we can turn our attention to an analysis of the dimensions in which colleges differ. For the purposes of our analysis, we will analyze colleges in terms of intellectual and social factors. Probably the most obvious way in which colleges differ is in terms of their intellectual demands upon the student. The adolescent must choose a college in which he will have a reasonable chance of passing the courses required for a degree. However, there are many more subtle differences among colleges as far as their intellectual climate is concerned. Serious consideration should be given to such factors as adequacy of the curriculum of the college, the ratio between required and elective courses, the adequacy of library and laboratory facilities, the ratio between faculty members and students, and the intellectual characteristics of the student body.

The last mentioned factor is one which is frequently overlooked when adolescents are selecting a college. They fail to realize that, even on the admissions level, colleges select their students so as to obtain a homogeneous or heterogeneous group in terms of intellectual ability and educational goals. Reed, Chicago, and Haverford are typical of institutions which attempt to attract a homogeneous group of students with exceptionally high intellectual ability and aspirations for graduate study. To attain this goal, these institutions emphasize intellectual factors in their selection of students (Karl, 1961).

On the other hand, most State universities and Junior colleges attract applicants with a wide range of intellectual ability and educational goals. Naturally, this fact is reflected in their relatively unselective admissions policies.

Information regarding the intellectual characteristics of a college can be obtained primarily from printed material such as catalogs, "view" books, and educational directories. A printed "profile" of the intellectual characteristics of the entering Freshman class of a college can be invaluable to a competent guidance counselor. Finally, the intellectual productivity of an institution can be approximated by ascertaining the percentage of graduates who pursue advanced studies and the number of graduate awards which they receive.

Obviously, counselors, parents, and students should take these intellectual factors into consideration when attempting to differentiate among colleges. However, they should not ignore the social factors which can have an equally important effect upon the college success of a student. Colleges differ in this area almost as widely as they differ in terms of intellectual characteristics (Pace and Stern, 1958).

In a relatively brief presentation such as this, it would be neither possible nor desirable to attempt to list all of the social factors which operate in a given college environment. However, we will point out several of the more important factors to take into consideration. Probably the most important decision revolves about the feasibility of residing at college or continuing to live at home. Naturally, a more marked social adjustment must be made by a student who, in effect, is entering a new community. A second factor of importance might be described in terms of a formality-informality continuum. The attire of the students, the nature of the social and personal relationships between faculty members and students, and the existence or non-existence of social pressure groups should be observed if possible.

Although the size of a college can frequently determine some of its social characteristics, it should be kept in mind that it is possible for a shy adolescent to be "lost in a crowd." A more important consideration than the size of an institution is the relative ease with which its students assimilate new members into their already existing social group. Many brilliant students drop out of college because they feel rejected by their classmates.

A final social factor to be maintained is that of the regulations of the college. It is well known that, in some colleges, the students, in effect, determine the code of conduct. As a result, the rules of behavior are amorphous and frequently subtle. Conversely, some colleges are best characterized as "authoritarian," in a sense that a rigid and well-defined set of rules and regulations is enforced. Since adolescents differ in terms of their reaction to authority, this factor should be taken into consideration in selecting a college.

In addition to printed materials, two other means of identifying the social characteristics of a college are available to the applicant. If at all possible, he should make a personal visit to the college while its students are in class. Casual observation of the behavior of its students is often extremely revealing. Secondly, he should try to discuss the college with some of its students in order to obtain their evaluation of its social climate. Naturally, the dangers of selective sampling should be kept in mind when evaluating information obtained in this manner.

## SUMMARY

In summary, many different educational alternatives are available to the adolescent. He must decide to finish high school, or to drop out. If he graduates from high school, he must choose between a formal or informal continuation of his education. He should take into consideration "on-the-job" training programs and the programs of study offered by vocational schools and technical institutes. If he decides to attend college, he is faced with a problem of selecting one college from almost nineteen hundred institutions with different intellectual and social characteristics. In making these decisions, he should be guided by the advice of counselors, teachers, and his parents.

## REFERENCES

*Changing Times, the Kiplinger Magazine.* Wash., D. C.: Kiplinger Washington Editors, 1961, *15,* No. 7, 36-39.

Irwin, Mary, Ed. *American Universities and Colleges.* Wash., D. C.: American Council on Education, 1960.

Karl, S. D., Ed. *The College Handbook.* Princeton: College Entrance Examination Board, 1961.

Lovejoy, C. E. *College Guide*. New York: Simon & Schuster, 1959.

Pace, C. R. and Stern, G. G. *A criterion study of college environments*. Psychol. Res. Center, Syracuse Univer., 1958.

Super, D. E. The multifactor tests: summing up. *Personnel Guid. J.*, 1957, *36*, 17-20.

Thompson, R. B. *Enrollment projections for higher education:1961-1978*. American Association of Collegiate Registrars and Admissions Officers, Sept., 1961.

# The Problem of Vocational Choice

## JAMES J. CRIBBIN

*James J. Cribbin received his baccalaureate
(1941) and his master's (1943) degree from
St. Louis University and his Ph.D. degree from
Fordham University (1951). He taught in the
Fordham University School of Education from
1947 to 1957. In 1957 he left Fordham to be-
come Associate Professor of Management and
Industrial Relations at New York University.
At the present time, Dr. Cribbin is Professor
of Management in the Graduate Division of the
School of Business at St. John's University. Dr.
Cribbin is, jointly with Brother Philip Harris,
O.S.F., and Rev. William J. McMahon, the
author of the four volume* Insight *series, de-
signed to provide guidance for Catholic youth.
The volumes in the series are:* It's Your Life
(1957), It's Your Education (1959), It's Your
Personality (1960), *and* It's Your Future
(1962).

When putting pen to paper, it is essential to establish a frame of reference with respect to the purpose of the writer. Has he but recently
visited the mountain and now stands ready to dispense the WORD?
Is his intent to raise appropriate questions rather than to proliferate
infallible answers? Is his aim to focus on certain key problems and
to propose admittedly incomplete answers in the hope that the reader

will agree or disagree, with a view to evolving qualitatively superior solutions? It is this last approach that is basic to the present discusson. Secondly, the logic of the situation requires that any consideration of the problem of vocational choice be oriented about an understandable theme; the difficulties involved are far too complex to be jacketed in a single discussion. The theme of this paper is threefold, each aspect being geared to a quotation. The first idea has its roots in the Bible where it is asked: "If the trumpet sound an uncertain note, who shall rise up to battle?" The second point is taken from St. Thomas, who stated: *"Semper autem defectus principii est pessimus."* The last idea seeks to reduce theory to the linoleum-level of practicality and stems from the words: "Theory without practice is as useless as practice without theory."

### IMPORTANCE OF VOCATIONAL CHOICE

The entire field of vocational guidance represents something of a dilemma. The issue is crucial. Few things in life are more important than developing that lifetime career pattern in which an individual will provide for those who will depend on him, in which he will contribute to the Church and society, and in which he will enjoy the highest possible degree of self-realization and self-fulfillment. It is a commonplace to say that one's occupation represents the watershed down which the rest of his life tends to flow. Where one lives, whom he marries, how he spends his leisure time, the friends he makes, the status he enjoys in the community, the respect he receives at his place of work, the satisfactions he derives from his job, the type of education he can provide for his children, whom his children associate with and ultimately marry, his opportunities to play the role of a Christopher, the manner in which he will spend his twilight years—all are a function of the way in which he earns his daily bread or cake.

When one appreciates the fact that the average person is likely to work for approximately 40 hours a week, 50 weeks a year, 45 years of his life—a total of some 90,000 hours—the matter of vocational choice is crucial, indeed. When one reflects that the average man is likely to spend as many or more of his waking hours in and around his job than he does with his wife, the matter is important. When one ponders the truth that an individual's position is often his most potent lever for moving the world in the direction of that which is wiser and better, the matter is critical. In fact, one wonders why those vocational counselors who are but casual and routine in the manner in which they provide occupational guidance do not have nightmares.

If occupational problems are crucial, they are also extremely difficult to resolve. In 1843, Henry L. Ellsworth, U. S. Patent Commissioner, could state with aplomb in his annual report: "The advancement of the arts taxes our credulity and seems to presage the arrival of that period when human improvement must end." In this year of Our Lord, we are much more likely to agree with the words, "So marvellous is U. S. technology today that practically any good idea can be turned into a product. . . . The pace of research is such that man's next great discovery may come next month, next week—or tomorrow" (*Time*, 1960, pp. 100-102). Between 1790 and 1838 only 11,008 patents were granted. In 1959 patents were granted for 50,545 inventions, and there is a backlog of nearly 200,000 patents pending! Is it any wonder that someone has claimed that nearly half of the things that we will be buying and using by the mid-seventies do not now exist! Where industry used to spend a dollar on research, it is now not unusual to find that hundreds of dollars are being expended. Where research and development used to be the last topic discussed at the annual shareholders meetings, it is often at present one of the very first on the agenda. Already the cornucopia of results is beginning to spew forth a variety of products that makes one's head spin. Fuel cells, miniaturization, transistors, tranducers, data processing equipment, automation and similar developments promise a new industrial revolution that will make the one with which we are familiar seem like three high school students tinkering with a hotrod.

### COMPLEXITY OF VOCATIONAL CHOICE

This sunburst of technological advance will serve only to complicate further an already complex process. Vocational guidance is largely a venture in prophecy, at best a very fallible undertaking. There are at least 40,000 occupations. Like cloud formations, some wax while others wane; some simply cease to exist, while others spring up almost overnight into a sturdy maturity. All are sensitive to changing economic conditions, social pressures, scientific progress, cultural values, and similar social phenomena. This ebb and flow, coupled with the democratic ideal that "everyone is as good as anyone," and that "the sky is the limit" for those who are willing to work and strive for it, is likely to cause the student to become hopelessly bewildered. Occupational information by itself, research has shown, serves only to add to the confusion.

The young person is confronted by at least two additional difficulties that merit some attention. In the first place, he is often an innocent in the storm so far as occupational choice is concerned. His reading is academic, devoid of any background of experience. Even if he works part-time, an excellent form of education, he is likely to get a buttonhook view of the occupation and of the business in which it is found. His job is lowly, his areas of exposure limited, his attitude too often one of earning rather than learning. As a young adult, he is often shunted by his own ignorance into a career which he later comes to regret, because he entered it for the wrong reasons and with the wrong expectations. An immature or distorted value system has betrayed many an individual into a career field that was unsuited to his personality. Secondly, and the reader may well disagree with this point of view, the guides of young people at times sound an uncertain note so far as vocational choice is concerned. Basically, and rightly so, they are *school* people who are chiefly interested in educational and spiritual guidance. In fact, all school guidance is fundamentally educational guidance, the other so-called guidance types flowing from this primary function and returning to it for the benefit of both school and student. This granted, the fact is that most school people have had little genuine experience in business; they lack a "feel" for an industrial situation; their knowledge of the workings of business life, like that of the married state, is likely to be largely conceptual and second-hand. At times, their training and experience prompt them to allot to industry a second-class status, except perhaps during a fund-raising campaign.

It is not my intention to criticize, since no man can be all things at once, or even sequentially. My point is that, as the French would have it, we tend to see what we look for; unconsciously we stress what has been or is meaningful to us. People who live differently are likely to think differently; they are likely to see things differently; they are likely to have at least slightly different concepts of what is important and what should be stressed in guidance; they are likely to be sensitive to different situations in terms of their significance. It is natural for a Religious to emphasize the primacy of the religious vocation. As a matter of fact, it was interesting to note that more than 95 percent of all the questions proposed by the clergy present during the discussion period following the panel presentation* dealt with problems of the religious vocation. Since nine out of ten students, however, will not enter any form of religious life, it is important that the guide not violate commutative and distributive justice by neglecting the nine for the one.

Since practically every study with which the writer is familiar has indicated that, to the mature student, the question of vocational choice is commonly one of his most perplexing difficulties, it would seem prudent to give this problem the attention it deserves. Although the entire area of job satisfaction is far too complex to consider at the moment, one might bear in mind that a summary of some sixteen years of research studies in this field indicated that approximately one in five workers is dissatisfied (Hoppock and Robinson, 1951). A study of some 5,000 people at various occupational levels and in different types of occupations showed that four in ten of those sampled would choose different careers, if they could go back to the age of eighteen and start all over. Even among the professional workers, where presumably one should find a high level of job satisfaction, about three in ten would prefer to choose a different vocation (*Fortune,* 1938).

In view of these facts, vocational choice is not a matter that should be relegated to a quasi-guidance limbo simply because the counselor has determined his own vocation and may have little knowledge of others. Assuming that the guide gives to this form of guidance the important, though secondary, status that it deserves, and assuming that he keeps in tune with the occupational times, it is essential that he have a clear idea of the nature of vocational choice. In a sense, the title of this paper is a misnomer. There is no such thing as *a* vocational choice, much less *the* vocational choice. The development of a stable career pattern is not so much a matter of choice as of maturing. One becomes occupationally mature as one becomes intellectually or emotionally mature; he gradually learns to make rational occupational choices as he does rational intellectual and emotional choices. Choosing the proper career is much like choosing the proper wife. The act of choice is important but it is a derivative of a slow maturing process. Unless one experiences this growth process, correct choices are difficult or impossible. It is for this reason that the counselor would be wise to emphasize development rather than choice.

* Certain portions of this paper were recast by the author subsequent to the original presentation.—Ed. note.

### DEFINITION OF VOCATIONAL GUIDANCE

Bearing in mind St. Thomas' admonition that to operate on the basis of incorrect principles is the worst fault of all, it might serve some useful purpose to comment on what is known about this process of vocational development. What is meant by vocational guidance? The traditional definition, sanctioned by the National Vocational Guidance Association (1937), has to do with efforts made to assist an individual in choosing, preparing for, entering upon, and succeeding in an occupation. The beauty of this definition is that it is so succinct as to be scholastic. Unfortunately, it suffers from certain limitations. What, for instance, do we mean by success? Shall one judge, as so many of our students do, by external frames of reference in terms of pennies, property, prestige, possessions, and power? Where in this definition is there a place for values, ideals, motivations, and similar realities? Where does the concept of self-realization and self-fulfillment find a place in it?

It seems clear that this definition is largely derived from a Protestant ethic of the Puritan species. It is well known that Puritanism, in the area of work, was geared to four principles: (1) it is a man's duty to know *how* to work and how to work *hard;* (2) success in work is evidence of God's favor; (3) the measure of success is money and property; (4) the way to success is through industry and thrift (Miller and Form, 1951, pp. 558 ff.) If the statement, "Without some understanding of Puritanism, it may be safely said, there is no understanding of America" (Miller and Johnson, 1938, p. 1) is true, then one can readily see that this definition of vocational guidance is a vestigial remain of a more puritanical day than our own.

Management theory used to be a rather simple affair. One analyzed the functions of a business, made appropriate provision for departmentation and scalar organization, abided by certain so-called principles of management, and externalized his thoughts in those dangling participles we call organization charts. But then the sociologists and the psychologists poked their camel's noses into the administrative tent and things have never been the same since. Now industrial leaders are bedeviled by the "corporate image," human relations, the fusion process, the informal organization, communications, frictions, morale, and a host of other concepts for which the tycoon of an earlier day could not have cared less. Much the same process has taken place in guidance. Parsons' (1909, pp. 4-5) original definition of vocational guidance as consisting of self-knowledge, understanding of the requirements and conditions for vocational success, and right reasoning between these two sets of facts now appears somewhat over-simplified. This is particularly true if, as happens in some schools, this process consists of the administration of tests and other devices, the dissemination of occupational information, and an occasional interview, often under the pressure of an approaching graduation day. Too often vocational guidance takes on the appearance of mechanically fitting assets and limitations to the jigsaw of career opportunities with too little attention being given to those ideas that are so dear to the hearts of the behavioral scientists, such as self-concept, values, aspirations, needs, drives, cultural pressures, societal demands, and so forth. Vocational guidance is but one aspect of the total guidance program, even as working is but one aspect of life. Both life and guidance are too multivariate to be reduced to a one-two-three formula.

If the contributions of the behavioral sciences have further complicated the guidance process, they have also made it more necessary for the counselor to evolve a definition of guidance that will direct his own efforts to assist others; otherwise, we are engaged in a game of charades in which the near-sighted lead the blind. Unlike most non-Catholics, it is not possible for us to consider the term "vocation" as merely applying to one's stable career. The *divine, universal vocation* for all of us is to save our souls and to continue the redemptive act of Christ; our *primary temporal vocation* is concerned with the state in life that one chooses; our *secondary temporal vocation* has to do with one's occupation or career. It is obvious that these distinctions are not merely a play on words. It is the experience of the writer that few high-school students really understand the relationships that these three vocations bear to one another. For the counselor to consider occupational guidance apart from the student's other two vocations would be a grievous mistake, yet it is my contention that precisely this is done daily in some schools and by some guidance workers. Secondly, it would help the counselor to blow a clear and certain note on his guidance trumpet and to give heed to St. Thomas' words, if a definition of guidance could be formulated which, with appropriate changes according to the formal object under consideration, would be applicable to all forms of guidance, and which would be more consistent with a Catholic view of the subject than most of the definitions that now are paraded before graduate students. To the writer's knowledge, no one in Catholic education has attempted such a synthesis.

Rushing in where perhaps angels fear to tread, the following definition of guidance is proposed for the critical analysis of the reader.*

> Guidance is the process of helping a person, in light of his relationships to God, mankind and the world, to develop and accept a mature, balanced and well-integrated concept of himself and of his roles in life; to test this self-concept against reality; and to actualize this reality oriented self-concept so as to attain the ends for which he was created, while achieving a maximum degree of self-fulfillment and contributing optimally to Church and society.

What appeals to the writer in this definition, despite its verbiage, is its wide applicability. In speaking of one's divine vocation, the definition as it stands would seem to define guidance. If, on the other hand, the formal object under consideration is one's primary temporal vocation, the substitution of the words "and of his roles in marriage" (and similarly for the other states in life) for the statement "and of his roles in life" would make the definition applicable. Clearly one can account for the various so-called types of guidance in the narrow sense, such as educational, occupational, psychological, and so on, by making appropriate substitution in the definition. The writer is not certain that this proposed definition touches all the guidance bases, but he is certain that it represents an advance over the mishmash that has so often paraded as guidance in the past.

### IMPLICATIONS OF THIS DEFINITION OF GUIDANCE

The meaning of this definition can, in the manner of Rodriguez, be best explained by an example. Joe, after graduating from college, accepts a position as a high school teacher with the intention of making it his career. Whether he perseveres in this intent depends on certain variables. Over the years, Joe has developed a self-concept that makes the idea of becoming a teacher both reasonable and possible. Intrinsic

* The writer expresses his indebtedness to the following authorities for many of the ideas expressed in this section of the paper: Caplow (1954), Roe (1956), Ginzberg (1951), Maslow (1954), Rosenberg (1957), Miller & Form (1951), and especially Super (1957a). The definition is an adaptation of Super's definition of vocational guidance (Super, 1957a, p. 197). The interpretation of their ideas is the writer's responsibility.

to this self-concept is a set of ideas, ideals, values, desires, motivations, and perspectives with respect to God, men and the world, which prompts Joe to dedicate himself to the service of the young. Inherent in this self-concept are certain drives, needs and a level of aspiration that make a teaching career attractive to Joe. He sees in teaching a means for attaining certain satisfactions consistent with his self-concept. Finally, he visualizes certain roles which he expects to play as an instructor; he anticipates a certain degree of self-fulfillment in his chosen career.

What happens as Joe lives the day-to-day life of a teacher? As time passes, four possibilities are evident. If the actualities and demands of teaching, together with the roles that they require Joe to play, are consistent with his self-concept and his role expectations, then the school will be fortunate enough to have a satisfied teacher on its staff. Should there be a gap between the variables already noted, then Joe may modify his self-concept and role expectancies so as to meet the reality demands of his environment. He may, on the other hand, either seek another position within the teaching field, which will be more in line with his self-concept and expectations. Finally, he may leave the teaching profession for some other type of work that is more consonant with his self-concept and expectations. If Joe belatedly comes to realize that teaching is not for him, perhaps at the age of forty-five when he is the father of five children, he may enter upon a forced compromise. At that time in life he may lack those skills that allow for an easy transition to another career, or the pressure of circumstances may make such a course of action almost impossible. At any rate, it is important to note that during the early years of his teaching career Joe is *testing* his self-concept and role expectancies against the realities of the teaching profession.

It would appear that a similar process goes on when one gets married. Each partner has a certain self-concept and a set of role expectations with respect to this state in life. Whether or not a marriage succeeds would appear, from a psychological point of view at least, to depend on the ability of those concerned to adjust their self-concepts and role expectations to the realities of married and family life. A few lucky ones may find that from the outset the role they expected to play, the satisfaction they anticipated, the values by which they hoped to live in this state are quite consistent with the requirements, rewards, and the price to be paid. Those who do not experience this happy fate have open to them the same alternatives as were available to Joe.

During the presentations of the panel, the writer was struck by the failure to consider two problems of the religious life which appear to him to be extremely important and which are germane to the present paper. He is well aware of his lack of competence in this area and wishes only to offer for consideration two ideas that religious guides may wish to think about. The first problem has to do with those who abandon the life of a religious or seminarian during their training period. It is common knowledge that many suffer from feelings of guilt, at least immediately after leaving the novitiate or seminary. Assuming that the individual involved has "left" with a good conscience, there would appear to be an element of the illogical in this reaction. Initially, this person chose "the better part"; eventually he felt that it was not for him. That he should feel disappointed is natural; it is not so clear that he should feel guilty. According to the proposed definition of guidance, this type of individual, during the novitiate or seminary period, was actually testing his self-concept as a religious or priest against the demands of this state in life. Since this process of reality-testing indicated that this way of life was unsuitable, and since he presumably abandoned it after having in vain sought to modify his self-concept and role expectations to meet these requirements, it would seem that he should no more have feelings of guilt than an engaged couple who ultimately decide not to marry, or a person who leaves a promising but unsuitable career.

It is the intention of the Church that the novitiate or seminary be a time for testing one's vocation. This fact brings us to the second problem. It is concerned with the kind of counseling, or the lack of it, that those who leave receive. Relatively little has been written on this subject, to the writer's knowledge. It would appear that the spiritual guide has a responsibility for providing "transitional counseling" which might prepare those who separate themselves for the new realities which they will encounter. It is not suggested that the guide become a therapist; it is suggested that he might be more psychologically perceptive and helpful with respect to the transitional problems that such individuals will face. If the proposed definition of guidance is valid, then such counseling might serve the excellent purpose, at the very least, of preventing disappointed applicants from pining after goals that are beyond their reach. It seems a shame that those who have tried and failed should feel worse than those who never even ventured to try. More positively, counseling of the type recommended might assist the disappointed in altering their self-concepts, their goals, levels of aspiration, and role expectancies, and to channel their resources in a different direction, in this "age of the layman," so as to minimize the wasted time and emotional energy involved in the transition. In discussing these two problems, the writer obviously bows before older and wiser heads than his own. The fact remains, however, that their omission during the panel presentations was somewhat remarkable.

It is clear from the proposed definition of guidance that the role of the counselor in school is not "to put square pegs in square holes." It is to help the individual to develop a realistic self-concept as a person who possesses a genuine sense of self-esteem and a feeling of adequacy in this world. It is to help the student discover his assets so as to capitalize on them, to be aware of his remediable limitations so that he may set about a program of improvement, to recognize his irremediable deficiencies so that he may learn to live contentedly with them. Over and beyond this, however, such an approach implies a greater emphasis on aiding the person to develop correct ideals, a true value system, an appropriate level of aspiration, a clear idea of those satisfactions that are worth striving for, and a proper set of motivations for attaining goals that are worthy of his time and energy. It requires, moreover, a developmental plan for achieving these ends, not merely in terms of specifying objectives, but also in terms of testing the reasonableness of these aims against the harsh realities of life. With such a rationale, guidance truly becomes a school-wide activity in which every faculty member plays a part according to his competence, area of responsibility, and interest. Such a view requires that pupil personnel work be organized throughout the school in terms of function and emphasis rather than be "delegated" to some overworked unfortunate busily engaged in catering to the educationally blind, the vocationally halt, the emotionally crippled, and the socially disjointed.

## THE PHASES OF VOCATIONAL DEVELOPMENT

If the guidance worker is to blow a certain note on his trumpet, while avoiding segmental guidance based on incomplete, if not erroneous, principles, his second task is to become familiar with what is known concerning the pattern of vocational development. In this area the studies are encouraging for the light they throw on the subject, frustrating because of their incompleteness.

One can divide a full life's work into five periods (Miller and Form, 1951, pp. 535 ff). The first, or *Preparatory* period, deals primarily with the work examples, the work models and the socialization process that takes place in the home, the community and the school. It is important for two reasons. First, students often make an artificial separation between school and "the real life" of work. Such a separation is a mistake. In essence, any school is supposed to see that the pupil: (1) is trained to stay on the job and learn his lessons; (2) is trained to obey authority; (3) is encouraged to develop initiative and to rise socially; (4) is enabled to develop character and a moral way of life; (5) is taught to get along with his teachers and schoolmates. Many students fail to realize that "in the very first jobs, the habits of home and school will be taken into work plants and their economic worth will be appraised" (Miller & Form, 1951, p. 533). Secondly, many young people are not so well aware as they might be of the fact that poor study habits and lack of motivation are not only barriers to success in school, but that they can also become stumbling blocks to success in business and industry. Ability to work independently and efficiently is rewarded in business as well as in school. Most industrial psychologists would agree with Pressey, Janney and Kuhlen (1939, pp. 601-604) that continuing job success depends on the individual's ability to do at least three things: (1) to perform his functions with increasing effectiveness; (2) to take care in a dependable manner of the routine work he is expected to do; (3) to get along with his associates. The first practical suggestion that might be made is for teachers and counselors to impress upon the student that those work habits, skills, understandings, and attitudes that are essential for educational success are also requisite for occupational success. The fact that this linkage is so rarely made effectively may well be due to the academic prism, already referred to in this paper, through which the typical teacher and counselor tends to view the world of industry.

The next three periods, *Initial, Trial* and *Stable* work phases, constitute one's "active work life." The *Initial* period is characterized by job impermanence, beginning when the worker seeks his first jobs during his span of school enrollment (part-time and summer work) and continuing until he has terminated his education. The counselor's task during this phase is formidable. He must persuade the student that it is better to work to *learn* rather than merely to *earn.* This learning can be multiple and profitable. First, part-time and summer work offer the student his first real opportunity to test his self-concept and role expectations against the demands of a real occupational situation —in a word, to secure some evidence as to whether or not he has "what it takes" to do a good job. Secondly, the initial work period supplies "feedback" against which the student can think through not only his future plans but also the ideals, motivations, expectations, attitudes, and goals that should guide him in such planning. Thirdly, work experience often is the student's first contact with the five American (external) success imperatives and the antimonies with which he will have to deal for the rest of his life. The success imperatives are: (1) to learn to accept responsibility; (2) to learn to work hard; (3) to learn how to get along with people; (4) to learn how to manage money; (5) to learn how to hold a job and build a reputation as a good worker (Miller and Form, 1951, p. 556). The antimonies include: (1) one must learn how to accept responsibility *but* the average worker may have very little responsibility; (2) one must learn the value of money *but* you cannot get rich by pinching pennies; (3) one must learn to get along with people *but* one must also be assertive, if not downright aggressive; (4) one should be loyal *but* one must also be opportunistic in climbing the success ladder; (5) one should be cooperative *but* to get ahead one must be a keen competitor; (6) one should respect every man *but* those who get ahead identify with the boss, think like the boss and act like the boss; (7) "everyone is as good as anyone else" *but* "rank has its privileges." Within the framework of the self-concept, the purpose of part-time and summer work, the American imperatives, and the antimonies of work life, the counselor has an excellent opportunity to help the student clarify for himself what is *essential,* what is *important,* and what is *incidental* in growing to occupational maturity.

The third work stage begins when the student "goes to work" and looks for a full-time position; it ends when he secures a position in which he remains more or less permanently (three years or more). This period is characterized by considerable change of jobs until the person either "finds himself" or "resigns himself" (Miller and Form, 1951, p. 536). Roughly, this period extends from the age of 18 to that of 35. When it is ended, workers can usually be classified into one of the following categories: (1) the *ambitious*—the strong, confident, highly-motivated worker who "must get ahead"; (2) the *responsive—*

the individual who fulfills a career which others expected him to follow; (3) the *fulfilled*—the worker who is satisfied with the attainment of his occupational goal and feels no desire to turn in another direction; (4) the *confused*—the patchquilt or erratic worker who is uncertain regarding the meaning of present and past work experience and indecisive concerning future moves; (5) the *frustrated*—the worker who feels thwarted or rooted in an occupational rut; (6) the *defeated* —the worker who feels helpless and hopeless and views himself as a failure (Miller and Form, 1951, pp. 639-650). The relationships that exist between these very genuine stereotypes and the proposed self-concept approach to guidance should be obvious. Another factor in the problem of vocational choice is highlighted by these actualities. It is the need for a student to develop a *time perspective*. Sooner or later, willy-nilly, each individual is likely to find himself slotted into one of these classifications. The counselor can use this realization as a strong motivational force to give direction and meaning to the process of planning.

The *Stable* work period is one of "job persistence beginning when the worker finds a work position in which he remains more or less permanently (three years or more) and continuing until retirement, death, or until he enters another trial period" (Miller and Form, 1951, p. 536). Although this stage is too remote to be of pressing importance to most students, it would be unwise to ignore it completely. First, it cautions the student to plan in terms of his total life rather than merely in terms of a career; it advises him to plan for immediate, inter-mediate and long-range objectives. Secondly, it offers an excellent opportunity for the counselor to inter-relate the student's three vocations, thus giving a unity to his guidance efforts that is often lacking. Thirdly, it gives meaning to the process of planning and reality-testing, for it is largely during this period that one will achieve a maximum of self-realization, while contributing to both society and the Church. Bluntly, the student should be aware of the cliché that if he is not someone by the time he is about 35, or at least well on his way to this end, then the chances are that he will be a nobody for the rest of his life. Fourthly, the question of values and ideas is crucial for any consideration of this work period, lest the student not only learn from the sons of Mammon but imitate them. The period of *Retirement* need not concern us at the moment.

Differing from the *sociological* classification of the stages of life-work that has already been discussed, but quite similar in many respects, is the *psychological* categorization of Buhler (1933) and Super (1953). The first of these stages, that of *Growth,* is of little significance in the present context, since it extends from birth to about the age of 15. The period of *Exploration* (ages 15 to about 25) involves a process of experimentation, floundering, and trial and error in which the individual develops self-understanding, tries his roles as a budding adult, tests himself in the world of work, and perhaps finds himself a mate and a place in the community. From the age of 25 to that of about 45 the individual is wrestling with the problem of *Establishment,* a period in which he establishes himself in his primary and secondary temporal vocations. The stage of *Maintenance* (ages 45 to 65) is devoted to "holding one's own" in competition and in making progress in one's chosen career. The period of *Decline* is the same as Miller and Form's period of *Retirement.*

Ignoring the problem of simple classification and more concerned with the "How" rather than with the "Why" of vocational choice, Ginzberg and his associates studied a "definitely privileged group" of males from the upper middle class (average income, $10,000-$20,000 —circa 1950). These subjects were chosen at age intervals of two years to include persons from elementary to graduate school. Their average intelligence quotient was 120 or more. A total of 91 persons were studied, including, as a secondary aspect of the study, 17 boys from the Hudson Guild settlement house and 10 girls from Barnard College (Ginzberg, 1951, chapter 5). From such an incomplete and skewed investigation only tentative inferences can be drawn. Ginzberg divided the *process* of vocational choice into three more or less distinct stages: (1) period of *fantasy* choices (ages 6 to about 11); (2) period of *tentative* choices (ages 11 to about 18); (3) period of *realistic* choices, which comes to an end when the individual completes his formal preparation and enters upon his first regular job (Ginzberg, 1951, p. 71).

The phase of fantasy choices need not concern us at the present. The period of *tentative* choice is divided into four stages. In the first, or "interest" stage, the person chooses on the basis of his likes and interests. This is followed by the "capacity" stage in which the individual becomes aware of the need to consider his capabilities and to introduce environmental reality elements into his thinking. During the "value" stage (about ages 15 or 16) the person becomes aware of the variety of factors, especially those of goals and values, that must be taken into account. He realizes that he must fit himself into the world, that he must use some goal or value system to order the multiple factors which must be considered, that occupational choice must be examined within the broad framework of a life plan, that the element of time is becoming an important consideration. But he does not know how to integrate these various elements in a coherent manner. In the final "transitional" stage, the adolescent takes a greater degree of responsibility for his own development, although he does seek the help of "key persons." In addition, he takes a more instrumental attitude toward work, being more concerned with working conditions, the length of preparation, the financial rewards, and similar specifics.

The period of *realistic* choices is sub-divided into three phases. The first, or "exploratory" stage, is that in which the student (now a college freshman) tries to acquire the experience he needs to resolve his problems of occupational choice (Ginzberg, 1951, p. 95). Although he expected college to answer his questions, too often he finds that it adds to his difficulties. This stage does, however, have certain advantages. The student seeks to broaden and deepen his understanding of reality and to test himself. He is clearer in his own mind concerning those fields that have no attraction for him. He is aware of a time perspective in terms of which he will have to make some decisions. Yet he is wary of making a definite commitment. In the "crystallization" stage, the individual is finally able to synthesize the many forces, internal and external, that have relevance for his occupational decisions (Ginzberg, 1951, p. 107). Finally, in the stage of "specification" closure is encountered as the person moves from a generalized choice to the specifics of a definite career. It is characterized by a willingness to commit oneself to a limited field of work and by an unwillingness to be deflected into another area (Ginzberg, 1951, p. 117).

### SUMMARY

To bring these considerations to the level of practical usefulness so far as the counselor is concerned, it might be well to summarize what has been stated or inferred concerning what is known of the problem of vocational choice:

1. The problem of one's secondary temporal vocation is intimately related to the individual's primary temporal vocation and to the divine universal vocation of all of us.

2. The problem of occupational choice is a *process*. This process involves the development of a self-concept (fantasied, tentative or

realistic) and the testing of this self-concept against the actualities of the world of work. In this process, the role of ideals, values, attitudes, motivations, needs, and desired satisfactions is at least as important as that played by abilities, aptitudes, interests, and occupational information.

3. The process of occupational choice involves a series of choices, each of which tends to open new areas for consideration and to make others difficult or impossible to attain. For instance, the choice of a liberal arts, business or engineering school curriculum tends to make available certain opportunities and to shunt others to one side.

4. The process of occupational choice is, to a greater or lesser extent, *irreversible*. That is, one can retrace his steps only at the expense of a certain loss of time and energy.

5. The process of occupational choice requires a sense of time perspective, if occupational decisions are not to be made by default, by accident, by impulse, or by the pressure of circumstances.

6. The process of occupational choice requires the discrimination between what is essential, important and incidental; secondly, it demands planning in terms of immediate, inter-mediate and long-range objectives, within the frame of reference of one's divine and primary temporal vocations.

7. The process of occupational choice is, to a large extent, a matter of compromise involving ambitions, ideals, values, assets, limitations, personality needs, motivations, social pressures, and environmental opportunities. This reality-testing situation should lead to the progressive delimitation of possible alternatives that are individually satisfying, morally right and socially acceptable.

8. The process of occupational development usually requires growth and progress through the stages of fantasy, interest, capacity, values, exploration, crystallization, and specification. During these phases, the individual tests his self-concept against reality and modifies it so as to evolve one that is realistic in terms of himself, as a person, and the social order in which he lives. Failure to do so is an invitation to occupational failure.

9. In the process of occupational development, the person seeks from work pretty much what he seeks from life. The degree of satisfaction that he ultimately secures from work is a function of the relative correspondence between what he looks for in his career and what the career has to offer him.

10. Satisfaction in a career involves a combination of monetary rewards, intrinsic satisfactions and concomitant satisfactions. The nature of the compromise which each individual makes with respect to the relative importance of each of these variables is a function of his self-concept and his reality-testing experiences.

11. "Success" is to be judged more by internal frames of reference in terms of self-fulfillment, than in terms of money, status, prestige, power, and other externals.

12. The aim of occupational development and intelligent occupational choice is self-realization—the ability to grow to one's full stature as a person, so far as unalterable environmental conditions permit.

The role of the school in general, and of the counselor in particular, seems clear. It is important that the student see the relationships that exist among his three vocations. Efforts should also be made to help the student to develop a time perspective, since the evidence is rather clear that almost inevitably his life will pass through certain definable occupational stages. Immediate, inter-mediate and long-range goals are important, but they should be planned in terms of that which is essential, important and incidental in light of the student's three vocations. The student should also be aided in distinguishing between an ambition and an objective, in the sense that he should appreciate the fact that finding one's stable career involves a series of decisions and choices.

While it is important that the student understand his assets, remediable deficiencies and irremediable defects, and be aware of the career opportunities that society offers him, it is far more important that he gain increasing insight into his ideals, values, attitudes, motivations, and desired satisfactions. It will also help if the individual can be persuaded to give some thought to the relative emphasis he places upon the intrinsic, the concomitant and the monetary rewards that he will look for in his career. There are some who are likely to say that the student is too young, immature and heedless to give serious thought to such factors as those which have been discussed. One suspects that if the typical student is that young and immature, it is probably because we, as school people, persist in thinking of and in dealing with him as young and immature.

What has been said, in essence, is that the counselor should not overemphasize the role of tests and occupational information in helping students but should rather stress the importance of attaining occupational maturity. As we speak of intellectual, emotional, social and other types of maturity, there is no reason why, as Super (1957a, p. 184) infers, the maturity alphabet should stop with the letter *s*. Vocational or occupational maturity, in its own way, is just as important as other kinds of maturity.

How, then, can the counselor help the student to attain to occupational maturity? Adjustment and maturity, as Schneiders (1955, p. 64) states, are very closely related. In fact, one could easily equate the characteristics which one authority applies to maturity with those which another applies to good adjustment. Adopting the idea that maturity is definable in terms of the types of behavior that an individual reveals, whereas adjustment is definable in terms of the outcomes of this behavior (Super, 1955a, pp. 186-187), it should be possible to apply the concept of maturity to the occupational behavior which a student should exhibit. In so doing, one can readily identify the role of the counselor in helping the individual to deal competently with his problems of occupational choice, thus bringing down to the level of practice what has been said throughout this paper. Since, however, different authorities present varying "lists" of traits that are characteristic of maturity, only a few of the more common ones will be given. The reader can readily supply other criteria from his own experience.

| *Maturity Characteristic* | *Student Occupational Behavior* |
| --- | --- |
| Cognizance of the external situation | He is aware of the importance of making intelligent occupational choices; he understands the importance of a time perspective is so doing. |
| A sense of goal direction | He integrates his three "vocations"; he has immediate, inter-mediate, and long-range objectives; he selects a field of work and an appropriate level within that field; he plans his future rather than having it determined for him by default. |
| A sense of personal identity | He has an adequate sense of his own worth as a worker and self-esteem as a person. He develops a self-concept that is realistic and wholesome. He is aware of the attitudes, motivations, and desired satisfactions that are peculiarly his own. |

| A scale of values | He has a value system that permits him to discriminate between the essential, the important, and the incidental so far as work is concerned. He places a correct emphasis on the monetary, concomitant, and intrinsic rewards of work. |
|---|---|
| Reality orientation | He understands the social matrix in which he must build his career; he is aware of the external resources that are available to help him. He appreciates the influence that sex, religion, parental influences, social class, education, and similar factors can have on his efforts. |
| Sense of responsibility | He is concerned with the problem of planning his career intelligently. He takes the initiative in seeking accurate information and counsel. He is "work-oriented" rather than "pleasure-oriented"; he is determined to work out his own occupational salvation and to accept the consequences of his own actions. |
| Self-insight and self-acceptance | He understands both his strengths and weaknesses, the pleasant and unpleasant aspects of his personality, his abilities, aptitudes, interests, and so on, while endeavoring to improve in those areas in which improvement is possible. |
| Good problem-solving techniques | He is capable of solving the problems involved in coping with his occupational development tasks and those created by a social order in a constant state of flux. |
| Flexibility and adaptability | He is able to modify his self-concept, attitudes, motivations, plans, level of aspiration, and so forth, in light of his reality-testing experiences and the vagaries of a changing social scene. |
| Concern for others | He has a "vision-finder," which enables him to see beyond himself and his own aggrandisement, whether this "vision" be one of excellence, service, the defense of the right, or some other manner of proving that he is "his brother's keeper." |

The advantage of such an approach to the problem of vocational choice, it seems to the writer, is that it includes all of the activities normally associated with vocational guidance, while being broader and deeper in content and outlook. It also seems to introduce a unity and integration in guidance that is often sadly lacking. It is concerned with abilities, interests, aptitudes, test results, occupational information, and planning; it is concerned, too, with the personality of the individual and his self-concept; it is concerned with his ideals, values, attitudes, and motivations; it is concerned with the realities of the world in which the student must live; it is concerned with these three "vocations." Finally, such an approach would seem to allow the counselor to deal with the student as a unified person, rather than to classify him as an educational, vocational, or other type of problem. The writer is not certain that this approach is the best way in which to view guidance. He is sure that it makes more sense than the atomistic approaches often adopted by counselors. It is his hope that the reader will be able to improve upon the writer's ideas for the mutual benefit of both.

## REFERENCES

Buhler, Charlotte B. *Der Menschliche Lebenslauf als psychologisches Problem.* Leipzig: Hirzel, 1933.

Caplow, T. *The sociology of work.* Minneapolis: Univer. of Minnesota, 1954.

Fortune Quarterly Survey. *Fortune,* 1938, *11,* 83-88.

Ginzberg, E., et al. *Occupational choice: an approach to a general theory.* New York: Columbia Univer., 1951.

Hoppock, R. and Robinson, H. Job satisfaction researches of 1949. *Occupations,* 1951, *29,* 572-578.

Maslow, A. *Motivation and personality.* New York: Harper, 1954.

Miller, D. C. and Form, W. H. *Industrial sociology.* New York: Harper, 1951.

Miller, P. and Johnson, T. H. *The puritans.* New York: American Book, 1938.

National Vocational Guidance Association. Principles and practices of vocational guidance. *Occupations,* 1937, *15,* 772-778.

Parsons, F. *Choosing a vocation.* Boston: Houghton, Mifflin, 1909.

Pressey, S. L., Janney, J. E., & Kuhlen, R. G. *Life: a psychological survey.* New York: Harper, 1939.

Roe, A. *The psychology of occupations.* New York: Wiley, 1956.

Rosenberg, M. *Occupations and values.* New York: Free Press, 1957.

Schneiders, A. *Personal adjustment and mental health.* New York: Rinehart, 1955.

Super, D. E. A theory of vocational development. *Amer. Psychologist,* 1953, *8,* 185-190.

Super, D. E. *The psychology of careers.* New York: Harper, 1957. (a)

Super, D. E. *Vocational development: a framework for research.* New York: Teachers Coll., Columbia Univer., Bureau of Publications, 1957. (b)

*Time,* New Products, 1960, *76,* 94-102.

# Religious Vocation in Adolescence

WILLIAM C. BIER, S.J.

*Father William C. Bier, S.J., received his
A.B. degree from Woodstock College, his M.A.
degree from Fordham University, and his
Ph.D. degree from the Catholic University of
America. He joined the staff of the Psychology
Department at Fordham University in 1948,
and since 1958 has been the Chairman of the
Department. He is a fellow of the American
Psychological Association and has been the
Executive Secretary of the American Catholic
Psychological Association since its inception
in 1949. Fr. Bier is the author of a number of
journal articles, dealing mostly with the psychological screening of applicants to the seminary
and religious life, religion and psychiatry, and
pastoral counseling. For more than ten years,
Fr. Bier has been conducting the psychological
screening of candidates for the New York
Province of the Society of Jesus. He has been
a member of the Committee in Charge of each
of the Fordham Institutes of Pastoral Psychology, and he has now assumed the editorship
of the Proceedings of these Institutes which
Fordham University Press is issuing as the
Pastoral Psychology Series.*

Religious vocation is only one of the vocational choices open to adolescents, but for the Catholic adolescent is it a particularly important
vocational choice.

Religious vocation is, of course, important for the Church, because without such vocations there would be no personnel to carry on the work of the Church. It is important, too, for the Catholic adolescent. Vocational directors are the authority for the statement that most Catholic adolescents, at least those who attend Caholic schools, consider the possibility of a religious vocation at some time or other in the course of their schooling. Thus, the boy thinks of the possibility of the priesthood, or perhaps of the brotherhood, and the thoughts of the girl turn to entering the convent. There was a time when I would have been rather inclined to discount such a statement as an over-enthusiastic generalization for which there was little if any empirical proof, but I am now inclined to believe, in terms of my own experience, that this is very close to being an accurate statement. At least in a study which we were conducting a few years ago at Fordham University (Sandra, 1957) we were unable to find a group of girls in Catholic schools who had never given any serious consideration to the possibility of entering the convent. We were compelled, finally, to eliminate this group from our study.

There are, of course, many adolescents who reject the possibility of religious vocation without any real trouble, but there are a significant number of others who find it difficult to reach this decision of whether or not to devote their lives to God's service. These adolescents need help, and they spontaneously turn to you, as priests, for the help which they need. Your function, of course, is to encourage those who, in your mature and honest judgment, have a vocation, but you have a similar contribution to make in helping other adolescents decide that they do *not* have a vocation. The latter can be a contribution to the struggling and mixed-up adolescent, no less than the former.

The term *religious vocation* is used in this paper to include all those who devote their lives in a full-time "professional way" to the service of God. The term therefore includes the diocesan as well as the religious priesthood, the brotherhood, as well as the sisterhood. It is employed in the same generic sense as used by Father Joseph Fichter, S.J. (1961) in his recent book, *Religion as an Occupation: A Study in the Sociology of Professions.* The essential point of this book is that for persons dedicated to the service of God "religion is an occupation," just as teaching, politics, the Army, or the law are occupations. This premise is the basis for the sociological study of religion as an occupation with which the book is concerned.

If this lifetime dedication to the service of God is an "occupation," it is evident that, in Catholic eyes at least, it is a special kind of occupation. One is "called" to this occupation; one does not simply choose it in the way one would choose any other occupation. But how does the adolescent know whether he is so called? The signs of vocation reduce to two basic ones: (1) fitness, suitability, aptitude; and (2) the rightly motivated intention. Fitness and suitability form the natural basis for religious vocation; the right intention is its supernatural aspect. No one without grace can be "rightly" motivated to dedicate his or her life to the service of God.

Why do young adolescents on the brink of manhood and womanhood, when life has the most to offer them, and when it beckons most enticingly, find the religious vocation attractive, a life which involves considerable renunciation and self-sacrifice? We do not attempt to explain this phenomenon on the natural plane at all. Our answer is that this is God's work, the work of grace. "The Spirit breatheth where he will" (Jo. 3:8).

Religious vocation remains, however, a matter of vocational choice, because God's call is an *invitation* to follow Him, not a command. Consequently, the adolescent is morally free to heed or not to heed this call, which means that, without sin, the young person may choose another career. The decision, however, is sometimes difficult, and it is to a priest, whether as counselor, confessor, or spiritual director, that the adolescent is likely to turn for help.

Out of the work which I have been doing for the past twelve years with applicants for admission to the New York Province of the Society of Jesus, during which time I have examined more than a thousand applicants, I will attempt to offer you something which may assist you in your work with adolescents in the matter of religious vocations. This program has been described elsewhere (Bier, 1953, 1954, 1960), so that I will restrict my remarks at present to three main headings: (1) the background of the applicant; (2) motivation for religious life; and (3) the uncertain applicant. In what I say, I will assume that you are functioning in your priestly capacity and attempting to help a young man or woman to settle the matter of a religious vocation.

## BACKGROUND OF APPLICANT

In his sociological study already referred to, Father Fichter (1961, p. 38) quotes research studies as revealing that seven out of ten of those with religious vocations have received all their training in

Catholic schools. The parochial school (with an estimated 50 percent of Catholic elementary school children) produces 70 percent of the vocations, while the Catholic high school (with an estimated 25 percent of Catholic high school students) produces 60 percent of the vocations (Fichter, 1961, pp. 41-42). It would seem, therefore, on a basis of these statistics that the Catholic high school is an even more crucial influence than the parochial school in producing vocations. By inference, however, the 50 percent of Catholic children in non-Catholic elementary schools, and the 75 percent of Catholic students in non-Catholic high schools are a largely untapped source of potential vocations. Another important influence, at least in the case of boys, is the experience of serving as an altar boy. Studies show that four out of five seminarians, and three out of five brothers, have been acolytes in their boyhood (Fichter, 1961, p. 40).

With respect to the social class from which vocations come, Father Fichter (1961, p. 84) quotes the following statistics, based upon two studies made at the University of Notre Dame in 1958:

| | SEMINARIANS | | BROTHERS | |
|---|---|---|---|---|
| | Number | Percent | Number | Percent |
| Above average income | 106 | 24.3 | 97 | 14.8 |
| Middle income | 275 | 62.9 | 452 | 69.1 |
| Below average income | 56 | 12.8 | 105 | 16.1 |
| Totals | 437 | 100.0 | 654 | 100.0 |

On the question of social class as a factor in vocations, Father Fichter writes as follows:

> One fact is quite definite, and this is that the main source of vocations is no longer the lower class, financially and occupationally disadvantaged, poorly educated segment of the American population. The reason why a large number of vocations used to come from this class is because the category itself was so large, rather than it possessed any peculiar virtues that helped to foster vocations. Now that vocations are coming mainly from the middle class, there is probably need for a re-examination of the concept of poverty and piety on the one hand, and of materialism and secularism on the other (Fichter, 1961, pp. 83-84).

So much for the sociological background of religious vocations, much more of which can be found in Father Fichter's well-documented work. What now of the psychological background of candidates for the religious life as revealed by the kind of work which I have been doing for the past twelve years?

One fact which emerges very clearly from this work is that the family is the nursery of the vocations, not merely in the spiritual and religious sense, as we have always known, but in the psychological sense as well. The favorable applicant for the religious life comes not only from a good religious home, but from a psychologically stable home.

Homes in which turmoil, bickering, tension, and quarreling are the rule, or homes in which the parents are deeply unhappy themselves and ill-suited to each other, are not generally the homes from which psychologically suitable applicants come. In such homes it is unlikely that the psychological needs of the child (needs for affection, security, identification, and so forth) will be met, and when they are not met, it is virtually impossible that the child's personality will develop in a psychologically normal manner.

Two home situations seem deserving of special mention in this connection. The first is found when one parent is seriously neurotic, or psychotic, or criminal, or alcoholic. These conditions differ in degree of severity and in their impact upon the child, but all of them are likely to create an unfavorable psychological climate for the children in the household. It makes a difference, of course, whether the ill or errant parent is the father or the mother. Where it is the mother, the children, especially the younger children, are likely to be much more affected because of the amount of time which the mother spends with the children. In the American home, the father is a more remote figure, but where he is seriously ill or delinquent, the children can scarcely escape the impact of his behavior on their upbringing. Such a home situation creates a presumption *against* the psychological suitability of the applicant for religious life. This is the case not because of the inheritance of any psychological disorder or criminal taint, but simply because of the environment in which the child is raised. A child raised by a neurotic or psychotic mother could hardly develop in a psychologically normal manner. Strecker has strikingly documented this proposition in his book, *Their Mothers' Sons* (Strecker, 1951), and in the companion volume, *Their Mothers' Daughters* (Strecker and Lathbury, 1956).

The second situation to be mentioned in this same context is the broken home. Divorce, at least in the sense of legal separation, is becoming more frequent among the Catholics, and even in the families of applicants for seminary and religious life. Separation or divorce, especially when there are children, and particularly when the parents are Catholics, does not occur abruptly. It is usually preceded by a period, and often by a long period, of growing disagreement and dis-illusionment on the part of the parents, a period during which fighting and bickering and turmoil and deepening unhappiness set the stage for the eventual separation of the parents. Those who really suffer in a divorce are the children. Both parents are needed for a child to develop a proper sex role and a proper sex identification. In a divorce a child is almost compelled to take sides in the dispute between the parents, and this can be psychologically very damaging to him, for how can he identify with a parent whom he feels he must blame?

A similar but less acute home situation is created by the death of one of the parents. Here at least the household is spared the bitterness of divorce, and the image of a deceased parent is likely to be quite different from that of a separated parent, while there is always the possibility of remarriage. Usually, however, the parent identification, which is psychologically necessary, is difficult for such a child, and the more so depending on the sex of the deceased parent. A boy will be more handicapped in his psychological development if his father is deceased, and a girl similarly would suffer greater impairment if it is her mother who is deceased.

If an applicant has a psychologically ill or delinquent parent, as explained above, or if he comes from a broken home, these conditions do not necessarily preclude a religious vocation, but they do, in my opinion, create a presumption against the psychological suitability of the applicant. This is a presumption which will yield to the contrary fact in an individual case, but this fact must be demonstrated and not assumed. It seems clear to me that such evidence can be secured only by an adequate psychological evaluation which should, therefore, be required of such applicants, even though not generally demanded of other candidates. The situation is less acute with the applicant whose parent is deceased. I would, however, recommend even here, especially when the deceased parent is of the same sex as the applicant, that more than usual care be exercised in determining the psychological suitability of the applicant. Individual circumstances will, of course, make a difference and should be taken into account as, for instance, the age of the candidate upon the death of the parent, the person who supplied for the deceased parent, and so forth.

We look into the background of the candidate and more specifically at his own past behavior because what the individual has done in the past furnishes the only valid basis for estimating what he is likely to do in the future. We inquire, therefore, into what kind of adjustment the individual has made in the significant personal relationships in his life thus far: at home, in school, at work, and so forth. In evaluating this behavior we must distinguish between normal, though strange, adolescent behavior on the one hand, and abnormal and pathological behavior on the other, as previous speakers have already indicated.

Positively, what we are looking for when we speak of the psychologically suitable applicant is for indications that the individual is a mentally healthy, reasonably well adjusted, and sufficiently stable individual. The National Association for Mental Health* issues a very simple leaflet giving some of the positive characteristics of people with good mental health.

First, the Association says in this leaflet, people with good mental health feel comfortable about themselves. This means, for instance, that they are not overwhelmed by their own emotions; they can take life's disappointments in stride. They neither underestimate nor overestimate their abilities, and they are able to accept their own shortcomings. They have self-respect, and they get satisfaction from simple everyday pleasures. The second chief characteristic of people with good mental health is that they feel right about other people. This means that they are able to give love and to consider the interests of others. They expect to like and trust others, and take it for granted that others will like and trust them. They respect the differences they find in other people, and they have a sense of responsibility to their neighbors and their fellow-man. The third chief characteristic of people with good mental health, according to the Association, is that they are able to meet the demands of life. This means that they do something about their problems as they arise and they accept their responsibilities. They plan ahead, but do not fear the future. They welcome new experiences and new ideas and they set realistic goals for themselves. They put their best efforts into what they do, and get satisfaction out of doing it.

The above description is suggestive rather than exhaustive, but I think that it does furnish a good picture of a mentally healthy person. These are the behavioral characteristics which, by and large, you expect to find in the applicant psychologically suitable for religious life.

* 10 Columbus Circle, New York 19, N. Y. The leaflets sell for $1.00 a hundred.

MOTIVATION FOR RELIGIOUS VOCATION

The person who has a vocation to the religious life is moved to embrace this state by a "right intention," to use the words of Canon 538, of the Code of Canon Law. Theologians in commenting on the proper motivation for religious vocation point out that no *purely* natural motive will be sufficient, such as the desire for honor, for prestige, or for security, but that on the other hand, *any* supernatural motive will suffice, such as zeal for souls, the desire to render one's salvation more secure, and so forth. It is certainly in keeping with the spirit of the Church that we should examine carefully the motives of those who present themselves for admission to the seminary or to the religious life. This is ancient wisdom, because the capacity for self-deception in the knowledge of one's own motivations is almost limitless.

The importance of motivation on the part of the applicant, and the need to scrutinize this motivation with care on the part of the spiritual guide is, I think, borne out by certain of our findings with our own applicants. We made a limited study of those who left religious life after entering for the ten-year-period—1949-1958. Focusing on the length of time spent in religion on the part of those who did leave, the following results emerged:

| Months in Religious Life | Percent of Those Leaving |
| --- | --- |
| 6 | 55 |
| 12 | 75 |
| 18 | 78 |
| 24 | 92 |

Since we have a two-year novitiate, the above figures mean that 92 percent of those who left our Society in the ten-year-period left during the novitiate. I might add further that this figure constitutes 28 percent of those who entered. On the basis of reports furnished by the Master of Novices, it can be said that the overwhelming number of those who left did so, not because they were found unsuitable, but simply because they did not wish to stay.

Why do young people choose a religious vocation? Human motivation is complex, even in very simple decisions such as: Shall I go to the movies tonight? It is inevitable therefore that the motivation would be complex in any really important matter such as the choice of a vocation.

In the matter of religious vocation, there is always a complex of conscious reasons, some of which are natural and others supernatural. While recognizing what theologians say to the effect that *any* supernatural motive will suffice for a genuine vocation, it must also be recognized that the mere presence of a supernatural motive is itself insufficient as an adequate sign of a vocation. In my experience, a supernatural motive of one kind or another is hardly ever absent in a candidate, yet not all of them are properly motivated as is proven, I think, by the large number who leave religious life so soon after entering. We must inquire, therefore, into the relative importance of the supernatural motive in the total complex of motives inducing the individual in question to embrace a religious vocation. If the really predominant motivation is natural, even though a supernatural motive is present, would one say that the candidate in question was drawn by a "properly motivated intention" to embrace a religious vocation? It is my opinion that the lack of a "properly motivated intention" is the largest single factor in early defections from religious life. Most of those who leave so soon after entering, do so because they never had a vocation, due to a defect not of suitability, but of intention. This fact could, I think, often be ascertained by a spiritual director beforehand, thus saving much heartache to the individual and trouble to the Community.

Because of the complexity and the personal nature of motivation, it is difficult to secure reliable empirical data on the reasons why young people embrace the religious vocation. It might appear at first sight that we could simply ask the question: "Why did you choose a religious vocation?" and that we could simply tabulate the responses of those willing to furnish this information. We can, of course, do this, but the approach suffers from at least two limitations. In the first place, if we ask the question of those who have been in a religious vocation for five or ten years, the individual may no longer recall exactly what his motives were on entering, or he may confuse his current motives with his motives on entering, or finally he may find it difficult to say which was his *strongest* motive. Secondly, data gathered in this way would miss those who chose this career, but who left in the early months or years of training.

Despite the difficulties mentioned above, data gathered in this way do furnish us with some insight into why young people choose a religious vocation. Father Fichter, in the book already referred to (Fichter, 1961, p. 24), furnishes the following information gathered at the 1958 Vocation Institute at the University of Notre Dame:

| REASON FOR CHOOSING PRIESTLY VOCATION | ENTERED SEMINARY AT AGE: | | |
|---|---|---|---|
| | (205) 18 yrs. or older | (235) 17 yrs. or younger | (440) Total |
| Attracted to priestly work | 10.7% | 35.3% | 23.9% |
| Surety of salvation | 19.0 | 9.4 | 13.9 |
| Strong sense of vocation | 16.6 | 8.5 | 12.3 |
| Love of God | 10.2 | 11.1 | 10.7 |
| Salvation of others | 7.8 | 4.3 | 5.9 |

The shift with age in the above table is worthy of note. Those entering the seminary at the slightly older age put surety of salvation in first place. In explanation of the above table, it may be remarked that the percentages do not add up to 100 because they were based on an open-end questionnaire, in which the respondent supplied his three chief reasons. The summation provided in the table represents only the first reason given by each respondent, and the table itself is limited to the five reasons most frequently given.

A word should be said about negative motives in relation to religious vocation. A religious vocation should be a positive choice, "Come, follow me" (Mark 10:21), and it should not be a second choice. The religious vocation becomes a second choice when negative motives become the dominant ones for embracing the religious vocation.

We are all familiar with the stereotype popularized in fictional literature, that it is only the girl thwarted in love who enters the convent, and that it is only when a male member of a noble family was not suited for a military career or for diplomacy that he was destined "for the Church." We tend to smile nowadays at these caricatures of religious motivation, but human nature has not changed, and similar motivations occur today. People are still jilted in love, and under such provocation a young man today, no less than his medieval predecessor, may think of the priesthood, or a young woman of the convent, but a wise spiritual director will know better than to accept such motivation as genuine or lasting.

We have already spoken of the candidate from an unhappy home and we may now observe in addition to what has already been said about him, that he is particularly vulnerable to negative motivations for the religious life. The basic motivation of such a young man is likely to be that he would wish to avoid in his own life the unhappiness he has seen in the lives of his parents. On the rebound, then, he considers a religious vocation, but his motivation is essentially negative, being the avoidance of the unhappiness of marriage. Similarly, the girl who finds sex and the idea of sexual relations repugnant, may find herself "attracted" to a life of celibacy, but in her case, too, the motivation is essentially negative. Candidates who present negative motivations of this kind should be examined with more than usual care, because such motivations are frequently a warning that the individual in question may not have a "right intention" for embracing a religious vocation.

Our discussion so far has been concerned only with *conscious* motives, i.e., those of which the individual is aware, or at least becomes aware if he reflects upon his motivation. In addition, however, to these motives there may be others of which the individual is unaware, but which, nevertheless, exert an influence on his choice.

Psychoanalysis, as you would certainly know, has called particular attention to the role of unconscious factors in human motivation. Some psychoanalysts have not hesitated to maintain that unconscious influences always operate and that they are moreover the dominant factors in human motivation. If one accepts this viewpoint, consciously appearing motives are reduced to mere rationalizations to justify the course of action dictated by the unconscious. Conscious motivations are thus always suspect, and are never the real motives.

The evidence which thus far has been adduced for the influence of the unconscious on human activity in no sense justifies the radical position sketched above. On the other hand, the unconscious is not a myth, and we are compelled to recognize the fact that it does *sometimes* influence human motivation. For this reason, the motives which people allege for their actions (excluding the case of deliberate deception) are not always the real motives, or the dominant motives. It has not been reserved to the twentieth century to discover self-deception. Is the girl who finds sex repugnant practicing virtue in embracing a life of consecrated chastity, or is she creating thereby an effective rationalization and indulging in considerable self-deception? Such questions are obviously very difficult to answer, and it seems that about the only generalization which can justifiably be made is that we must be prepared to chart a sensible middle course between the two extremes of *never* accepting at face value any motivation, and *always* accepting a person's motivation without question. This may be no more than ancient wisdom, but there is a new urgency to follow it in terms of the more adequate present-day knowledge about the role of unconscious factors in human motivation.

There is evidence for the existence of unconscious motivation when an individual feels more strongly attracted or repelled by a proposal than he is able to account for in terms of his conscious reasons. Not all such unconscious motivation is undesirable. It is my opinion that unconscious motivation frequently and perhaps even generally plays a part in a genuine religious vocation. The reason is because I believe that this is the way that God's grace normally works. Grace operates by rendering a religious vocation attractive to an individual to a degree beyond the ability of the individual to explain. He can give you some reasons and they are valid, but they are not quite the full story, and the individual vaguely knows this. The rest is God's free gift: "You have not chosen me, but I have chosen you" (Jo. 15:16). What other than the grace of God could make the lifetime renunciation of the religious state attractive to modern adolescents, to whom the world has so much to offer? The recipient of this spontaneous gift of God which is a religious vocation, does not know the reason for this predilection, but he does know very surely that God is calling him, and he knows that, above everything else that he might do in this world, he wants to respond to that call. In the light of such an invitation, human reasons are feeble. You may say: "Well, this is nothing but the grace of God." I could not agree more fully, but it is illuminating, I think, to realize that the action which we recognize as grace is an example of unconscious motivation in modern psychological terms.

Finally, it may be observed that the right intention in the matter of religious vocation is something that admits of degrees. A certain minimum is, of course, required, that minimum being defined as the presence of *some* supernatural motivation. But beyond this minimum there is almost no limit to which rectitude of intention can be developed. Actually, purification of one's intention in the service of God is a lifetime work. In dealing with the applicant to the religious life, then, it seems pertinent to observe that a right intention is not the same as a perfect intention. The latter may be expected to develop gradually through a lifetime in religion and to result from the cooperation on the part of the religious with the healing grace of God which improves, elevates, and purifies human motivations.

## THE DOUBTFUL APPLICANT

In terms of the desire on the part of a priest, as a spiritual director or confessor, to help adolescents in their choice of a religious vocation, the doubtful applicant presents a particular problem in which there is special need for prudent counsel. The clearly suitable and the obviously unsuitable applicant for a religious vocation present no special problem of direction, once the facts are known. The doubtful applicant, on the other hand, proposes a difficult problem of direction, and I would, therefore, like to offer some considerations which may assist both the director and the applicant in these cases.

When I speak of the doubtful applicant, I mean by the term to include two types of applicants: (1) the doubtfully suitable applicant; and (2) the uncertain applicant. In the first case, the doubt is in the mind of the director as to whether the applicant under his direction has the requisite qualifications for a religious vocation. In the second case, the doubt is in the mind of the applicant, who is uncertain as to whether or not to dedicate himself to God in this way of life. Let us consider each of these cases in turn.

*The doubtfully suitable applicant.* We have already referred to the two principal conditions which are likely to raise a doubt in the mind of a director as to the suitability of an applicant, namely, an unhappy or unfavorable home situation, and behavior on the part of the applicant himself which is strange, unusual, and difficult to understand. Doubts in these cases are not negative doubts, arising simply from insufficient knowledge, but positive doubts, based on reasons which at least suggest the unsuitability of the applicant. Whenever doubts of this kind arise in the mind of the director, whether they come from the above-mentioned sources, or any others, I would offer it as the proper general principle that they should *never* be disregarded. To dismiss them on the assumption that if the candidate is unsuited, this fact will emerge in the course of training, is to fail, I think, in the responsibility of spiritual direction and to create far greater problems subsequently both for the candidate and for the Community than would have been involved by facing up to this problem at the time of application.

It seems clear that the first step to be taken in the case of a doubtfully suited applicant is to remove the doubt by securing more information about the individual, if such is possible. In this way it could be ascertained, for instance, whether the applicant himself is a well-ad-justed individual, even though he does come from a broken home, or whether the general presumption of unsuitability is unfortunately only too amply verified in his case. It will be obvious that this kind of information requires the intervention of a psychologist or a psychiatrist. If the Community to which the applicant is seeking admission has a psychological testing program, it may usually be left to the results of this testing to determine whether the doubt of the director is justified or not. Depending upon circumstances, it may be prudent, and even indicated, for the director to manifest his doubt to the responsible admitting superior. I would feel that he should certainly do so, if he is asked for a recommendation, as is often the case. Doubts should never be presented as certainties, but the positive doubts of which we are speaking, which raise a real question as to the suitability of the applicant, should be manifested. If confidentiality would in any way be threatened by this communication, the director should secure the permission of the candidate to make the requested report to the superior. If a candidate should refuse such permission, this refusal may itself be a further indication that the doubts of the director as to the suitability of the applicant are well founded.

If the Institute to which the applicant is seeking admission does not have a program of psychological assessment, the responsibility for resolving the doubt may fall squarely on the shoulders of the spiritual director for whom this may then become an obligation of conscience. It is now possible to secure this kind of assessment on an individual basis from a psychologist or psychiatrist functioning in a private capacity. If the spiritual director must himself assume this responsibility, then the psychological report should be made to him, and he will then use it in his further direction of the applicant. On the basis of such a report, and perhaps after a conference with the psychologist or psychiatrist concerned, the director could tell the candidate whether or not to go ahead with the application for admission. If this seems to be placing too great a responsibility on the priest-director, I can only reply that this is a responsibility which, it seems to me, has been too little acknowledged and discharged by spiritual directors.

It will sometimes happen, of course, that the suitability of the applicant cannot be too clearly determined even after the most careful and most adequate investigation. If a doubt still remains, what should be the course of action? I would propose that in such a case the benefit of the doubt should be given to the Order and to the Church, and not to the individual. In such a conflict the common good should prevail over the individual good, although it is a very real question as to how much of a benefit it would be to an individual to admit him to religious life or the seminary under such conditions.

Some of those who look at religious life from the outside—lay Catholics, and particularly non-Catholics—have observed that religious orders are more tolerant of psychological deviation in their members than are other groups and subcultures in our country. The inference has sometimes been drawn that actually religious life is a *good* place for psychologically marginally adjusted individuals, because of the tolerant treatment which they receive in religion. In the factual sense, the above observation may be true, but it is hardly a desirable condition and certainly not one to be encouraged. Emotionally disturbed people are hard to live with, and one such individual may immeasurably increase the normal difficulties of religious life for an entire Community. Mentally ill priests and religious, since their behavior is characteristically irrational, are not infrequently a scandal to the faithful. While their conduct may not be blameworthy, it is scarcely edifying. It is likely that there shall always be a certain number of priests and religious whose psychological adjustment is precarious at best. In many cases these psychological difficulties may have developed only after years of faithful and effective service. It is one thing to accept what God's providence permits, but it is another knowingly to open the gates to such problems as we do when we admit to the religious life those who are doubtfully suitable from the psychological point of view.

The religious life and the priesthood make more demands on the psychological maturity and the adaptive resources of the individual than does life in a lay state. The reason is that the vows of religion involve the renunciation of the three most basic human rights: to possess, to marry, and to self-autonomy. Human nature continues to crave these things, and the lifetime inhibition of them makes considerable and sometimes extraordinary demands in terms of psychological resources. This is basically the reason why spiritual writers have traditionally referred to the religious life as a martyrdom and a holocaust. With these facts in mind, it seems imprudent to encourage candidates to undertake this way of life who have notably less than the average amount of psychological resources.

Many priests might feel that they should not "stand in the way of a vocation," if they are only doubtful. It would seem to me, however, that this attitude largely begs the question because we cannot properly speak of a vocation until the suitability of the applicant is established. Consequently, such a priest is helping to decide the genuineness of a vocation, rather than standing in its way. In my opinion, it is a false charity to approve for admission a candidate who is doubtfully suitable. Frequently these individuals prove to be problems in religious life from the day they enter. They take a disproportionate amount of the time of the Master of Novices or the Spiritual Father to the detriment of those who would profit more from this attention. Any Master of Novices will testify that one or two people of this kind in a novitiate are more of a worry and concern than the entire rest of the novices put together. Invariably these individuals leave religious life or the seminary in the end, but only after much heartache and soul-searching for the individual and subsequent superiors, and their departure is often an unsettling experience, not only for the individuals who leave, but for their former companions who remain. In the judgment of many, the number of ex-seminarians and ex-religious is already too large, and I truly believe that a significant number of them are drawn from the ranks of those who were doubtfully suitable prospects in the first place.

*The uncertain applicant.* The final point to be considered is the case of the applicant who is uncertain of his vocation. This kind of an applicant is especially likely to seek the help of a priest in resolving his own indecision with respect to his vocation.

It would be my viewpoint that the individual who is uncertain in his own mind as to his vocation does not yet have a vocation. According to theologians, the subjective sign of a vocation is the firm resolution to dedicate one's life to the service of God in the priesthood or the religious life, and for a proper supernatural motive, as already indicated. The individual who is uncertain as to whether he should seek admission or not, does not have such a firm resolution, and hence does not yet have a vocation.

In trying to help an applicant of this kind, it seems to me that a distinction should be made between the minor seminary, juniorate, or aspiranture on the one hand, and the major seminary and the novitiate on the other. I would propose that the individual who is not yet sure of his vocation, and who feels that he should "give the life a try" might be encouraged to enter the minor seminary or the aspirancy, but not the major seminary or the novitiate. Father Fichter

(1961, p. 187) reports that less than one-sixth of those entering the minor seminary are ordained to the priesthood. Burke (1947, p. 2) reports that less than 25 per cent of the students entering the minor seminary are ordained. Aspirantures have a better record, one national survey indicating that 57 per cent of the girls in them persevere into the sisterhood (Fichter, 1961, p. 188). If these and other figures which are in substantial agreement with them are accurate, they would seem to imply that the minor seminary and to a lesser, but still significant extent, the aspiranture are places in which the majority of candidates are unsettled in their vocations and are "giving the life a try."

These findings are in keeping with psychological studies on the development of vocational choice. Both the minor seminary and the aspiranture deal with vocations during the high school years, and psychological studies indicate that vocational choices are usually not realistically made until the end of the high school years. Ginzberg (1951), for instance, distinguishes three stages of vocational choice distributed as follows:

Fantasy choices up to the age of 11
Tentative choices up to the age of 17
Realistic choices from age 17 up.

Psychological studies such as those of Ginzberg and others (v.g. Super, 1953), together with the figures quoted above, combine to suggest that young people in the high school years are still in the process of determining their vocational choice and that the choice which they make in this time is likely to be no more than a tentative one. It would seem to me, therefore, that a candidate who is not yet settled in his own mind about his vocation may be permitted to enter the minor seminary (and a girl the aspiranture), because this period of training embraces the time when vocational choice is still tentative, and this fact must be taken into account in the training which is offered to the candidate at this time in his psychological development.

As indicated above, I think, however, that the case is quite different when it comes to the major seminary and the novitiate. Here I would say that the candidate who is uncertain in his own mind as to his vocation should be encouraged to wait, to consider the matter more fully, to pray further, but not to seek admission.

The work of the novitiate is training in the spiritual life, which is rendered extremely difficult, if not actually impossible, if the attitude of a novice is such that he is constantly questioning his presence in the novitiate. How can one build, if the foundation is constantly wavering around one? How can one make progress, if every time one lifts a foot to move in a forward direction, the question intrudes itself as to whether one should be on the road at all? Day-to-day difficulties arise in every life, and when they arise in the life of the novice uncertain of his vocation, they are a fresh invitation to him to reassess his whole position. This continual re-appraisal is a soul-searching, emotionally disturbing process, and it seriously distracts and detracts from the thought, energy, and attention which should be devoted to the work of spiritual progress.

Apart from the lack of progress, there is another kind of danger faced by the individual uncertain of his vocation. The person who is unable to decide about his vocation is frequently a person indecisive in general. If such a characteristically indecisive person is permitted to enter religious life, there is the danger that he will not have the courage to leave, even though it subsequently becomes quite clear that he should do so. It requires distinctly more courage to leave the seminary or the religious life, than it does to enter. If this type of individual cannot bring himself to make the easier decision, is it likely that he will be able to make the harder one? It is even possible for a person of this kind to drift into the priesthood or into final religious profession, not electing these states by any positive choice, but rather arriving at them by default of any decisive action and by the circumstance that the individual finds himself in the seminary or in religious life.

It is obvious that the preceding remarks on the role of the priest in helping adolescents in the matter of religious vocation are selected and limited. They have been chosen, however, because they relate to problems frequently encountered by the priest in dealing with the adolescent who is giving serious thought to the possibility of a religious vocation.

## REFERENCES

Bier, W. C., S.J. Psychological testing and theology of vocation. *Rev. Religious,* 1953, *12,* 291-304.
———. Practical requirements of a program for the psychological screening of candidates. *Rev. Religious,* 1954, *13,* 13-27.
———. Testing procedures and their value. In J. E. Haley (C.S.C.) (Ed.) *Proceedings of the 1959 sisters' institute of spirituality.* Notre Dame: Univer. Notre Dame, 1960, Pp. 263-299.

Burke, H. R., S.S. *Personality traits of successful minor seminarians.* Washington: Catholic Univer., 1947.

Fichter, J. H., S.J. *Religion as an occupation: a study in the sociology of professions.* Notre Dame: Univer. Notre Dame, 1961.

Ginzberg, E., *et al. Occupational choice: an approach to a general theory.* New York: Columbia Univer., 1951.

Sandra, Mother M. Elaine. Identification with the Catholic religion as related to selected personality indices. Unpublished doctoral dissertation, Fordham Univer., 1957.

Strecker, E. A. *Their mothers' sons.* (Rev. ed.) Philadelphia: Lippincott, 1951.

Strecker, E. A. and Lathbury, V. T. *Their mothers' daughters.* Philadelphia: Lippincott, 1956.

Super, D. E. A theory of vocational development. *Amer. Psychologist,* 1953, *8,* 185-190.